T0064549

Journeys With My Mother's Ashes

Healing Grief Through Travel

HÉLÈNE JERMOLAJEW

BALBOA.PRESS
A DIVISION OF HAY HOUSE

Copyright © 2020 Hélène Jermolajew.

All rights reserved. No part of this book may be used or reproduced by any means, graphic, electronic, or mechanical, including photocopying, recording, taping or by any information storage retrieval system without the written permission of the author except in the case of brief quotations embodied in critical articles and reviews.

Balboa Press books may be ordered through booksellers or by contacting:

Balboa Press
A Division of Hay House
1663 Liberty Drive
Bloomington, IN 47403
www.balboapress.com.au
AU TFN: 1 800 844 925 (Toll Free inside Australia)
AU Local: 0283 107 086 (+61 2 8310 7086 from outside Australia)

Because of the dynamic nature of the Internet, any web addresses or links contained in this book may have changed since publication and may no longer be valid. The views expressed in this work are solely those of the author and do not necessarily reflect the views of the publisher, and the publisher hereby disclaims any responsibility for them.

The author of this book does not dispense medical advice or prescribe the use of any technique as a form of treatment for physical, emotional, or medical problems without the advice of a physician, either directly or indirectly. The intent of the author is only to offer information of a general nature to help you in your quest for emotional and spiritual well-being. In the event you use any of the information in this book for yourself, which is your constitutional right, the author and the publisher assume no responsibility for your actions.

Any people depicted in stock imagery provided by Getty Images are models, and such images are being used for illustrative purposes only.
Certain stock imagery © Getty Images.

Print information available on the last page.

ISBN: 978-1-5043-2284-3 (sc)
ISBN: 978-1-5043-2288-1 (e)

Balboa Press rev. date: 10/26/2020

Dedication

To my sons, Ginski and Nikolai - You were there

'When you find a foul in the game change the direction of play.'
Nikolai Jermolajew: 22 November 1997 – aged 12

Acknowledgements

To my parents, you gave me life and raised me with love.

To my sons Nikolai and Ginski for being the incredible human beings that you are, for your hilarious humour and your quiet support.

To my daughter-in-law Kirra, you came with us on this journey, through you and your love our family continues.

To my new daughter-in-law Kristin you have joined our family since this event and even though you weren't there for that trip you have added so much love and joy to our on-going journey.

To Ewa Konecka you supported me through the saddest 24 hours of my life and were a wonderful support to my parents.

To Garry Tongs dear friend, Editor in Chief and esteemed collaborator, my profound gratitude.

To Judy Bielicki, you showed me the way to my prose journey and convinced me I could write, without you this memoir would have remained as random blog articles and social media snippets.

To all my friends old and new who supported me on my journey and joined in the fun, personally and via social media, too numerous to mention individually but you all know who you are.

And a particular thank you to all my Angels, Guides and my Universe, my wings have grown stronger.

I have to also mention and thank singer-songwriter Rowland Salley. The chorus of his brilliant song Killing the Blues reflected my life story and spun in my head every time I sat in an aeroplane seat, thank you. And special thanks to my wonderful late friend Stephen Hindy for introducing me to the album.

Contents

Part One

Part Two - The Other Side of the World

Part Three

Part One

My mum, Tamara Nikolaevna Jermolajew, chef on Lord Howe Island 1970

Introduction

This is the story of my journey after my mother passed away. A story of grief, of drama, of stress and a little of my past. It is also the story of my Gap Year of travel around the world and how this travel lifted me up and helped me along my path to emotional healing.

I know grief is a very individual experience. There are no rules for when it should start, when it should end and what you do about it in between. Each of us is an individual with our own ways of being, so no one can tell us how to 'be' around our grief. There are many platitudes out there about losing loved ones. Some of them are helpful others are not. One thing is certain and that is, we change regardless of whom we have lost. For me, it was an even deeper change when it was Mum who passed. Suddenly my entire support system was gone. I became an orphan. I've heard it said that our mothers are our first home for it is she who carried us for nine months. When she dies our first home is gone. It's like our house and all our possessions and memories have burnt to the ground, never to return, at least not in the same format. We need to be gentle on ourselves at this time.

I also learned that we have to be very aware of ourselves and our well-being. I have listened to psychologists speak about grief and they often say that even though there is no 'end' time to the process, we need to be aware of the stages. Many say that if our very deep grief lasts more than a year we risk sliding into depression. Many cultures and religions have traditions around death and grief. It seems to me that these tend to follow the emotional voyage through the unknowns of bereavement. The important thing is to take care of ourselves on this journey, listen to our internal needs and surround ourselves with caring, uplifting people.

I chose to not follow any prescribed traditional path and now, eight years later, I can honestly say that I am glad I did it my way.

Prologue

I am OK now, but I wasn't...

A Facebook memory appeared on my screen, a photo from 2009. I looked closely at the image. A slim, colourful, smiling me hugging a tree at Floriade in Canberra, surrounded by beautiful spring daffodils. Little did I know then what was ahead of me in 12 short months.

Behind me were ten years of getting my mother free from her fears of Dad. The last time he attacked her and then tried to burn the house down, I finally said to Mum 'Enough!' and called the police. He was placed in hospital where he was diagnosed with morbid paranoia. Given his horrific childhood - living through a revolution in which he lost his entire family and ending up in terrible orphanages by the age of seven - the diagnosis was not surprising. I now suspect that he was suffering from PTSD. But that is another story. Mum was struggling with accepting that her husband would never be allowed home again and she would never have to have a little bag packed ready to jump out the window if an attack came in the night. With help from counsellors, the ACT Government's Art for Health course, friends and family, she began to slowly loosen up.

Her first action at the age of 79, was to learn the English language properly. She hadn't previously been allowed to do so. Through her close friend Ewa she was assigned a teacher who would come to her house. This lady was so enthralled by Mum's life story that she asked her to write about her life and through that, they would correct and discuss English grammar.

Mum and her teacher became close friends. At age 85 those stories were published by Ginninderra Press as a memoir titled 'It Can't Be Forever'.

On the eve of the year 2000 Mum and I climbed Mount Franklin, an elevation of 1646 metres and part of the Brindabella ranges on the border of the Australian Capital Territory and New South Wales. Mum was 79. It took an hour and a half of driving and two hours of climbing but we made it to the top by 4am and drank champagne to welcome the dawn of the new century accompanied by the morning mist and a solitary bird singing.

The following year 18 days after my 50th birthday Dad died. As his health worsened Mum had the Domestic Violence Order reversed and she sat by his side in the nursing home. My mother, no matter what, cared about people and lives. Despite all the life-threatening episodes she always acknowledged my father's part in saving the family during and after World War II.

Once Dad passed, Mum could really believe she was safe. So began a whole new life for her. She joined the U3A, studied all manner of subjects and developed new friendships.

By 86 Mum's Parkinson's disease was starting to take hold. Other health problems were beginning to set in. However, being the stoic she was, Mum was still helping a charity with their Christmas work, still hosting an open house every Saturday morning, for her friends to drop in for coffee, and still being my loving mother and grandmother to my sons. Luckily my younger son Nick was living with her so I could sleep at night knowing someone was at her house in case of emergencies. There were quite a few of those.

Hospital visits became more frequent and by age 89 she must have had a real sense of not being around for much longer. She was actually quite psychic. While living in Bosnia for a while, soon after her marriage, Mum had been taught to read coffee cups by the Turkish women. In the 1960's she predicted the younger of my two brothers leaving home. He did. One day he walked in and told Mum he was throwing in all his studies and going to New Guinea with a mining company. Mum was horrified. In later years she saw my older brother's death. He died in 1980 from leukaemia just before his 35th birthday. She swore to never read another coffee cup again! Was it intuition that caused her, early in the year of her death, to call the solicitor to her home and change her will, little realising what drama this would cause me? Unfortunately, she wouldn't listen to my advice and her legal advisor didn't help.

The words, 'She's gone' tore my life asunder. I had spent many years taking care of my mother with the last four slowly becoming more and more difficult for both of us. Mum was suffering physically and I could see her slowly fading away. It was devastating to watch as her body weakened, frustrating the still very clear mind. The last year was the worst as she became weaker and sicker eventually having a stroke and passing on to a better world.

What next?

After the stress and trauma of Mum's passing, I started thinking about what I would do. I had no plans as my whole life had been work, marriages, children then looking after parents. I focused on dreams of travel.

Then, more drama. The last surviving member of my family of origin took legal action on Mum's will. Being stunned is an understatement. We had lost our brother way back in 1980, a musician with great talent and passion for music, gone too early. Then our father in 2001 and our mother in 2010. I thought that perhaps being the last ones left would have drawn us closer, but no. Then, a bit more than a year into the legal action this brother suddenly died. This really threw me. Now there was no-one left from my family of origin, no-one who knew me as a child, no-one from my family of origin to love or even be angry at! I felt so alone and cheated.

Six months after Mum's passing I finally admitted to myself that I couldn't handle the deep grief and legal drama alone anymore. I took the offer of counselling from the hospice. It was the best thing I could have done as the counsellor started me on my long journey of healing.

Everyone needs to find their own way to deal with sadness in life. The grief of losing a loved one affects each of us in different ways. Each of us needs to find what helps us get through to a point where we can cope with life again. These ways could be all sorts of things; the support of friends and family, counselling, reading books or watching movies about others who found a path, to name just a few. My way became a combination of counselling, friends, and overseas travel.

The drama of legal action continued for two years. I almost lost my house. Just as that drama came to an end another family member tried to do the same.

I have a huge sense of injustice. I'm a reasonably nice person, most of the time, but I have a phrase that I borrowed from a personal development course leader 'Don't fuck in my space'. That means don't accuse me of things I haven't done and don't abuse me in any way, because then everything can turn very ugly. Too many people either hadn't listened, were unaware or thought they'd try it on anyway.

I wasn't handling all of this stress very well and I felt that there could easily be a breakdown brewing – serious decisions had to be made.

What was I to do?

Yes, I have two sons, but they each have their own lives. One was building several businesses and had a life partner with business ventures, busy creating their lives - exactly as it should be. The other had kicked off his shoes and was travelling somewhere in the wilds of Central America - when would I see him again? No idea! And that is as it should be too. Sometimes I wish I'd done the same – but then... I wouldn't have these two incredible sons and I wouldn't be who I am.

Then I took a long hard look at my life; no life partner, no family of origin left, no-one available to travel with outside Australia, a house that wasn't earning me any money. To all intents and purposes no future with much fun in it. Except on those odd occasions when I would get together with friends. Yes, I have amazing friends who will always be there for me and I love them dearly, I have my writing and connections with fellow poets and writers, but they all have lives, responsibilities and families of their own. It seemed that I was the only one with no good reason to stay in one place.

So many people get to this point in their lives, a vague future with little or no purpose, nothing to do except gardening and reading and a few other hobbies here and there. There is a time and place for that, but I wasn't ready for it yet. I was an emotional mess after many years of stress. Sitting around at home wasn't going to help.

So...

Once all the legal problems with family were over I re-assessed my situation. I could continue sitting around waiting for someone to be available for social time but, there were too many memories and too much sorrow, too much grief and way too much thinking time to do that. Not only was my entire family of origin gone to greener pastures but so were many dear friends. Life is short, life is unpredictable, and yet life should still be fun.

I became the Golden Oldie traveller.
I packed my bags.
I rented out my house.
I hugged my friends farewell.
I started writing a blog.
I took off on a life mission for 12 months to see the world and realign my body, mind and spirit.

I was travelling after dreaming of this all my life. Much later than I wished and for reasons I didn't like. Perhaps it would also have been nice to have a travelling partner. However, I was darned if I was not going to have my adventures just because there was no-one to share them with. Anyway, travelling with others can be a tricky business as I found out in some earlier, shorter travel overseas. Sometimes it is better to just go alone especially when needing to heal.

Off I went, initially with my two sons and future daughter-in-law to take my mother's ashes home to Dalmatia, then on my own, exploring the world.

Over a period of time I had recognised my interesting system for dealing with drama and stress. When emotions would rise to almost breaking point, I would somehow deal with them and settle down until the next one came along. Sometimes it was an ugly event other times a silent internal process.

Mostly this worked, even in the days of teenage depression when the black cloud would descend and envelope me. Only one friend knew about these times and would sit with me, saying nothing. Just being there on the school verandah.

No-one knew about the two suicide attempts, except my first husband. Foolishly in those days I was in that un-enlightened, fairy tale phase of thinking that external factors – at that time my now late ex-husband, could make me happy. When he revealed himself as an abusively jealous man I thought there was no way out except death. The resulting mockery from him didn't help. I had many lessons to learn about expectations but they were in my distant future.

Both times I was saved. Not by a person. I didn't know what it was but I started thinking about other forces being at work. I later called them my 'Angels' - I'd been kept alive, it wasn't my time. Why? I had no idea.

I started paying real attention to the inexplicable when my favourite brother, Victor, died at age 34 - why did he have to go? And what were all those strange happenings after his passing? I began reading books on the psychic, went to the Spiritualist church a few times and later, through my second husband, did some psychic classes with the late Lew Carrington-Russell. For three months after my brother's passing I was in a fog. I have no memory of how I went about daily life and how my one-year-old son survived, I guess I was on automatic pilot. It was only after a friend came to dinner one night and must have said something profound that I shook myself out of that state.

In 1988 I discovered NLP (Neuro-Linguistic Programming) and although that is a model of communication, through that intense experience and the people I met I learned a lot about myself and all sorts of healing modalities. A different journey began. I became a Reiki channel, dabbled in Holistic Pulsing and massage and eventually became a Life Coach. Bit by bit I found that which most resonated with me.

Fifteen years after my brother's passing, my second marriage was breaking down. I was standing at the kitchen sink my hands in the sudsy water when suddenly I was overwhelmed by a wave of sadness and wanting to talk to my brother. We had been quite close, in fact, I saw him almost as a replacement parent as our parents were working so hard trying to make a living as market gardeners. The sobs escaped and I fell apart. I thought I had finished with grieving 15 years earlier, but I realised then that grieving never really ends - a scab grows over and it doesn't take much of a scratch to make it bleed again. Ironically, the only person who was there and could hold me while I sobbed my heart out was my soon-to-be-second-ex-husband.

After that episode I soaked in even more 'personal development' courses and books. I eventually found 'The Secret' DVD, the Abraham books and then Mike Dooley.

All of this exploration stood me in very good stead when it came to sorting myself out after relationship crashes, deaths of dear friends and loved ones and every other stressful situation I encountered. I thought I had dealt with them but now, as I look back, I think that I had only partially done that. The tools I had were not enough to do a proper job, whatever a 'proper job' might be and so when the big crash came it was really big.

Never Prepared for Death

Funeral hustle and bustle over. Guests gone. Left to my own devices in my house where my mother had her stroke. The first of a long line of cathartic emotions struck.

Three weeks earlier I had brought Mum home from the hospital where she had landed after her cat bit her. Then internal bleeding started.

Doctors suspected it was caused by blood thinners. At her age and stage of frailty, the only thing to do was take her off the drugs and see whether the bleeding would stop. Her doctor took me aside to tell me that without the drugs there was a 50/50 chance of a stroke. Unfortunately, he didn't tell me what symptoms to look out for and I didn't know what questions to ask.

She pulled through, was placed in the rehabilitation ward and after a few weeks, sent home. We decided she would move into my place, as there was no way I could leave her in her own house now. We walked into the lounge, she looked through the window and saw my red roses blooming and all the trees. I saw her beautiful smile, the smile I hadn't seen for a long time because her Parkinson's was at the point doctors call the 'Parkinson's mask'.

'We should have done this a long time ago,' she said.

'Yes,' I thought, 'but you were talked out of it.'

I settled Mum in and she was happy. We agreed my son and I would paint and renovate her house and she would stay with me. The very next day we started the painting while Mum stayed at home and pottered around. I should have known there was something brewing when she insisted that she never ate rolled oats for breakfast. I began doubting myself so checked with Nick, yes, of course, she always made herself a porridge for breakfast! But I didn't know what symptoms to look for.

Two days later while painting, my phone rang, my son's voice telling me to get home. Mum had had a fall. A friend of hers had come knocking when Mum was asleep. Being in an unfamiliar house she went the wrong way and tumbled down a couple of steps into the sunroom. We picked her up, checked her over, settled her on the lounge and my son went back to painting while I stayed to keep an eye on Mum.

Some of Mum's thoughts and doubts became clear to me from one phrase she repeated when I would tuck her into bed at night. She would look at me and say 'I never thought you would take such good care of me.' To me that doubt was incredible - why would she think I wouldn't care for her? As I thought about it I remembered all the early adult arguments, typical mother and child individuation episodes, the raging argument we had before I stormed out and moved into my future mother-in-law's house. Do most parents have that doubt?

Two days later I was out buying paint when the phone rang - my son - Mum had another fall. I dashed home to find she had had a stroke not a fall. We had no idea when it happened as no one else was home at the time. My son found her when he had dropped by for lunch.

It was heart-breaking seeing my mother taken away on a stretcher, her frail little body all scrunched up. There are no words to describe my feelings and there was no time to succumb to them. I followed the ambulance. My wonderful son Nikolai turned up and we sat with her in Emergency. Eventually, she was moved into a room by herself. This was a catastrophic stroke. Although her entire left side was severely affected Mum started telling us one of Krylov's Russian fables I'd heard many times, about a dragonfly and an ant. This fable, written in rhyme, is based on Aesop's fable The Grasshopper and the Ant.

After repeating the story about 10 times in Russian, Mum suddenly switched to French and continued re-telling the fable. She hadn't spoken French since arriving in Australia sixty years earlier in 1950, except to teach me bits and pieces. If the situation wasn't so dire and sad it would have been funny.

After a few hours Mum was moved into a ward.

She would say some amazing things, like 'tell Nick to come here and help me walk. I can hear his voice and if I can put my arms around his neck I can walk'. There was no convincing her that Nick wasn't there. One day she said that she had something important to tell me. She had a serious look on her face. 'A doctor has made a mistake I have found a severed hand in my bed. Obviously', she said, 'a doctor has cut off someone's hand and hidden it in my bed. I have hidden it under the pillow'.

There was no point even trying to convince her otherwise. I knew what had happened. As a result of the stroke affecting her left side, her left hand was immobile while her right hand was constantly moving as if searching for something. At some point, when feeling around, she must have come across her cold, immobile, left hand and thought it was a severed hand.

The story continued one day when all the family was there. I had told them about Mum's 'severed hand' so they were all aware, however, she expanded a little this time and as we listened intently she suddenly said '...and it is such a good young hand, someone could still use it'! We all looked at each other and burst out laughing. How like Mum, here she was suffering from a massive stroke, yet still thinking about other people and doing the right thing - an amazing woman!

After a stroke, many things become impossible for the patient, one of them for Mum was swallowing. She hated the hospital food and hated the thickened water even more, but she wasn't allowed anything else because of choking on both proper food and liquid water. I wondered if baby food would work. I only bought three to test whether she would eat them. Mum really liked the fruit ones, it seemed to be refreshing as well as filling and Mum loved sweetness, so I bought a whole lot of them. Unfortunately, we never got through them all as she took a turn for the worse and was moved to the Hospice.

The doctor called me to her office to explain what was happening. There was nothing more they could do medically, from this time on it could only be palliative care. Mum's wishes for no resuscitation or life support were very clear - including extending her life in any way if there was no cure. Both legally and morally her wishes had to be adhered to.

I knew all of this, I tried so hard to be a big girl but there wasn't enough space in my eyes to hold the tears and the dam burst. It was impossible to control my emotions knowing this was definitely the beginning of the end. The doctor was understanding and as gentle as possible with me.

Stoicism kicked in. I'd learned how to deal with bad times from my mother. She modelled a way I have followed. How did she deal with many years in Nazi labour camps? How did she deal with bombs; the loss of her first pregnancy at 8 months; sick children; the life of a refugee; life-threatening situations at home? Strength of mind and body, that's how, so I followed suit not always in my best interests.

The problem was I wasn't my mother, so my created external strength covered a bowl of jelly on the inside. Perhaps she was the same but was very careful in never showing it.

After Mum's passing, I had to call on all the strength I had so I could believe I would get through. At the forefront of my mind, I kept the thought that my mother would be very disappointed if I fell in a heap. That wasn't our way.

Hospice

As well as the severed hand story Mum did and said some interesting things after her stroke. Hospice nurses told me that Mum was ordering coffee in French. One day she was talking to me about Easter and that it was time to colour the Easter eggs. Another day she asked me to sing Russian Christmas Carols. That was very hard. Singing was one of the many special things we did together. In childhood, I would join her in the tomato plantation or in the milking shed and we would sing. I stumbled, because without Mum singing I had no chance of doing a decent job of it, but I did start and told her that she had to join in. She did a bit in spoken words and even corrected me when I got stuck. The hardest thing was to even think of a carol to sing when my mind was taken up with watching my mother suffering and slowly dying.

Mum had stopped eating but one morning she really wanted coffee. Thank goodness for the invention of special sponges you can soak in a drink for the patient to suck on. She was so hungry for her coffee that morning. Mum loved her coffee. She came from Yugoslavia where Turkish coffee was an essential part of the culture and taught me very early how to both prepare and enjoy it. In the hospice there was no Turkish coffee but the vending machine produced a reasonable drop. Her face lit up with satisfaction as she relished the taste.

Clare Holland House hospice in Canberra is a beautiful space on the shores of Lake Burley Griffin. The very first time I walked in to visit a friend years before I could swear that the walls were painted with love, such is the positive energy.

Once Mum was moved to the hospice I spent most of my days there, well into the evening. My doctor had already put me on Carers' leave before the stroke so I was free to do whatever was necessary. Mum's friends would visit. I would leave and let them have their time together. Although all the staff and volunteers are amazing and care for their patients beautifully, I wanted to take some of the pressure off them by making sure I was there as much as possible especially at mealtimes.

Slowly, slowly Mum faded to a point where she could no longer speak but could communicate with us by nodding or slowly moving her head from side to side. I asked her if she wanted me to read poetry, that was a nod. Mine? That was a nod too. So for a few days, I spent a little time each day reading my poems. Without Mum's support, beginning in my childhood, I may never have continued writing.

I was asked to get her some smaller clothes that could be cut off when changing her, she had become so tiny and frail that the staff didn't dare move her arms and legs to remove clothing. While shopping for those I became fiercely obsessed in finding exactly the right clothes for her funeral, knowing they'd soon be needed. At least one item had to be green, her favourite colour.

The day came when the doctor told me that she could pass at any time in the next 24 hours. My brother had been over from Perth to see her, her grandsons had been to see her, all her friends had been and time for her to leave was drawing near.

Mum had a very close friend, Ewa. She used to call Ewa her 'other daughter' but I think they were more like sisters, not in age but in their closeness. I am sure Mum shared many more secrets with Ewa than she did with me. Although Mum talked about many experiences in life she didn't open up too much about her inner feelings to her children. I think that was her way of protecting us. She had an aura of strength. I only saw her crying twice in my childhood, but I knew there were many occasions I didn't see. This is why I am sure she felt more at ease talking to a sisterly friend than a daughter. However, by the time she reached her 80s I had witnessed many more tears. We had a routine that after work I would drop in to check on her, massage her legs and cook dinner. It would break my heart to see her crying so many times. The answer to my question was always the name of one family member or another who had just been on the phone.

It is strange to realise the things I have forgotten of that awful period. Stress is a strange being. Ewa reminded me recently about my floral efforts. In amongst the stories of her childhood Mum had told me about her birthdays at school when her classmates would cover her dormitory bed in lilac blossoms for her birthday. I had always wanted to recreate that for her but as her birthday is the 5th of May, it is Autumn in Australia and no lilacs. As she was preparing to leave the Earth in October 2010 it struck me that it was lilac time. The day before she passed I stripped Mum's bushes of all blooms, raided my friend Magda's lilacs and brought them all into the room. To quote our friend Ewa in her recent email which reminded me of the event 'The thick bouquets filled out the whole room and the sweet perfume of the flowers could be easily detected on the other side of the door. The nurses commented on the beautiful perfume and how uplifting a gesture it was.' Without Ewa's reminder, those flowers would have remained forgotten.

Ewa stayed with me and we spent the last 24 hours with Mum. We were too scared to go to sleep that night, even though the nurses had brought in a cot and suggested we take turns, we couldn't. We kept an all-night vigil by her side. When my mother did take her last breath on the following afternoon it was within a cloud of lilac perfume and to the sounds of her favourite opera singer, Maria Callas. We had been softly playing Mum's favourite music all day. Mum loved the opera. She had a beautiful contralto voice. In school, she was not only in the church choir but also sang arias from Tchaikowsky's Queen of Spades.

Now, left to my own devices. Everything was over. Five years of being a hands-on carer always on alert for emergency phone calls, over. Guilt and tears set in. Guilt? Over and over the thought of Mum being on her own when she had the stroke. Why didn't I insist on the neurologist seeing her earlier than the appointment he had booked for many weeks after her release from hospital? Why didn't I recognise the signs while she was still in the rehab ward, telling me some very strange stories of what went on that I just took to be dreams? Could they have been signs of her brain function being affected? On it went. The sound reel just wouldn't stop. I slept on the lounge with the TV on for 3 months because I couldn't face the silence of my bedroom, I needed something to stop the guilt reel. Mum wasn't there to advise me.

Then suddenly anger from toxic relationships, the resulting stress of emotional abusers, sadness of being on my own, grief for my mother and yet unaddressed bullying from my last job all crashed in on me. I obviously still had much to address.

Within a couple of weeks my brother, the last surviving member of my family of origin, received a copy of Mum's will and instead of talking to me immediately took legal action. Another horror stretch began. Overnight a streak of grey appeared in my blonde hair. No-one knew what was going on inside me and the damage being caused. A trait I picked up from Mum; don't whinge, whine or complain while everything is hitting the fan, deal with it, then you can talk about it later as a 'fait accompli' if you want to. I was still on sick leave. My doctor looked at me when I went back to her after the funeral and said, 'you have no idea how stressed you are or will be, you're not going back to work'. Sick leave ran out just as I turned 60 and I chose to retire, I just couldn't face going back to a job where I'd been bullied for 12 months. This caused all sorts of problems of course as that was the end of my pay packet. I had two mortgages.

My solicitor advised I apply to the bank to stay one of my mortgage repayments until my brother's legal action was completed.

I stood at the bank counter, tears pouring down my face. Feeling humiliated, angry, hurt and a total failure through no fault of my own. I had never cried in public, crying was done in my own private space, yet here I was unable to control myself amongst total strangers. The unfeeling voice on the other end of the phone sounded so far away as it told me that all my cards would be cancelled while my mortgage payments were on hold. The teller looked at me with understanding but could do nothing. I passed the receiver back and have no recollection what happened between that moment and somehow driving home.

I had been through many dramas in my life starting from birth and managed to deal with them and move on. A traumatic birth, which of course I don't remember but my mother told me about. How she survived is beyond me. Physical injuries from a jealous brother; emotional injuries from seeing the violent episodes from my father; teenage depression; two suicide attempts; two failed marriages, (the first of which ended in death threats from my husband, the other when I discovered that the marriage was not based on honesty); an eight-year toxic relationship; and having all but one member of my family of origin dead by the time I turned 60 - and he was gone in the following year.

How was I going to get over this latest humiliation?

Six months later the bank told me that my time was up, I had to start paying again or lose my house - could life get any more stressful?

The next 12 months are a blur. Somehow I got up every day, I did things, saw friends, travelled, went to weddings and funerals. Photos I took are my memory of those events. Then I received a phone call from Sydney in January 2012. It was my close school friend, Helen, ringing fifteen months after Mum's death.

'I can hear from your voice you haven't heard' she said.
'Heard what'? I was thinking that something had happened in her family.

'I hope you are sitting down' I sat down, just in case.
'Alex just died'.

I was stunned. Alex, my brother, my last surviving family member, was dead? I didn't even know he was ill! Nobody told me. If it hadn't been for Helen and her husband Ray, who were also very close friends with my brother, I wouldn't have known of his death. They also hadn't been told of his illness. It was a shock for all of us

CHAPTER 1

Tripping Around in Australia

The legal action was over, I could breathe, I hadn't lost my house. A friend lent me the money for airfare and accommodation so my son and I managed to attend my brother's funeral.

Then the second wave of attacks started, even more personal and even more vicious, from the same source that had hurt my mother many times over the years and whom she had forgiven many times against all advice. I knew I had to do some serious thinking and make some important decisions. My nature was to put up with abuse and maltreatment for as long as I possibly could, giving the other person every chance to stop their behaviour and resolve our challenges. I did this in all three long term relationships, with some friends and with all the challenging members of my family. However, my very strong sense of injustice eventually rises when the final straw is reached and my shutters come down.

This way of protecting myself worked for most of the unpleasant events in my life but this time it was only a partial fix. The effect of the new attack was so deep I had to do something else. I needed to not only distance myself from those family members, but I had to also find something that would help me regain my equilibrium. My sense of guilt about my mother's stroke was overpowering and no amount of logic would shift it. These new attacks were not helping my already low self-esteem and confidence.

My 60th birthday was four months after Mum's passing. I was determined to have a party - my mother would have wanted it. She was the one, after all, who started me off on fantastic birthday parties at age 13. My 60th arrived, the backyard was full of people and we all had a great time. I became more than a little alcohol affected. For a reason I don't remember, I gave my bedroom to my visiting son and slept in the room Mum had occupied for a few weeks before her stroke. I awoke the next morning in a massive panic attack. I tried to go back to sleep but it kept coming in waves every time I closed my eyes. I had never had a panic attack before. The only thought I had was fear of death. It was awful, I got out of bed and went outside.

A few months later I realised I couldn't handle everything on my own. I had spent several years juggling work, caring for Mum and dealing with the last relationship. Fortunately, that relationship ended before Mum became really ill but there was no time to deal with the fallout before needing to pay more attention to my mother and to continue working.

The immediate legal action after Mum's funeral meant that I didn't have time to grieve for my mother properly and so six months later I finally gave in and took advantage of the offer of counselling from the Hospice. The counsellor was a gem, she truly understood what I was going through and helped me get a little balance back so I could continue dealing with unfolding events.

I needed to be gone.
I needed to go to places I had never been before.
I needed to find myself.

So in 2012, almost 2 years after Mum's passing, the main legal actions were finally over, I decided the only way I could sort myself out was with travel, to get away from all the negativity and leave Australian shores. I decided 12 months should do it but before leaving I would need to prepare.

I fully expected people overseas to ask questions about the Outback and I'd feel quite foolish having to admit I'd never been there. Off I went. My close friend Shirlee was living 'Back o' Bourke' at the time so a week with her sounded like a good idea. Needless to say, it wasn't without some challenges.

The trip seemed straight forward enough. Easy compared to finding my way around Bangkok earlier in the year when a friend and I went there for dental work. But, as I learned a long time ago 'always expect the unexpected'. The train was held up on the outskirts of Sydney for an hour, so instead of taking us all the way to Dubbo to change to a coach for Bourke, we were transferred to a coach at Orange, taken to Dubbo, transferred to another coach which should have reached Bourke at 7pm. The last coach broke down several times and we arrived at 9pm, well after dark. The official bus stop was at the disused railway station. I was the only one who didn't have anyone picking me up. The coach driver refused to take me closer to my hotel and I had no idea where the hotel was. I was left alone in the dark at the disused station. Those who know the area also know it is not a good idea to be out on your own after dark. So here I was, an obvious middle-aged tourist with touristy luggage having to walk through one of the most dangerous areas of the town on my own to an unknown destination.

Luckily, over the years of various courses and reading, I had developed the habit of talking to my Universe. I fully expected I would be cared for and be safe no matter where I was. This had already been proven many times including several times on the road when dangerous situations arose. Once, a car drove straight through a red light at high speed and my uncharacteristic delay of a couple of seconds when the light turned green meant a difference of inches between safety and certain death. My Angels are with me and they certainly were that night after a Holistic Pulsing class.

So, I set off in the dark in Bourke knowing I'd be looked after but staying vigilant anyway. After being followed for a short time by a young undesirable fellow, I came across the police station and asked for directions. The policeman's eyes opened wide as he asked, 'Are you on your own? And you are walking?' The police car was out on a job so I had the option of waiting around for them to return and give me a lift or follow the directions to the hotel. It wasn't too much further and most of the way was along the well-lit main street, so I walked. I was rather puffed and tired by the time I got there, my legs were starting to shake as I realised the risk I had been forced to take. I opened the door into the bar and as my foot caught on the carpet, I fell face-first into the room. Oh dear, such embarrassment! Suddenly there was a man beside me saying, 'Hello, are you Helene?' I turned toward him and grinned, he helped me up. The guys at the bar couldn't believe where I had walked from to get there. My adventure and entry into the bar were the main topics of conversation that night.

The next morning Shirlee arrived and we started my holiday by watching the local schools' soccer tournament and a barbecue. My week with Shirlee driving me to all sorts of places was great medicine. I loved the Outback and I began to understand a little about the red centre of my country. A poem about my visit probably describes it best.

Farewell Outback

Farewell Outback of open spaces
Of coolabah, mulga, and broom,
Farewell to dusty red-earth traces
My leaving came too soon.

They say there's not a lot to see,
They say there's nothing there,
I'll now dispute when they say to me
'You'll get bored, the place is bare',

For I've seen life at variance
To what you see in towns,
I'll let you know the difference
Of places of renown,

I've seen opal mining,
Dugouts underground,
Had a go at an excavator
That didn't make a sound,

I've been to Cameron Corner
Straddled three Aussie states,
I travelled roads that bumped and shook
I've opened station gates,

Paddy melon bowling
On roadside bulldust red,
Emus, 'roos, goats and sheep
With rains were then well fed.

We caught a shingle back to feel
It's dinosaur rough skin
And climbed the rocks at Tibooburra
To prove where I had been,

We drank and ate at every pub
That we found on our way,
We talked and laughed and swore a bit
With folks we met each day,

I cruised upon the Darling,
I crossed the great Paroo,
I walked upon the little bridge
Across the Warrego,

So out in Lawson country
I saw things as they are,
Remote and dry and hardened,
The land quite often bare,

So every city person
Who thinks they have it tough
Should come out to the Outback
To learn what's really rough,

See how men and women
Work with flood and drought
Manoeuvre roads of dust and rock
Yet still, they have not a doubt

That where they really love to be
Is Outback on the land
Where those who know this hardened life
Will lend a helping hand.

Helene Jermolajew
Laughter, Tears and Coffee – Balboa Press 2017

Renovations

Meanwhile, I had also decided that it would be a good idea to renovate the kitchen and living area of my house. Luckily my younger son Nikolai is a very competent building tradesman so he agreed to manage the project. I am so grateful he did, as it became a massive drama. Suppliers were getting everything wrong. The wrong kitchen ordered then the right one had wrong measurements and pieces were missing. This began dragging on. My kitchen was demolished with the expectation that the new one would be in place in a few weeks. Oh no! I ended up without a kitchen for over 6 months. Ewa had been staying with me but two people in one house without a kitchen and cooking on the barbecue just wasn't working. Eventually a few days after Christmas the installation was complete, but there was more work to be done.

I decided to leave the tradesmen to it and went off on more short trips with my friend Magda. First a few days in Parkes at the exhilarating Elvis Festival in January. I coined a new word after that weekend - I was 'youthened'. A few days of pure fun, singing and dancing in the streets, with thousands of other people all doing the same was very cleansing. Then a week in Tasmania, with Magda again, exploring a state I had never visited before. Tasmania is a stunning place. Magda is a fantastic travel companion, so easy going, nothing is a problem and always eager to explore.

I came back to the challenges of the renovation. I needed to start getting organised for my 12 months away and the house had to be ready for tenants.

In amongst the chaos I managed to take some meditation and thinking time. I thought about the purpose of my trip. There were several. Firstly, as a family, to take Mum's ashes home to her birthplace. Secondly, I promised myself that by the time I returned in 12 months I would have found something to reconnect my body, mind and spirit and arrive healed. Thirdly, to have fun. I asked all my angels and my entire Universe to keep me safe and help me find what I needed. I knew that on the 30th of April 2013, when I stepped into the uncertainty of the next 12 months, all would be well.

Eventually, the night before my son and I were to fly out, we completed the finishing touches at 3am! We had to be at Canberra airport at 6am.

CHAPTER 2

My Gap Year is Launched

3 0ᵗʰ April 2013. My journey began. We waited to be called on board at Sydney airport. We were tired. Kirra had flown in from another part of the country. Nick was in charge of the scattering tube containing my mother's ashes. Ginski would join us in London.

I wanted my sons with me on this first leg. They were very close to their 'Babi' having spent a lot of their childhoods with her and 'Deda', their grandfather, my Dad. Mum adored her grandsons and spent a lot of time telling stories, teaching them Russian, singing, walking them to school. I didn't have grandparents as a child, sadly both Mum and Dad were orphaned very early in life and all extended family were either dead or lost when my parents migrated to Australia as refugees.

My sons didn't talk much about their experience of their beloved 'Babi' passing. They spoke beautifully at her funeral but the rest of the time it was all practicalities. I wanted to provide them with an opportunity to do something meaningful for themselves in connection to their grandmother.

In 2011, before a year had passed since Mum's funeral, the decision to take Mum's ashes back to her birthplace was made with my sons. I had no idea the legal actions would continue for as long as they did nor what else had to happen before we could fulfil this last act.

My mum was born in Split, Dalmatia in 1920. In those days Dalmatia (the Adriatic coast of Croatia) was part of the Kingdom of Serbs, Croats and Slovenes, later it became Yugoslavia and much later everything changed again. I had grown up with parents, and many of their friends, being known as Yugoslavs. However, my father was born in Russia and although Mum was born in Dalmatia her mother was Russian and father Serbian. Both spent their youth in Yugoslavia and part of their hearts were still there.

When I talked with Mum about her wishes, she said she wanted to be cremated. This was totally against our church's religious beliefs but she didn't care.

'So, Mum, why do you want to be cremated?' I asked.

'Two reasons; 1) it will be too expensive to dig up your father's grave to put me in and 2) I DON'T want to lie on top of your father for the rest of eternity!' I wasn't sure whether to be shocked or to laugh as Mum was rather 'proper' with perfect manners. However, I understood her wish.

'OK, so what should I do with your ashes?'
'Throw me to the sharks'. Mum loved the sea and so this request wasn't out of character.

'Where shall I throw you?'

'Wherever you like', was her only reply.

My first idea was to take her ashes to a village just north of Split, Bakarac on the Adriatic coast. She had fond memories of school holidays there. While researching, it looked like there was now an oil refinery across the bay! Perhaps the area was no longer the pristine piece of coast my mother had described.

After that discovery, I had an amazing dream. My mother came to me. I remember the details clearly. She and I were walking along a road, crossing a bridge. She was dressed in a white 1950s style frock with a wide white belt and looked like she did when I was young although she never wore white. A white car was following us. I had no idea what was under the bridge. As we reached the other side we suddenly appeared inside a room, the walls covered with cream and green tiles, it seemed to be part of a college. Through the open small window, high up the wall, I could hear a choir singing. I asked Mum if that was our church choir and her answer was 'actually it's the Ukrainians'. I turned away and when I looked back Mum had vanished, replaced by an old priest with a long white beard leaning on the most beautiful 4 legged wooden walking stick. The stick seemed to be made from rosewood. He took my hand and placed it on the handle of the walking stick. The texture of the wood reminded me of the night I fell down the wooden staircase of my ex-partner's flat. That night I woke up halfway down and the first strange thought was 'gee, the wood of these stairs is smooth!' The priest blessed me and vanished. I knew then that Mum had led me to a blessing and all would be well, she was also showing me where to take her ashes. The location wasn't as clear as the blessing so I needed the wonders of the internet again.

Using the very few clues from my dream I searched up and down the coast of Dalmatia for suitable places. I came across a village called Omis 25kms south of Split. It looked like it had potential. The Cetina River flows from the mountains for 100kms through forested slopes and craggy cliffs to the Adriatic Sea.

As it happened, just as I found this village on the map Ginski communicated that he was in Split. Coincidence? I don't think so. As he is a wonderful, amenable young man I asked him to hop on his scooter and take a trip to Omis and let me know if he thought it a suitable place for his Grandmother's ashes. He did.

We messaged after his little side trip and he started describing the place 'It's lovely Mum, as you drive down the road and round the corner you cross the bridge.......' my jaw must have hit the ground at that point – 'as you cross the bridge....' Well! Thank you Mum, and thank you son, we found a place! It took close on two more years to get there with the ashes but we made it.

Our flight had been called and we wandered off. On the way to the gate, Nick suddenly dashed back to our seats, we had left the ashes there. That was the first time we nearly lost Mum.

Thankfully our flight to London was uneventful, spent dozing and watching movies. I wished I hadn't put on so much weight after Mum's death - the left arm of my aisle seat was biting into my hip. The weight was one of many things needing attention.

We arrived in Heathrow in the morning, still tired, found coffee, and then the coach to take us to Gatwick where we picked up the hire car. We were too early to check into the hotel so we searched for food in the lovely village of Horley.

Finally, we checked in, Nick and Kirra had to go into London for business and I stayed to wait for Ginski to arrive from Central America. Once he was there it was onto the train to meet the others. I had never been to London, my three companions had. We met on the bridge near Big Ben, walked all the way to Leicester Square via all those familiar places from the traditional Monopoly board, had a beer at an Irish pub and then walked all the way back because that's where the car was! My little 62-year old legs and back struggled but I enjoyed seeing all those famous places.

A night's sleep in the charming Gatwick Belmont and the next day we were off on our mission.

Super excited by London

My Mother's Birthplace

There I was with my family in my mother's birth city, Split. My boys had been there before so it wasn't new to them. I expected to be much more emotional. Was it because I wasn't alone and being with my sons always meant we had a lot of fun? After their first visit, Nick and Ginski created a collage of photos for their beloved Babi which touched her deeply. I wondered how she would have felt about all of us being there at the same time. Was she watching over us?

We arrived in Split on the airport bus and not knowing where our rooms were, we thought we'd take a cab. The driver's response was, 'no, it close, Radunica closed to cars'. So with map in hand and two sons to orientate us we set off on foot. OK, so it was closer than any cabbie would be prepared to drive but a bit of a hike for someone like me - then there was the alley and steps. We managed and I made it.

We had two apartments, one had two rooms, the other had one room with two single beds. Each had its own bathroom and entrance. I'm not sure how it would work if unrelated people were staying in the rooms as the hot water governor is in the two-roomed apartment as is the modem. However, it was lovely and spacious.

Split is a fascinating place. Part of the old town is built within the crumbled walls of Diocletian's Palace and in some cases parts of the palace form parts of apartments. Diocletian was a Dalmatian Roman Emperor, who only ruled for a short period, then abdicated and spent the rest of his life in his Dalmatian summer palace. I am always in awe when I walk on the ground where ancients walked. In Split that was doubled knowing that both my parents also walked here. Sadly, there was no way of finding the old orphanage where my father had spent a short time or where his brother might be buried after being killed in a fight in the same orphanage. No way of finding where my mother's family lived either. We have no records and trying to find anything would take much longer than the time we had.

I had heard about an international flower show held in the substructures of the Palace and wanted to find it. Easier said than done. My parents loved all flowers and always had pretty gardens, which they tended with great care, so I thought that experiencing this flower show in my mother's birth town just a couple of days before her birthday would be a wonderful experience. The first challenge was finding the entrance to the substructures. The palace was built in a rectangle and has four gates - Silver, Bronze, Gold and Iron. The southern gate facing the water is the Bronze and the entrance to the substructures, but it wasn't very obvious. We finally discovered that the flower show had been cancelled!

I was the most excited. It's interesting travelling with 20 and 30 somethings. My older son made a statement much later in our travels that floored me, 'We don't do museums Mum, everything is on the net'. To his credit, he went with me to every museum while we were travelling together.

After exploring with amazement the way the substructures were built I wandered through the cathedral while the kids lounged like lizards waiting for me.

We wended our way on to the Golden gate, where a statue of Grgur Ninski (Gregory of Nin) is located. It is said that if you rub his big toe your wishes come true – well what did we find? Good old Grgur was all boarded up for renovations. Did that mean some of my wishes wouldn't happen now? Of course not! Superstition is not my game.

It struck me that I had no idea about this Bishop and his connection to my mother's birthplace when I named my firstborn Grigori, his christened Russian name – funny little fine threads appear in life.

There were basic cooking facilities in the apartment but we didn't bother, the spectacular green markets were close by and foraging for food was an adventure. Grapes were the size of plums, bright red tomatoes and strawberries winked at us. The local cooked food was wonderful and my sons discovered burek. I was shocked to realise that Mum and I had never introduced my boys to this taste sensation.

I love being around my boys, they are so much fun. They were always comedians and there was a time we couldn't have dinner around the table as Nick, the younger, was a clown and Ginski, the older, his straight man. I used to be in gales of laughter, to the point that I couldn't eat. I so wish I'd thought of recording their shenanigans. Here we were in Split, their Grandmother's birthplace and one stopping place of their Russian-born Grandfather, evacuated from the 1917 revolution by the Red Cross. My boys were playing cards, laughter rang within the stone walls of the apartment courtyard and we were getting through a lot of local beer. Unfortunately, their card games are not ones I can keep up with, but watching them my mind flew back to when I was younger and Mum, Dad, my brothers and I would play cards as a family. Good memories.

The next day was Ginski's birthday. His birthday and my mother's birthday were only two days apart and whenever we could we held a combined celebration. Mum would always come up with something surprising for her oldest grandson. She had saved his very first tiny school uniform shorts and given them to him on his 21st birthday! That cracked us up completely.

So what to do on his birthday in Split? We had Mum's ashes and I was sure she was looking over us but oh, how I missed her presence. We discussed the possibilities and decided to catch a ferry over to the island of Hvar to celebrate. Both boys had been there some years earlier and loved the island. It was still low season so the partying hadn't started, and that meant very good attention in the restaurant we chose for lunch. The local food was delicious. We had the best stew-thing with prunes and were plied with samples of shots and cocktails. Low season is sometimes much better in tourist destinations. Ginski and I found gorgeous little stone nooks, alleys and steps for photos while Nick and Kirra did their own exploring. The island was once part of the Venetian trade route; you can feel the antiquity. I loved having my professional cameraman son with me, he understands the yearning for that great shot. A beautiful island and well worth a visit.

Omis

Two days later it would have been my mother's 93rd birthday. I had booked an apartment in Omis, the plan was to decide what to do with Mum's ashes when we arrived. We took the bus from Split to the little seaside village. We were met by the woman who owned the apartment and a friend of hers. Initially, I couldn't understand why, knowing there were four of us, she only had space for two and had to make two trips and why she insisted that the boys were second. I found out later.

The lady took my daughter-in-law and me inside then returned for my sons. The boys had strange looks on their faces when they arrived. 'You wouldn't believe it, she was offering us young girls' they said. I was aghast. I hadn't liked the apartment's energy from the minute I'd walked in, this revelation made it so much worse.

Decisions had to be made. Firstly, where to take the ashes. Originally I wanted to spread them in the waters of the Adriatic in response to Mum's 'throw me to the sharks' comment. We wondered if it would be better instead to spread them in the river leading into the Adriatic. From the bus window as we crossed the bridge we had noticed signs for boats for hire. Nick and I walked through the pretty little village to explore the possibilities. We found a place and organised a boat and captain.

Our plan was to go up the river checking for suitable places for the ashes then stop on our way back in whichever was the prettiest spot.

The river was stunning. It carved through high grey cliffs topped with stone buildings here and there. Some were old monasteries, some had been pirate hiding places and others were used in WWII by both the Germans and Italians. We sailed on, the river an emerald green reflecting the trees growing wherever they could find a foothold amongst the rocky crags. Past reeds and snags, little coves with a boat drawn up or a sculpture on the bank. Finally, we couldn't go any further for ahead was white water. In this spot was a restaurant; a resting place for hikers, white water rafters and tourists. I think our captain was hoping for a nice relaxing time with some mates and a drink but we decided not to stay, we didn't have time. He tried to hide his disappointment.

On the way back we were wondering how to explain to our captain what we were doing. After all who knows what peoples' attitudes are towards cremation and spreading of ashes. Nick had some Serbian he'd learnt from his mates and a bit from my dad. As that language is so close to Croatian we chose him to talk to the captain. We discovered that our Captain was originally Italian and also spoke some German and Russian, so between all our languages we managed to get him to stop the boat at our chosen spot.

We took turns in pouring some of Mum's ashes into the gently rippling river. Mum loved rivers, even though she had almost drowned twice in rivers as a child. She loved the sea and the ocean, she loved nature and all creatures great and small.

We had chosen the perfect spot. Low bushes clutched desperately to the grey rocky cliffs, a meadow of reeds along the water's edge framed a low forest of trees. So many shades of green, my mother's favourite colour. Amongst the lighter greenery a dark green, stately pencil pine pointed to the sky and marked the spot. The scene, reflected in the water of the river, was one Mum would have loved. After all, she did lead me there in a dream didn't she?

On the Cetina river a pretty spot for some of Mum's ashes.

Before setting off up the river we had discovered that the ferry I wanted to catch the next evening, to Ancona, wasn't scheduled. We had two choices, leave that day or stay an extra night and be late for my booking in Bari. It wasn't a difficult decision as none of us liked the energy of the apartment, even though I loved the village itself and the accommodation was fully paid for. We chose to leave after our river trip and catch the ferry that evening.

After a short rest, we walked to the bus stop. In no time at all, we were back at the harbour waving goodbye to the beautiful city of Split as the lights of the town twinkled in the water. We and the rest of Mum were on the next leg of our journey.

Family on board the overnight ferry from Split to Italy

Bari

It's a long train trip from Ancona in northern Italy to Bari in the south. The boys were still playing cards. Not much was said about our experience of leaving part of Mum behind in Omis. We still had half of her with us in the scattering tube decorated with a sunset over the sea.

Arriving in Bari one night early caused a bit of chaos. The bill ended up higher than anticipated but that's all part of travel and 'expecting the unexpected'.

I had been in Bari briefly in 2006 on my whirlwind European trip and discovered that St Nicholas, the saint I named my younger son after, was buried there. I didn't have time to find the church then so this trip was a good opportunity.

I had started on my path of spiritual exploration in 1980 after my beloved brother died and I had many strange and interesting experiences. I was pointed in various directions, to numerous courses and books leading me to where I am now. The Law of Attraction, thanks to 'The Secret' and the Abraham books, 'Thoughts becoming things' thanks to Mike Dooley and his Notes from the Universe and so many other books, authors and courses that opened a whole new world for me. Serendipity is no stranger.

I'm not religious and prefer the word 'spiritual' for my belief system, although these days this word seems to be both overused, misused and, like the word 'love,' misunderstood. But I haven't found a suitable alternative yet. I firmly believe in maintaining cultural ties to our forebears. It's not easy to understand others or yourself without understanding the culture and the roots from which we come. Often those ties include some parts of religion. They also include language, music, food, drink and every other aspect of life. I was born in Australia but christened into the Russian Orthodox church, I was brought up on three languages Russian, Yugoslav and English and surrounded by Italian, Greek, German and Ukrainian. I went to the Church of England Sunday school for a little while and learned the Lord's Prayer in English. At the same time, my mother taught me the Lord's Prayer in Russian.

I didn't know too much about our religion until I went to high school and discovered that priests and ministers of all Christian denominations came to the school to teach scripture. I became fascinated by the Russian priest's lessons, topped the class and won a prize, but this didn't make me religious, it made me more educated. My mother taught me to question everything before making choices. Apart from my christening, I didn't step inside one of our churches until I was 16. There were many reasons for that, distance was one but mainly Dad wouldn't allow it, one of the many challenges and dramas created by my father's morbid paranoia.

To maintain our culture I chose to name my sons after Russian saints and christen them into the Orthodox church. Those saints are not exclusively Orthodox, most overlap other religions particularly the Catholic and so here we were about to experience an Italian Catholic festival of a saint claimed by so many and after whom both my son and my maternal grandfather were named. If only we could all recognise how alike we all really are.

Before leaving Australia, I discovered we could be in Bari during the annual festival of St Nicholas the patron saint of Russia and all children. There are many historical reports about this saint. The relevant piece here is the story about stealing him from his grave in Myrna. It is said that a group of sailors from Bari sailed to Turkey and stole part of St Nicholas's skeleton and brought the bones to Bari. Every year there is a three-day festival commemorating that event which took place on May 9, 1087.

We were there on the first day of the festival. Bari was decorated like a fairyland. The top of the city wall, now a road, was filled with myriad stalls and street entertainers. The festival starts in the morning with priests going out in a boat with a huge icon of St Nicholas, spending some time at sea. The painting returns in the evening and a Mass is held by the water at 6pm. Afterwards, the painting is paraded through the town on a boat-shaped float accompanied by people in 11th-century costumes. At midnight the painting reaches the church of St Nicholas where, with much celebration in period costumes, the story of St Nicholas ends and the painting is taken into the church.

I am glad that we, as a family, managed to have this experience. We visited the crypt of the church of St Nicholas where the remains are entombed. The silence was palpable. The space glistened in the candlelight. We sat for a while with our private thoughts.

Our time in Bari was over, the best ice cream ever was devoured, arguments with the hotel owner resolved and we were on the train heading towards our next adventure on the other side of Italy.

Naples

We arrived at Naples central station, took our luggage, and were walking to the exit when Ginski said 'who's got Babi?' Oh no! Mum was still on the train! Luckily Nick had become quite the runner. He took off to our carriage and returned valiantly holding Babi. That was the second time we almost lost her. Mum was having quite an adventure.

I'd been in Naples for a few days in 2006 and wasn't very impressed. All the negative stories I'd heard were true. It didn't help that it was during the garbage strike, but I had always loved their music. The beautiful lilting sound that is unmistakably Neapolitan. Unfortunately, neither the first time nor the second did I hear any of that beautiful music. In fact, in my travels, I noticed there wasn't much music in the streets of Europe at all. However, if you want to see Pompeii, Herculaneum or Capri it's easier to stay in Naples.

My choice of hostel was a good one, with a kitchen, of course. My sons disentangled the Italian supermarket vegetable shopping system. Older son and I had a vegetable cook-off – he won - I liked his mix much better than mine. Thank goodness I'd taught him to cook. Younger son didn't need many lessons from me, he was a natural from a very young age starting by raiding my pantry and making 'potions' for killing flies and ants. My mother noticed his skills and interest so she enrolled him in children's cooking classes. Both my sons have ended up good cooks, able to care for themselves and to eat healthily.

I knew it would be a struggle to make this part of the trip as much fun as possible. Not one of us was keen on Naples. It didn't help that Nick came face to face with the infamous type of person in this city, the pickpocket. Nick had his hands full with bags and backpacks when we boarded the bus to the ferry terminal from Corso Giuseppe Garibaldi. There was a lot of jostling with a fellow, 'Gee, after all that, he didn't even stay on board!!' Ginski laughed. 'Check your pockets.' When Nick did he found his phone was gone. Luckily that was all as he also had his camera and wallet in his pockets. Although we weren't keen on Naples, I knew what was ahead - Capri!

But first...Pompeii and Herculaneum.

The train to Pompeii was most unpleasant, old, unkempt and covered with graffiti. It looked and felt awful! However, it was the best and cheapest way to get to Pompeii. On the way back, given the condition of the train, the boys decided they could use the overhead bars as gym equipment, as we suspected nobody cared.

Pompeii was first destroyed by an earthquake. Just as they were rebuilding, Vesuvius erupted, making the destruction complete. It was interesting to see what has been excavated and how the people would have lived in the town and gone about their daily lives. Homes, markets, pubs, toilets, produce storage all excavated and, luckily, labelled.

Herculaneum was somewhat different, smaller and further away from the main impact, it had a lot more detail preserved. I preferred Herculaneum. There were almost whole buildings in places and even some of the wall decoration and floor mosaics still visible. There is much more of Herculaneum but part of Naples is standing on top of it, so excavation is impossible. Perhaps because so much survived I felt as if I were inside peoples' homes and this place felt more alive. My imagination was captured.

Capri

Excitement reigned as the day for Capri and the Blue Grotto arrived. We only had a day so my fingers were crossed for calm weather and low tide. As we boarded the ferry I remembered Mum's story of leaving for Australia from the Port of Naples. Twelve hundred and ninety-two refugees, four of whom were my parents and brothers, boarded the American ship General Stewart bound for a country they knew nothing about. How strange that must have been. The island that we would soon experience was only seen by my mother as their ship sailed past, she watched until it became a tiny speck.

We arrived at Capri, hired a boat and headed off around the island. Ginski had some experience driving boats in the Caribbean so he took the wheel. I was seeing one of my favourite destinations from a totally different angle. From the land, you can't see the craggy cliffs, the statue of the welcoming waving boy perched on a rock or the goats tiptoeing on the Jurassic limestone. The Faraglioni Rocks I had seen at sunrise from my hotel balcony in 2006 were right there as we sailed past. The only way to see the green grotto is also by boat. It has a charm and beauty of its own and the water is definitely a stunning green.

We returned to the point where you anchor your own boat and transfer to a small wooden rowboat which is manoeuvred by a rower through the small entrance into the Blue Grotto. It appears pitch dark, I was facing inwards and wondered when the blue would start, Ginski was facing outward and I heard him say 'turn around Mum'. I was stunned! The exquisite blue of the water was indescribable! I had dreamed of this moment since the age of 18 when I was a guest at an Italian wedding anniversary at the Grotta Capri in Sydney. The inside of that restaurant was built to resemble the Blue grotto and here I was, in the real thing!

We had circumnavigated Capri, fulfilled a dream and it was time to return the boat, take a quick trip up the hill to Anacapri on a cute little bus and then back to Naples. From Anacapri you can take a chairlift to the mountain. I knew my fear of heights would never allow me to do that but my three companions went off. I stayed on terra firma and enjoyed re-visiting the shops in the village. On seeing the photos I was relieved I had listened to my intuition. The chairlift is a series of single chairs, I would never have coped hanging in mid-air on my own.

Nick and Kirra were flying home the next day so they relocated to a hotel for a good night's sleep. We said our sad goodbyes over dinner and Ginski and I were left to our own devices.

Our next stop was Serbia. After much research, I discovered that the cheapest option was an extra night in Naples then a flight via Istanbul to Belgrade.

I've always found the best way to get around and see a city is the Hop On Hop Off buses. We had time to kill so on the buses we went. It was on that day I began discovering what a fun and patient travelling companion my firstborn is. He put up with the bus ride and followed me to the

National Archaeological Museum. I wanted photos of everything and that's what I got.

And so our Italian holiday was over. It was time to move on to the research part of our journey, in Serbia. With Nick gone I was in charge of Mum's ashes so I had to pay attention and keep her close by.

Ginski and Nikolai sharing the driving at Capri

CHAPTER 3

Why Serbia?

At 79 my mother decided to learn English properly. She had been in Australia for 49 years. My father wouldn't allow her to learn English from a teacher. She picked bits up from us children as we learned the language in school, which sometimes worked against her. When we learned the word 'derringer' she thought it sounded rude and wouldn't allow us to use it. So, what did we do? We said it whenever we were in her hearing – kids can be so cruel. She would listen to the marketing reports and news on the radio and, whenever we could get away with it, the radio serial Blue Hills. Other bits she learned from neighbours or people who would come to buy our tomatoes. It must have been excruciatingly difficult but my mum was not one to give up. Having studied French, German and Latin, as well as her own languages of Russian and Yugoslav in school, helped a little, but not much.

Mum's English improved through the process of writing her memoir. She wrote about her life and my father's life, the early years of which were spent in Yugoslavia.

Mum was born in Dalmatia in 1920 of a Russian mother and Serb father. She was told that her father was a doctor but the rest of his family were well-known delicatessen meat producers who are still to be found in Dalmatia. Her mother's side was connected to the Russian military and society. My maternal grandmother died in childbirth and my grandfather vanished. Mum was given to her Russian auntie who had a daughter one year older than Mum. They were both eventually sent to the elite Russian schools evacuated from Russia during the revolution. These schools were given monasteries, castles and other buildings by the royal family to continue educating the emigrée girls.

Two of the schools Mum attended were in Serbia and one in Slovenia. After finishing secondary school with honours she began a medical degree at Belgrade Medical University.

My father was born in Russia in 1912. In 1917 the revolution broke out and all of his family, except for his older brother, were killed. Eventually, he and his brother were evacuated by the Red Cross and taken to Dalmatia via Turkey and Montenegro. They ended up in an orphanage in Split where Dad's brother was pushed down the stairs and died during a fight between the Catholic and Orthodox boys. Dad and the other Orthodox boys were then taken to a Serbian orphanage. He was seven years old. His life from that point became even more horrific.

As fate would have it, one day Mum missed her tram from university and took a cab, my father was the driver.

Serbia was where my son and I needed to be.

Belgrade

There we were in Belgrade, via Istanbul airport. In Istanbul, we had to go through security. As Mum's tube of ashes came through the screening process the lady looked at me quizzically.

'That is my mother', I said. She looked at me sadly and motioned she would need to test the ashes.

'Yes, fine, go ahead' I answered. And so, my mother went through her first-ever drug test. I could see her deep blue eyes twinkling. She would have been delighted at experiencing something new and possibly naughty. After all, this was the woman who, during the early days of the war, took part in minor subversive activities to confuse the invaders.

We arrived in Belgrade at about 7.30pm and checked into the Hedonist Hostel. What a fun place to stay. While searching for a hostel in Belgrade I kept coming across this one and kept pushing it aside thinking that a place called 'The Hedonist' would be far too noisy for me. Eventually, I gave in. For some reason, it was calling me. The perfect choice.

We were hungry. The hostel staff recommended Tri Shashira ('Three Hats') restaurant so off we went. It is in the cobbled street Skadarlija in the old quarter, a street filled with restaurants and music. The meal we had was enormous! We went a little overboard. Ginski ordered Chevapi and chips, we had a Shopska salad each and I had a Karadjorge (rolled veal stuffed with ham, butter, garlic, crumbed and deep-fried). Next time we would order one meal to share.

My next challenge was to manoeuvre myself to a top bunk. I hate top bunks. That's when I learned to contact hostels before booking, to ask for a lower bunk.

Beograd! (Belgrade). First the orientation walk. When we entered the massive pedestrian plaza, Knez Mihailova, we stopped, looked at each other and exclaimed in unison 'This feels so chilled out!' There are heaps of restaurants, cafes and every store you can think of. I remembered my mother saying that when she was young living in Belgrade, the city was considered the Paris of Yugoslavia.

In my parent's day, it was fashionable to promenade at dusk, Knez Mihailova was one of the main streets to walk along, as it led to the fortress and the rivers. This was where you went to see and be seen or to meet friends and neighbours. As I looked up what is now a pedestrian plaza there were crowds of modern people strolling, people at cafes, buskers and street performers. For a moment I imagined my mother, dressed in late 1930's style and my father in suit and hat amongst the crowd.

The first discovery was a public fountain. A simple but beautiful white marble drinking fountain with multiple outlets of perfectly clear water for all to use. The locals, the tourists and definitely the homeless. A marvellous public service, so I only had to buy one bottle of water and then refill it at the fountain.

We walked all the way up to Fortress Kalemagdan. The place where, in 1456 The Ottoman siege of Belgrade ended in a major battle led by (John) Hunyadi, a Hungarian. The place my parents often mentioned in their reminiscences.

We looked out at the confluence of the Sava and Danube rivers. A broad expanse where the waters of the Sava and the Danube flow on either side of the densely treed Great War Island, then re-join before flowing on to the Black Sea.

Fruska Gora

Friday, our search for Mum's history in earnest began. We hopped into the little green machine we had hired and drove off to Fruska Gora, 95 kilometres from Belgrade towards Hungary. Without my son this just would not have been possible, driving on the opposite side of the road isn't something my brain can cope with.

Novo Hopovo monastery in Fruska Gora Serbia is where Mum went to school from age 5-10. It was easy to find, the highways in Serbia are well sign-posted.

The area is stunningly beautiful with green rolling hills, vineyards and forests. We found Novo Hopovo, but as there were signs to Staro Hopovo three kilometres further on we chose to explore that first. The road wound through the forests where my mother walked as a child. I could understand why she loved the colour green so much, there was a multitude of shades of green in the dense forest.

The beautiful little white stone church of Staro Hopovo stood out starkly amongst the green. Originally there had been a log church built between 1496 and 1520 and dedicated to St. Nicholas. It was ruined by an earthquake in 1751 and a new one of cut stone and brick with a ten-sided dome was built. It was dedicated to St. Panteleimon. The current church looks very new because, sadly, the one built in 1751 was damaged during WWII when the living quarters were set ablaze.

The inside is decorated with stunning, colourful Serbian religious murals. We wandered around the grounds taking photos. It would have been nice to have time to walk in the woods but we needed to go to Mum's school.

So back up the three kilometres of winding forest road to the other monastery, a large yellow edifice. We came across a monk walking along the cloister. Communication wasn't easy but we understood enough to conclude that he knew nothing about the Russian era of this monastery but was happy for us to have a look in the church.

Entering this church was so very different to the one down the road. As I stepped over the threshold I felt history envelop me. I entered in awe. The walls of frescoes, all badly damaged, exuded an aura I couldn't quite place. Part of me was bouncing with excitement while the other part was just wanting to be still and soak up the feelings. The still part won. I stood in the centre of the church imagining my mother as a little girl standing there. It still brings tears to my eyes. I was standing where my mother stood, I was looking at the walls, the frescoes, the iconostasis just as my mother had and I had my son with me. I wondered if my beloved, departed mother was with us at that moment. Was she happy that we had found her first school, had she led us there? What part of me was being healed at that moment?

I had heard Mum's stories of all her schools so many times. I created my own images from her stories and dreamed of visiting these places not entirely believing that I'd get there, let alone with one of my sons. How I wished my mother could have been with us in the flesh standing there telling us her stories.

It is hard to explain how much I missed her at that moment. How I wished she could tell me where she stood, which friends stood next to her, what thoughts went through her head. When did she join the choir? Was it in this school or in the next one? All I could do was imagine and try to remember as much as I could of her stories.

My wonderful son kept taking photos - he knew I needed as much photographic evidence as possible for reminders and memories.

I thought about how children don't pay attention to their parents' stories and histories. I remembered the many times I had thought in my youth 'yeah, yeah Mum, lovely stories but I've heard them all!' No, I hadn't.

I didn't ask questions, I was only partially listening and only partially interested. I now had so very many questions that could never be answered, my heart broke.

It was time to leave. We walked around the church and along the surrounding cloisters. Again the overwhelming feeling of walking in my mother's footsteps descended on me. What an incredible life it must have been. A little girl who had lost both parents and had been given to her auntie to raise. Sent, along with her cousin, to boarding school at age 5. She was fortunate her auntie had the financial means to send both girls to these elite schools. There, they both received an outstanding education. From the beginning, classes were held in both the Russian and Yugoslav languages.

Mum only found out at age 16 that her auntie was not her mother and that her surname had been changed. In her memoir, she mentions how she felt she had lost something important when she discovered her surname had been changed from her father's Yugoslav name. This had been done by her auntie and uncle so she could go to the Russian schools. Supposedly, without the change, she would not have been allowed to attend.

We walked around the grounds and found a copse of 10 trees not far away from the buildings, there we took turns in scattering some of Mum's ashes in silence with our own private thoughts. We drove back to Belgrade. Did we talk? I can't remember. Did we listen to music? I can't remember. I was lost in time, space and inner thoughts.

Back at the hostel, it was time to shake myself out of the events of the day and become an extroverted social being again. Crepe night. Gathering with all the other guests around the kitchen table munching on crepes filled with Nutella, crushed Plazma biscuits and other assorted goodies. The room filled with laughter and chatter. This was one of the brilliant ideas at the Hedonist – gathering people together around food to share stories of lives and travels.

It was Eurovision weekend and I had booked the TV for that night and the next for the finals from Malmö. Amidst groans of dissent, I stood my ground. Here I was in Europe at Eurovision time – there was no way I was going to miss it. Luckily everyone else went clubbing and I had the TV to myself. I was amazed the next night when everyone joined me for the Grand Final, I guess even the dissenters watch that.

Bela Crkva

Before the Eurovision Grand Final we had a long trip planned to Bela Crkva to track down Mum's third and final school - her second school was in Slovenia. Well, that day was a surprise and an adventure wrapped into one.

But let's start at the beginning. We'd gone to the Russian House on Thursday to see if we could find any information before setting off for the 100km trip to find the school, only to find that the library was closed on Thursdays. The receptionist didn't know anything about the old Russian schools - it seems that this history is so long ago that no-one knows and no-one cares. However, she did give me a phone number for a lady who had something to do with the old Russian cadets.

I rang the woman and had a strange conversation. She wouldn't talk to me until I had given her my full Russian name - my first name wasn't enough, it had to be first, patronymic and surname! Australian casualness wasn't going to work in this conversation, it had to be Russian formality. She had no information herself but did give me the name of a gentleman in Bela Crkva who apparently had a 'museum' based on the Crimean Cadet Corps in that town. I did know that Mum's school had close associations with this Corps. My hopes were raised.

The trip there was an adventure. My son Ginski is fun to travel with, laid back, just as photo mad as I am (only he is a professional with much better results), entertaining conversationalist and a good driver. Travelling distances in other countries is always fascinating. We came across trucks, tractors hauling various loads, horses and carts, hay wagons - all a challenge on the road. No wildlife but dogs and cats play chicken with the traffic.

There had been lots of red poppies along the side of the road so I mentioned to Ginski I would really love a photo of a whole field of them not just bits by the road. Some time had gone by when the car came to a screaming halt, son jumped out of the car grabbing the camera on the way. As I turned to look there was a field of poppies. What a son!

When we first arrived in Bela Crkva I became a little concerned, I thought it would be a wild goose chase. But we struck gold!

The town initially seemed run down. It had been a large centre but a lot of people left or died and many buildings are abandoned and have fallen into disrepair. My hopes were fading. We came across the Russian church but it was locked.

I wasn't sure whether the address the Russian woman had given me was real, she wasn't even sure of the street number. So we drove down Partizanskaja street, found the number but all the doors looked locked. The street looked deserted. There are no front yards, all the houses open right onto the footpath with large double gates leading into the yard.

I had the window open as we drove further down the street and noticed a frontage that looked like a shop, I could hear voices. We thought perhaps we could go in and ask, after all the Belgrade woman said that everyone knew this man. We entered, to find it was a restaurant. I asked the waiter if he knew Mr K. He immediately turned to a gentleman at a table of people having lunch and said 'I think this is for you'.

Yes, it was the man we were looking for! You could have knocked me down with a feather. He was as amazed as we were. After a brief explanation of what, who and why we were there, apologising for interrupting his lunch and offering to come back at another time, it was agreed we would stay in the restaurant, have a cup of coffee and wait till his lunch was over. It was, in fact, a 12-month memorial lunch for one of their friends. How appropriate. Here I was on a mission with my mother's ashes searching for her school and where should we find the man with information but at a memorial lunch.

So, I had my first restaurant Serbian (Turkish) coffee along with some really nice traditional cake. I had been looking for 'Turkish' coffee ever since we arrived in Dalmatia three weeks earlier and had been told no-one serves it in cafes, particularly in the cities. I was very fortunate that my new friends at the Hedonist would make it for me. The waiter in Bela Crkva told me it is no longer called 'Turkish' coffee, it's Serbian coffee in Serbia, so I guess it's Croatian coffee in Croatia. The two slices of cake must have been from the memorial lunch – awesomely yummy rich cakes, taking me back to my youth and Mum's baking. I love that some traditions continue and although progress is good, our roots are very important. Traditional food is one way of staying connected to our origins.

Mr K proved to be a mine of information. He took us back to his house where we met his wife. They both speak perfect Russian although born in Serbia, so communication was easy. The 'museum' (he prefers to call it a memorabilia room) was chock-a-block full of photos, paintings, books and all sorts of paraphernalia related to the Crimean Cadet Corps that had escaped the Russian revolution and based themselves in Bela Crkva. The Kingdom of Serbs Croats and Slovenes (later the Kingdom of Yugoslavia) was very generous to the (politically) white Russian migrants who escaped and settled in the area. Individuals starting with the king and his family and other royal relatives donated (or lent) buildings, monasteries and castles to the Russian schools to set up their educational institutions.

Two of those schools were the Crimean Cadet Corps and the Marinski Donskoi Women's Institute. They were housed in massive buildings in Bela Crkva and the two schools shared important occasions like religious festivals, balls and choir performances. At other times communication between the boys and the girls was strictly forbidden - needless to say, they managed to get secret written messages to each other.

Mr and Mrs K had associations with the Cadet Corps through their families, particularly Mrs K whose grandfather was an artist and documented their escape from Russia in paintings and carvings. Her father was a cadet at the school. As a result of all their memorabilia and the connection between the two schools they also had quite a bit of information about Mum's school. Mum may be in some of those photos – impossible to know because she had no photos of herself as a young girl and the photos in his collection are very grainy.

One of the sad things about wars and migration; my parents had no evidence of their youth, no photos, no papers, nothing. Sadly, I didn't get to do this trip until after Mum passed away, so I can't show her the photos to find out if she is there. War messes up lives for many generations. I wish human beings could resolve their differences without violence and I wish that my parents had been able to save something of their early days for me to read and hold. But that had not been possible. Having to escape from invading forces, first in Serbia from the Nazis and later in Germany from the Soviets, meant they had to destroy or leave behind all evidence of their backgrounds.

After telling me everything he could, Mr K took us to see the building where Mum's school had been. It was massive, sad and falling into disrepair.

As we walked around we found someone had made a large hole in the corrugated iron fence that was supposed to protect the back of the building, so in I went. After his first shock that I was going through the hole in the fence, our guide decided to join me. The dear man was like a kid again, eyes sparkling at doing something 'naughty'.

I clambered through the fence and walked in the courtyard where Mum's footsteps echoed. There is the remnant of a basketball court. I don't know if it was there in her time or was created later, whatever, this area was her playground. Possibly they had a tennis court, she used to tell me how she loved playing tennis. Because of that one of the pastimes I shared with my parents was watching television broadcasts of major tennis tournaments.

Our guide showed us around and we even had a bit of a look inside, but it is all falling apart and way too dangerous to go too far in. I would have loved to have seen the place the way it was when Mum was there. I always find it disheartening when beautiful old buildings are left to crumble.

After the school he took us to the Cadet Corps school which is still used by the Serbian Military. The best we could do was stand at the boom gate and look at bits of buildings through trees while he spoke with the guard. We weren't allowed to take any photos.

That done our next stop was the cemetery where many of the Russian migrants are buried - some are people of the Tsarist court. The cemetery is also in a state of disrepair, but now cadets from Russia go there annually for tours and do some volunteer work. Piece by piece the cemetery is being restored.

I am ever so grateful to Mr and Mrs K for spending time with us and helping me piece together a little more of my mother's life. Without these two very generous people we could not have found this part of our history.

That experience brought back Mum's stories of her school years and what was, in essence, a charmed life. This school marked not only the end of her childhood years but also, unknown to her at the time, almost the last of the charmed life she knew and expected to continue. Being there brought on bitter-sweet feelings. Knowing how different her life was meant to be and how it ended up. It underlined how we never know what tomorrow will bring and how we need to be grateful for what we have today.

Sitting at the kitchen table back at the hostel playing around on social media, I could hear German, Spanish, English, Russian and a touch of Serbian now and again. Some of the people speaking those languages were from the relevant countries, others not. I loved the multicultural melding. The best part is that all these people are young. Perhaps there is hope for our world through all of these enterprising people sharing lives, languages and traditions.

The next day we drove out to Novi Sad and Kikinda. Novi Sad was larger than I expected and it would have been nice to explore properly but we discovered that Kikinda (our final destination) was another 80kms away. So we couldn't stick around.

Along the way, I noticed a fellow shepherding a flock of sheep along the road and then a couple of young lads minding another flock in a field. My mind immediately went to the stories I'd heard Dad tell of his young days in Milocaj, Serbia, minding his boss's cattle and sleeping with them in the barn. For some people, little has changed. He did say that sleeping with the cattle was good because he was never cold - one positive for an orphaned Russian boy surviving as a refugee.

Kikinda itself looked interesting but we couldn't make head nor tail of the civic maps and heritage signs. It was Sunday so the information centre was closed. We asked a few people sitting at cafes but no-one had ever heard of a Russian church let alone a school and we couldn't get hold of a city map either. Oh well, I suppose I wasn't meant to find Mum's cousin's school. The day was getting on and we had a long drive back so we gave up on our search. We stopped at the horse-driven mill we had seen on the way in. There was a strong smell of horses so I assumed it was still used, but it was Sunday so no way of finding out. A few photos and we were on our way back to Belgrade.

Our last two full days in Belgrade were taken up with wandering. We ate a traditional lunch from the bakery, Goulash y Lepine (goulash in a large bread roll, the middle dug out and filled with a stew). Unfortunately, not to Ginski's liking, he preferred the burek we had also bought. The stew was made of kidneys another tasty reminder of my childhood and my mother's offal stew. As a result, dinner was organised by my son. He hunted down all the ingredients he needed and cooked up a storm with his vegetable dish that he had created in the Caribbean and this time included the local cabanosi – tasty local flavours. Good one son.

Final Frontier for The Golden Oldie and Son

Our day to leave Belgrade dawned. The online timetable said that there was a 5.30am train to Zagreb so I suggested we catch that one instead of the 10.30 as there is only a half-hour connection between the Belgrade train arriving in Zagreb and the Ljubljana one leaving. So after a night of no sleep - Ginski I could understand he got up at 4pm, but why me? I'd had three bad nights of sleep in a row! We rose, organised ourselves in the dark of the dormitory and caught a cab to the station, bought our tickets and waited and waited. Ginski went off to buy food for the train while I stayed with the luggage. The beggars appeared, several approached me, I was glad when my son returned. We waited some more and the train on Platform 1 started making warming up noises. Ginski asked someone about the train that was there and it turned out to be the one for Budapest. Finally, the information office opened and I found out that there was only the 10.30 train! So back to the hostel, we weren't going to hang around the station for 5 hours.

When in Naples the first thing the hostel told us was the places not to go because they were too dangerous. In Belgrade, when we asked the question, we were told that it is a safe city, but to beware of the taxi drivers. So we were ready.

The first drive from the hostel to the railway station cost us 400 dinars. When we needed a cab to take us back he loaded our luggage in the boot, then told us that the charge was 1200 dinars just for the luggage! Well, we weren't going to put up with that, then they started the game cabbies often play. Three or four of them will try to convince you the quote is correct and when you still say no and go to walk away another one will pop up and offer to do it for half the price. Both of us were familiar with that trick from trips to Asia, where I had to argue with every taxi driver and if you weren't on your toes you got done big time! My son is also a very experienced traveller, so these guys weren't going to get the better of us!

We ended up agreeing to 600 dinars even though I wasn't happy, but of course, our luggage was already in the cab so we couldn't just walk away. Our return trip to the station five hours later only cost 350! Yes, you have to watch those cabbies pretty much all over the world. Booking the cab through the accommodation was always cheaper because the drivers know you will have been told how much it should cost. Very useful information during the rest of my solo travels.

Finally, we were on our way. Very slowly. The train stopped at almost every station between Belgrade and Zagreb as well as a lengthy stop at the border.

There are several things needed for a smooth exit from Serbia as it isn't part of the EU. Your accommodation provides a slip of paper to prove you are a legitimate tourist and that you stayed in proper accommodation. Without that bit of paper you could have problems at the border we were told - although I have spoken to people who have visited and stayed with family and they didn't need the slip of paper and didn't have any problems at the border, go figure. Keep your tickets and passport handy on the train, just in case. The first check is on the Serbian side of the border when they check your ticket, take the precious piece of paper and stamp your passport with the exit stamp. On the other side of the border, the Croatians check your ticket and stamp the passport with an entry stamp. That whole process is repeated on the Zagreb to Ljubljana leg. So we had 6 ticket checks and 4 passport checks.

We arrived in Zagreb and, as we couldn't get passage through to Ljubljana from Belgrade, it was a mad dash off the train to go and buy tickets with only minutes till the train left. It was the same train we had come in on, so I really don't know why we were told that we couldn't get a through ticket. It's worth double-checking that information, along with timetables, because I don't recommend doing that dash travelling solo with luggage. We only succeeded because Ginski was with me. He did the dash while I watched the luggage. The alternative is to plan to spend some time in Zagreb before moving on. We didn't have that luxury.

The scenery changed dramatically after the border to Slovenia. I had become accustomed to the flatness of Serbia. Slovenia introduced itself with hills and mountains - forested, green and beautiful. The train travels through the valley alongside the Sava River all the way to Ljubljana. I fell in love with the country there and then. I was listening to my iPod and can highly recommend soft saxophone music to accompany the view. That music proved to be perfect for sitting on a train watching the Slovenian hills get taller and greener while the river just did its thing rushing over rocks creating little rapids in places and in others just smoothly flowing minding its own business. I wish I could have heard the gurgle of the water. However, I have a good imagination so the gurgle was there in my mind, behind the saxophone.

Ljubljana

We arrived in Ljubljana at dusk – it is light there for a lot longer than it is back home - and headed to the hotel only a few blocks from the railway station. We checked in and went to our room on the eighth floor. An overpowering smell of stale cigarette smoke hit us when we opened the door. We rushed back to the desk to sort this out. I had booked a non-smoking room. My son doesn't smoke and I had given up during the time Mum was dying. Even as an ex-smoker I couldn't handle the stench. Luckily the clerk was a nice guy and fixed the error immediately by moving us to the fifth floor.

So here it was 10.00pm and we hadn't eaten properly all day, cold burek and a couple of packets of crisps didn't count, so we went in search of real food. It was easy getting around the centre, it is one massive pedestrian area along the river with what we thought were restaurants all along the way. We did notice something peculiar - we couldn't see anyone eating dinner. They were all either drinking or eating ice cream. We finally found a restaurant with real food and sat down only to be told that the kitchen closed at 10pm. The waiter did say he'd check, maybe the kitchen could rustle up a salad, but we wanted real food. He suggested 'maybe the pizzeria around the corner'. Oh no, not pizza! We found the place and discovered that not only do they stay open till midnight but they had local food as well as pizza. Not knowing anything about Slovenian food it was a bit of a lottery, but we ended up with very nice meals, tasty and satisfying. I liked the taste of Ginski's meal better than mine. I had chosen a dish with smoked pork, although nice it wasn't spectacular. I later found out that Slovenians have a 'thing' about smoked pork, it's everywhere.

In the morning we picked up a rental car – an Opel Corsa – luckily they found one with GPS. Ginski was a happy lad, loving the feel of the car and it had some speed. And so, GPS sorted, we drove out to Hrastovec.

Our destination was part of our search for my mother's schools, a Slovenian castle gifted to the Russian refugee schools by the Kingdom of Serbs, Croats and Slovenes. Having found her first monastery school in Fruska Gora in the Novo Hopovo Monastery and her third school in Bela Crkva in Serbia we were on a mission to find Mum's second school. She was too young to move on to the Marinski Donskoi Institut in Bela Crkva after her first 5 years in Novo Hopovo and so was enrolled in the school at Hrastovec in Slovenia. She only spent one year there but her amazing memory retained the information clearly, just like everything else in her life.

In the distance from Ljubljana were the snow-capped mountains, a beautiful sight. We drove the 141 kilometres along the highway, through tunnels and villages with the view of the mountains every now and then.

Excitement - we found the castle - then disappointment when we discovered it had become a psychiatric hospital. We couldn't even get out of the car let alone see inside. Mum said that in her time, the ceilings were covered with cloth. As an adult, she suspected that perhaps the ceilings were painted with art 'inappropriate' for young eyes. As most castles and palaces in Europe have very ornate paintings on ceilings, often of nudes, I think she may have been right. I would really like to see what is on those ceilings.

It was a delight to picture my mother's stories more clearly. I was excited to have found this place. When Mum had talked about her 'castle school' I imagined the typical fairy-story castle, but Slovenian castles are different.

Hrastovec castle is located in north-eastern Slovenia in the green Slovene hills about 15 kilometres from Maribor, Slovenia's second-largest city. There it stood in all its Romanesque glory, white walls and red-tiled roof sparkling in the sun. One of the largest surviving castles in Slovenia its three round towers can be seen from a distance.

As we couldn't see inside we drove around and found places to take great photos outside. There is a lake at the bottom of the hill providing water for a vegetable garden - I wondered if once that may have been part of a moat.

We drove on and found a spot on a hill for my son to take photos of the castle while I concentrated on the village. I'm not sure if the village was for the workers or for 'outpatients'. They had little gardens and cute village cottages. We were closely watched by a lady sitting on a stool outside one of the cottages. The castle is surrounded by both forest and cleared farmland - was it like this when my mother was there?

It was May, not long after Mum's birthday, the European spring. The forest was bright green and the earth abundant with wildflowers, white, yellow, pink, purple. Tall feathery grasses nodded in the gentle breeze acknowledging the beauty. I felt the roots of my mother's love of nature. Being surrounded by such colour and the peace of forests must have left an indelible effect on her. I wandered a little way along a track at the edge of the forest and also understood why European fairy-tales are so graphic in their imagination. The contrast of the colourful clearing, where fairies no doubt abounded, to the darker inner regions amongst the trees lend themselves to all sorts of images of possible demons, witches and goblins and those Russian rotating witches' houses that stood on chickens' legs. Ah Mum, thank you for all your stories.

Eventually, we had done all we could do, photos taken from all angles, from close up and distance. Sadly, it was time to move on.

Lake Bled

I watched the receding castle until it vanished from view. We reached Lake Bled at 4pm. It struck me how short distances are in Europe compared to Australia. We found our accommodation, on the second floor! No lift, eek! 55 steps! Yes, I counted them! I was becoming used to the physical pain. I climbed those stairs at least ten times over our three days there, not bad for an overweight 'middle-aged' duck with a painful back and hip. Luckily Ginski was there to carry my luggage. The hosts were nice - young and friendly. I hadn't followed the travel tip from Hitchhikers Guide to the Galaxy – '...a traveller always has a towel with them, they are so useful...', so towels were an extra cost. Breakfast was 2,50 euros but worth it - a 'health jar' of muesli with yoghurt and banana and a glass of raspberry drink.

Bled is very hilly, luckily we had the car. We drove around the lake to see if Ginski could run all the way around – there was a path so he could have. My initial impressions were a little disappointing. For me, it has become too commercialised with many modern hotels on the foreshores. I would have preferred the architecture to reflect the landscape rather than the rectangular white and glass boxes, but then, that is just my opinion. We stopped for a wander at the medieval castle on the precipice overlooking the lake. The water views, complete with white swans, were so very pretty.

We woke up the next morning to a grey drizzle. Neither of us is great at sitting around all day so we decided to drive to Lake Bohinj. That lake is three times larger than Bled and three-quarters of it is in the national park so I thought it would also be less built-up.

We decided warm clothes weren't necessary and that as I had my camera Ginski didn't take his. We regretted those decisions. Halfway there son said, 'that rain is hitting the windscreen like snow' I looked and replied 'probably because.....yes! It IS snow!' This we couldn't believe, it was the 24th of May for goodness sake! A quick U-turn, back to the Vila to get Ginski's camera and whatever we had in warmer clothes. I was so glad we did. By the time we neared the lake, the snow was falling heavily and we had a ball taking heaps of snow photos. I don't know how much fell that day but there was enough to turn Lake Bohinj into a Christmas card scene and make the 24th of May 2013 memorable!!

Cows in spring snow

You never know who you will bump into when travelling. That evening, back at Lake Bled, we met some of Ginski's friends at the Kult Klub. A lovely group of young ladies, who just happened to be in the same place at the same time. It was a fun evening and a bit too much wine went down, not to mention the first shot of local Slivovic-type spirit to warm us as we were freezing. It was an evening of thumb wars, pizza and silly shenanigans - all overseen by a wall crammed with photos of famous performers. It started a pattern of meeting amazing people who would become good international friends.

It was Towel Day, 25th of May 2013. No, we didn't wander around with a copy of The Hitchhikers Guide to the Galaxy in our hands and a towel on our shoulders but gee, it was tempting to do so. It was time to leave Bled and head back to Ljublana. Ginski had to fly out to London on his way back to Utila where his filming skills were needed.

We returned the car at the airport, had a meal and sat around waiting for a few hours for Ginski's flight. The poor man was so very tired, there had been way too much partying the night before. Finally, his flight was called. I had been ignoring the coming of this moment. Having had such a wonderful time, sharing so much both spoken and unspoken and now I was fighting back tears as I took a photo and waved him goodbye.

On my Own

The airport shuttle took me back to Ljubljana and my new accommodation. The hostel was interesting. An old bank building transformed. To maintain the concept of the bank, my room (a 10 bunk dormitory) was broken up into cells of one double bunk in each cell. Every dormitory door displayed a symbol of a world currency. Mine was the Dinar, how fitting. A fascinating place, very difficult to describe. The only drawback was, that because of the segregated cells it wasn't easy to meet the people in the dormitory.

The first part of my travel was over. It was amazing how much my sons, my daughter-in-law and I had done and shared in that short month. Now I had to prepare for the rest of my travel, Mum's ashes still with me. I had to be ready for rising emotions. No need to hide them as there would be no-one to hide them from. I was on my own for the first time on this trip.

Phase two began on Sunday 26th of May 2013 - alignment of Body, Mind and Soul. Spending almost three years in the doldrums and a year before that in total stress from work and the passing of my mother, followed by several years of legal stress, had done me no good. I had put on weight, ruined my back and was totally unfit.

It was time to find my way to me.

Stumbling across the Law of Attraction and Abraham books was one good thing that came out of the previous few years. Thanks to a friend I saw 'The Secret' and decided there must be more to it. There was. I travelled to Sydney to see Esther Hicks live. I liked her, it suited my belief systems and I started working with those principles even before I'd left home on this trip. Now it was time for me to follow the advice on re-alignment more closely. I decided, for the rest of this journey, I would spend the last minutes of every evening and the first minutes of every morning doing gratitude exercises. Having already asked for help from the powers that be, I trusted in the process.

It was Sunday, I thought the markets would be open but unfortunately, they weren't. Except for cafes and restaurants, most of the town centre was closed. I stood in the square and understood my son's words when we first arrived there four days earlier. On our search for dinner that first night Ginski stopped, looked around and said 'this town feels as if it is a Hollywood set'. On my walk that Sunday I understood the feeling but couldn't quite put my finger on why the beautiful city felt that way. A little later I understood.

In 1895, there was a massive earthquake and 10% of the 1,400 buildings in Ljubljana were destroyed. Many areas were then rebuilt in the Vienna Secession style. Such an interesting mix of clean yet ornate lines giving the city a feeling of being perpetually new. There is an historical Austrian influence in Slovenia as it was part of the Austro-Hungarian Empire. It was only in 1918, after the First World War, that Slovenia joined the Kingdom of Serbs, Croats and Slovenes.

I love hostels, always full of useful information. In reception, I read the legend about Jason and the Dragon and then excitedly scurried off to find the Dragon Bridge.

The story goes that after stealing the Golden Fleece from the king of the Black Sea, Jason and the Argonauts were blown off course and ended up at the mouth of the Danube. They sailed on until they reached a marshy lake at the mouth of the Ljubljanica river where the dragon lived. They camped there and Jason had to kill the dragon before they could carry their ship in pieces overland to the Adriatic sea. Don't you just love myths and legends? The dragon is the symbol of Ljubljana.

As I write my story I realise that another of the many fine threads of my trip was beginning to form.

The sculptures I found didn't make sense and it was only the next day I realised that what I thought was the Dragon Bridge was in fact, the Butchers Bridge! I had misread the map. This explained the gruesome sculptures I found there. I would have to go in search of the dragons.

Walking around the centre of Ljubljana is easy and calming. The old town straddles both sides of the river. Lots of good musicians busk in the area. A band near the market, a small band near a bridge and a really good saxophonist near the tourist train.

There are 17 bridges in Ljubljana that I know of. I didn't find all of them but I did manage to cross quite a few. Every bridge has a theme and associated sculptures. The four best known - the ones I crossed the most - are the Dragon Bridge with its breathtaking dragons, the Butchers Bridge, the Cobblers Bridge and the Triple Bridge. All are pedestrian bridges connecting the city on both sides of the river.

The architecture of each bridge and the sculptures are spectacular. They alone make a trip to Ljubljana worthwhile, but then there is everything else. The walking is easy. The castle overlooking the city is reached via the cute little tourist train. I spent some time up at the castle wandering around - sadly I discovered my height 'thing' hadn't cleared up, as I climbed stairs to high places. The hypnotherapist back home was a waste of money.

The castle itself was interesting, the cells where they locked people up must have caused great trauma to the prisoners. It was apparently built as a fortress and at various times was a military base, a prison and the seat of the lords of Carniola, but never a residence for any ruler. Unlike the sparkle of Hrastovec, this one was dark and foreboding. The gardens around the castle, however, are very meditative and pretty with a wonderful view of the city below.

After spending a little tranquil time in the gardens, I caught the tourist train back for lunch. By the time I went out again it had rained and turned cold. I still went for another walk in a different direction and eventually ended up back at the river. It was ice cream testing time.

I came across the Russian Cultural Centre and decided to visit the next day. I also happened upon the Church of St Nicholas. I noticed its magnificent heavy bronze door with carvings of bishops' heads and a handle with a patina resulting from hundreds of years of hands. Saint Nicholas is a very popular saint. I was amazed at how many Saint Nicholas churches I came across. Having a son named Nikolai meant I kept feeling his presence.

And so ended my first day on my own. I had been trying to figure out which country or city to go to next but nothing was making itself clear to me. Finally, I decided to go next door to Austria.

There was so much to do the next day. I didn't want to go out until I had done my washing and booked the train to Vienna. Booking the train online was all too confusing so, instead of fighting with computers, I went to talk to the people at the Russian Cultural Centre. I walked via the markets. Oh, those beautiful strawberries and cherries! They reminded me of the markets we visited in Split. I missed my children and their laughter, wishing they could still be with me.

I had a wonderful long chat with the people at the Centre, including the director. The ladies didn't know much about the history I was looking for but the director was quite informed on the happenings in Maribor before and during the revolution and the first world war. It sounded as if the communist era in Russia obliterated all memory. I went away having shared some information with them. They gave me the website for the

Russian House in Moscow which collects lots of information on the earlier period and I promised to send them the information I had received from the Professor at Maribor University, which I did. I also sent photos to Bela Crkva as promised. Then I went wandering to see Parliament and find the Orthodox church. I was hoping it might be Russian but it was Serbian. The beautiful cream coloured church of Saints Cyril and Methodius stood out from the green of the gardens.

After a rest back at the hostel, I was off again, on the other side of the river. I ended up at Republik Square. The University student bands were performing all day in front of the Philharmonicorum building. I just caught the end of one band that sounded pretty good, unfortunately, the next one was doing way too much screaming for my liking. But it was rather cool watching these guys right in front of the University buildings with the castle up on the hill overlooking it all. I continued on and found the BMW art car in front of another museum. That whole area seems to house parts of the University. The architecture faculty building was nearby. At the end of the street, I turned for home.

On the way, I found a sports store and bought a headlamp. While at Lake Bled, rummaging around in the dark one night I heard my son's voice 'Mum, you need to buy a headlamp, they make life a lot easier in dorms'.

Back at the hostel, there was a young man at reception. I asked him if he knew anything about the trains and when he looked it up there was heaps of information. There were some special tickets for 29 euros and I could also get a discount, being retired. But that meant hoofing it up to the railway station. I was already suffering from all the walking, but it had to be done so off I limped. Yes, there were specials but the 29-euro price was for the 4pm train, I wasn't keen on arriving in Vienna at 10pm, so I opted for the second special 47 euros at 8am, even better than the discounted seniors one at 54 euros and certainly better than the full price of around 72 euros.

On the way back to the hostel, I bought a Doner kebab for lunch, normally I love those things but from the first mouthful I was coughing and spluttering! Thank goodness I'd said 'only a little chilli'!

The train was booked, Vienna accommodation was booked, my bags were packed and the next day it was farewell to Ljubljana. As always I hadn't managed to see everything but then, as I repeated many times to myself, you can't do it all. The main reason for coming to Slovenia had been achieved and it was time to move on. I had decided I wanted to get to Vienna then Dresden and, hopefully, Oppach in Germany before heading to Poland.

And so another country, city and week on the Great Trek came to a close. Next stop – Vienna.

CHAPTER 4

Austria to Poland via Germany

'Wien, Wien, nur du allein' wrote Rudolf Sieczynski in 1914. I wanted to know what led poets and composers to write such romantic words and music about a city.

My train left Ljubljana at 9.30am for Maribor where I had to change trains. I hoped to get a glimpse of Castle Hrastovec for the last time but it wasn't visible. The next part of the trip wound through pretty countryside which gave way to foothills and mountains. Green forest-clad mountains dipped into valleys and charming red-roofed villages huddled together as if keeping warm in the spring mountain air.

My stop was Wien Meidling, a major suburban station being used in place of the Hauptbahnhof which was being renovated.

The hostel was huge, just a two-minute walk from Westbahnhof. I began in my usual way, orientating myself through maps and questions. Relaxing was called for after all that walking the previous day and dragging my suitcases on and off trains, I wasn't ready to go exploring just yet. Luckily I was first into the dormitory so grabbed a lower bunk. My angels were with me.

Like most hostels, this place had a kitchen, dining room and bar but I still couldn't be bothered cooking, so it was over to the railway station shopping centre to rustle up some food.

The hostel was located a little further from the centre of the city than I realised. This meant figuring out the underground train system. Success!

Exploration began with a WOW! I didn't know where to look next. All the buildings were spectacular; beautiful old architecture. I walked past one that took up what seemed like an entire block; I couldn't take my eyes off it. When I rounded the corner I found that this building was the Art History Museum. Facing it was the matching Natural History Museum, with the largest collection of meteors in the world. In between lay Maria-Theresia Platz, a beautiful symmetrical area dominated by a massive statue of Maria Theresa, the only female ruler of the Hapsburg Dominions.

I started heading towards the Spanish riding school, there were horse-drawn carriage rides as well as an antique-looking tourist train. Then I saw the Hop On Hop Off sign. Although one of the girls at the hostel said not to bother, that it was useless, those buses are my preferred orientation transport. For 20 euros, I bought a ticket for all three lines and off we went.

I was immediately thrilled that I hadn't listened to the girl. One of the first buildings we passed was the Parliament – a massive Grecian temple. By the end of the third line, I knew that four days in Vienna would not be enough. On returning to the hostel I wanted to extend another week, but they could only do till Sunday. I booked at their sister hostel closer to the centre.

The beauty of the Hop On Hop Off buses is that this is exactly what you do. If you would like to spend time somewhere you get off and then catch another bus later. This became my first activity in every city where the bus service existed.

First stop, a closer look at the statue of General Radetzky – I guess it's not for nothing that Johann Strauss Senior composed the famous march, which of course started playing in my head.

Then St. Stephen's Cathedral (German title - Stephansdom), the church of the Roman Catholic Archdiocese and the seat of the Archbishop of Vienna. It stands in all its Romanesque and Gothic glory in Stephansplatz. The funeral of the Italian composer Antonio Vivaldi was held there. Inside I was amazed to be greeted not by silence, gloom and candles but a vibrant, colourful light show. Beautiful colours playing on the walls accentuating the grand interior. The outside was in the process of being restored so it was very difficult to get a clear photo of the ornate exterior and the stunning roof. Vienna is not a place you visit in a hurry.

Thursday dawned cold and wet, a day to rest and catch up on writing and reading.

I had heard that there was a free philharmonic concert on the lawns at Schönbrunn Palace that night but if the weather was bad it would be moved to Friday night. There wasn't much clear information but from what I could gather the concert would be moved.

I awoke the next morning to another cold and wet day. The five girls sharing the dorm left and I was thrilled to bits. They either couldn't or didn't want to converse, all their belongings covered the entire floor so getting to the bathroom was an obstacle course. I had to smile to myself wondering whether they were scared they'd catch 'old disease' if they spoke to me. I found out much later that young girls from that particular part of the world tend to be like that when travelling. Oh well, there went my personal joke. As it was cold, wet and windy all day it was nice to have the whole room to myself and be able to see the floor!

That night two South Korean girls turned up and very quickly we began chatting. Even with their limited English, we talked about their visit to Vienna. What a difference - respect and conversation.

During the day I went downstairs to find out when the concert would be only to discover, although the weather was bad, it had gone ahead the previous night. The weather forecast had predicted that Friday's weather would be worse.

So what does one do on a cold damp Friday in Vienna? Go to the Art History Museum (The Kunsthistorisches Museum) of course. Well, was I impressed!

The Museum was commissioned by Emperor Franz Joseph to house the massive Hapsburg collection of art. The exterior of this spectacular sandstone building is topped with a stunning 60-metre octagonal dome and a series of statues personifying the arts as well as real artists and their sponsors.

I stood awestruck, amazed by the drama and elegance of the foyer. The marble, the magnificent walls and ceilings. At the top of the first marble staircase stood the most stunning pure white sculpture of Theseus defeating the centaur. On either side at the top of the stairs were two massive white lions. Oh, I could rave about this art gallery forever. Not only does it house wonderful works by artists such as Rubens, van Eyck, Tintoretto, Caravaggio and many, many more - the building itself is a work of art.

The Museum allows artists to set up easels and copy some of the Masters. A fellow was doing just that while I was there. They also allow photography, believing art belongs to the people and should be seen whether people can get there in person or not. Even if not a museum or a gallery-type person you will be stunned by the Kunsthistorisches Museum.

It was time for a break so I went in search of coffee in the Museum café. Not just a modern afterthought attached to the Museum, it is in the magnificent Cupola hall. Black and white tiled floor, red velvet sofas and chairs and the food! It took ages to decide what to have with my coffee. I finally settled on the bright green Mozart Bombe. The base of the Mozart Bombe is Sacher torte, chocolate, pistachio and to top it off a covering of green marzipan.

Surprise! I awoke to a dry morning, even the sun was trying to shine. This was my opportunity to go to Schönbrunn Palace a few train stations away. The palace shone in the sunlight. The obligatory sparkling, golden living statue of Mozart met me at the entrance. Two magnificent gilded eagles atop two high columns, their wings outstretched, greeted the visitor.

The time came for me to enter the dazzling edifice. Sadly, no photos allowed. Inside, the palace was even more spectacular. After the Art Museum, I didn't think that one could get more ornate, but oh yes, you could. To think, how many architects, artists, painters and builders were required to create this world of art, glamour and brocade for the imperial summer residence.

The palace visit over, it was time to explore the grounds. Walking along the tree-lined avenues with horses and carriages passing, I was swept back to another era. If it wasn't for the noisy tourists in modern dress it would have been easy to imagine myself surrounded by princes, courtiers, kings and queens.

I came to the treillage which skirts the privy garden and as I walked in its shade the poet in me was finally inspired. I sat and pondered awhile, imagining the comings and goings of royalty, the peace in the shade and the future colours of autumn.

Schönbrunn Treillage

Arched treillage, cool and green,
Oasis from summer heat,
Matted ornamental grape
Surrounds this wooden seat,
Visions clothed in cloaks and gowns
Tiptoe through your arch,
Perhaps a lover's secret kiss
Before he must depart?
Powdered wigs and skirts that rustle
In satins, silks and lace,
Red waistcoats, matching roses
A smile upon the face.

Then I picture you in autumn
When the sun will lose its fire,
Green summer leaves turning crimson,
Herald winter's desire.

Helene Jermolajew
Laughter, Tears and Coffee – Balboa Press 2017

The geometry of the Privy Garden was beautiful and quite a sight from the viewing platform. The rose gardens, the Orangerie, and there were the giant lemons, the same as we had seen in Naples almost as big as my son's head. A young Russian couple was wandering around taking photos of each other, I offered to take a photo of them together (as you do when you travel) and they very kindly took one of me with the lemon tree.

It was time to move up the hill to the Gloriette. Built in 1775 it is both a focal point and a lookout. To get there I walked through a massive expanse of gravelled estate flanked by Romanesque statues, along treed avenues past the 'Roman ruin' folly, past another expansive geometric garden, along a winding track up the hill, past the astounding Neptune fountain to the grand Gloriette. From there the view was awe-inspiring, Schönbrunn and Vienna at my feet.

The next day dawned cold and wet again. What to do? I had discovered that 'The Third Man' movie had a cult following in Vienna. I hadn't realised it was filmed there. The 1948 Orson Welles original is shown at the Bur Kino three times a week one session is at 2pm on Sundays. I don't know why I went as early as I did - it's one thing to be early to find a place but quite another to arrive three hours before the start of a movie. Mind you it did take me a while to find the cinema but I was still two and a half hours early. So I wandered on and found a South American restaurant called Maredo. The interior is appropriately decorated with booths, tables and a curved stained glass ceiling. Lots of wood to give it a very warm South American ambience. A little expensive for my meagre budget but after living on salami and cheese for quite a while it was time to shout myself a proper lunch. Their specialty is Argentinian steak, but they also had lamb and it came with pan-fried veggies and potato, so, although torn between the two, this excited lamb-crazy Aussie just had to order the lamb. Very nice. I shouted myself a dessert and coffee as well stretching time as long as I could before heading back to the cinema.

I had forgotten so much of the movie. There it all was, all the bits of Vienna I'd seen from the bus; the Ferris wheel, the streets. OK, I hadn't been in the sewers although there is a Third Man sewer tour.

I thoroughly enjoyed sinking back in the red velvet seats in the balcony. It reminded me so much of going to the movies in the 1960s as a teenager, with my mother. We always sat in the front row of the Cremorne Orpheum cinema balcony to watch a movie and munch on scorched peanut bars.

Back at the hostel, to my horror, I discovered that this hostel sends an online message at 7pm that the wifi will be shut down from 7-8 and everyone has to go to the bar to socialise. Well, you can imagine that this was not going to sit well with me. Off I stomped to reception where all I got was a shrug of the shoulders, the explanation being 'it is the company policy'. When I said that the other hostel in the chain didn't do this the answer was 'they will'. So there I was, no wifi and not wanting to go to a noisy bar with lots of people getting drunk. I love socialising and do enjoy the odd bar but I don't like being forced into it and I dislike large noisy bars where it is impossible to talk to anyone and all I end up with is a headache. I understand the theory behind this policy but not everyone wants to spend every evening in the bar. A very inconvenient policy indeed, they could learn a few things from the Hedonist. So out came the book and the iPod - by 10pm I still couldn't access the wifi.

The next day the cold and wet weather continued, still, I headed out for my own history walk around the old town. I had the map and I knew what I wanted to see. Clothed in my new weatherproof jacket, Bundaberg rain poncho (bought at the Canberra country music festival) and a souvenir umbrella clutched firmly in my hands, I began my personal tour. I might as well not have taken the umbrella, the wind was ferocious, in no time the umbrella was turned inside out. My clothes felt clammy as the wind blew them against my body, but I wasn't going to be deterred and still managed to get to most of the places of interest.

I stopped to photograph the Roman ruins in the middle of Michaelerplatz. Photos were my diary, without that visual reminder much would have been forgotten. I also posted on Facebook every day so my friends and family knew I was safe and my impressions were recorded.

The next goal was to find the Volksgarten laid out by Ludwig Remy in 1821. Success! A beautifully symmetrical garden of mostly roses. In there I discovered the Theseus Temple. This is what I love about not knowing too much about a place. I need just enough to bring the explorer out to stumble across amazing finds that cause me excitement. This temple, completed in 1821, was created by Pietro di Nobile in the neoclassical style. It is a small replica of the temple of Hephaestus in Athens (which I had been thrilled to see back in 2006). The Theseus Temple was originally designed to house Antonio Canova's statue of Theseus which was moved to the Kunsthistorisches Museum in 1890. Yes, that same attention-capturing sculpture of Theseus slaying the Centaur placed at the top of the stairs of the art museum.

So, through the park, stopping to take heaps of photos of beautiful roses, across Doktor Karl-Renner-Ring to the spectacular Parliament House built in the classic Grecian style. What an amazing structure! I thought it was rather unusual to find in Austria. However, there is a reason for the architectural choice. When the Imperial Commission was appointed to consider the design it was influenced by the industrialist/politician Nikolaus Dumba who preferred the Greek classical style. After all, it was appropriate for a parliament, given its connection to the seat of democracy.

Rain and wind notwithstanding I continued along Rathausplatz to City Hall, a gothic style building designed by Friedrich von Schmidt and built between 1872 and 1883. I loved the arches and spent quite some time trying to get a few good shots, I'm not sure I succeeded but it was fun and at least I was under cover for a little while.

Playtime amongst the arches over, it was forward again up Reichsratsstrasse, past the university, across Universitätsstrasse to the Neo-Gothic Votivkirche. The concept for this church came from a failed assassination attempt on Emperor Franz Joseph by the Hungarian nationalist Janos Libenyi on 18 February 1853. The Emperor's brother, Ferdinand Maximilian Joseph, asked for donations from everyone in the Austro-Hungarian Empire to build this church in honour of the rescue of the Emperor.

The weather was worsening and I'd had enough of being cold and wet, it was time to return to my room.

The Spanish Riding School was Tuesday's entertainment. My seat was on the second level, which is quite high up in the arena. I was fascinated watching those elegant horses being trained. Half-hour sessions with five horses at a time. The riders and horses look so smart and regal.

The arena is huge. It is part of the Hofburg and was built between 1729 and 1735, originally for ceremonies attended by the royal family. A portrait of Emperor Charles VI hangs above the royal box enhancing the mostly white arena.

We were treated to the horses going through their paces to the music originally played for the Emperor. In the afternoon I went on the guided tour. The horses are all born grey - except the throw-backs to the original breeds which can be brown or black. As the grey horses age, they turn white, which can happen any time after the age of four. The superstition, apparently, is that as long as there is one black Lipizzaner, the school will always exist.

It takes about 6 years to fully train a horse and almost double that to train the rider to full competency. What a commitment! The horses are trained using relaxing exercises focussed on strengthening and building their muscles. They are careful with the horses and make sure not to put too much strain on them. Again memories of Mum flooded back. The day my parents and I took my firstborn to El Caballo Blanco on the outskirts of Sydney. My son was enthralled by the dancing stallions. Close on 30 years had passed since then and that venue no longer exists.

What an awesome day the next day was, still damp but I decided that I just had to get to the Vienna Woods, I desperately needed some nature. Thanks to a fellow Queanbeyan Bush Poet I had the directions to the Lainzer Tiergarten in the Vienna Woods. Not far from the Hutteldorf train station, at the end of a cul de sac, is a wall with a wooden gate. This is the Nikolaitor with the old, tiny, St Nicholas chapel close by. My St Nick again.

Lainzer Tiergarten started life as a private hunting ground for Frederic I when he decided to wall off 6,054 acres of the Vienna Woods for his personal family hunting ground. Now it is a protected nature reserve where the only threat to the animals' peace and quiet are joggers, picnickers or tourists with cameras.

The first animal I saw was a Mufflon (Mouflon), a wild sheep. He stood there, beautiful and majestic amongst the trees, silently watching me as I carefully and slowly changed lenses on my camera. Just as I lifted the camera to take a photo he took off. I didn't see him again. Further along, a herd of wild pigs with lots of piglets came into view. I never realized that wild pigs have a spotted pattern in their bristles, I was familiar with the domestic pigs we used to have on the farm. As I wandered along there were beetles, birds and squirrels. There is a whole lot more wildlife there, but unfortunately, I wasn't blessed with all of them.

I certainly knew there were lots more birds, the twittering grew louder and more varied as I moved further away from the noise of the traffic. The small area I saw in the few hours I had was stunning. It was a cool misty day, on the verge of more rain. The bright green woodland had a rain-forest feel and earthy aroma. Again I understood how woods like these lent themselves to amazing fairy stories. I really did expect Little Red Riding Hood to come skipping out of a clearing, or the wolf to come loping along the brown damp woodland floor. I was glad it wasn't sunny and warm, sun would have spoiled the mysterious atmosphere. That little nature break was balm to my soul.

That night I met a remarkable woman - 71 years old, also from Australia, doing what I was doing, for similar reasons. She was also on her own going where the wind blows. We shared stories and connected at a level of understanding, both feeling lost, both feeling misunderstood and both feeling very alone and emotionally assaulted. She was a fascinating person to chat with, so full of life and adventure and determined to find her way back to herself.

It's a tough gig this getting beyond the stress and grief of a loved one dying and family members showing their true colours. The night we bumped into each other at the hostel reception was the 33rd anniversary of my favourite brother's passing. A fine thread?

The next morning was taken up with a sleep-in after 2 sleepless nights, and packing. The train was booked for the next day. It was almost time to leave Vienna.

I bumped into my new-found friend at breakfast and happened to mention the last thing I wanted to do before leaving was to go to the Central Cemetery to find the graves of composers. She asked if she could join me. After getting directions from the reception staff we set off. U4 to Karlsplatz, then tram 71 all the way to Zentral. A lengthy trip and there were moments we wondered if we were on the right track, but trusted all was well. It was.

On arrival, we first wandered a little through the Jewish cemetery. How sad it was to see so many who's death was just listed as Auschwitz.

On our search for the composers' graves, we noticed a stage being set up. A lady told us that there was a free concert starting at 5pm. It was 4 o'clock so we rushed off to find the composers, and by 5 were settled into seats for the concert.

Now, seriously, opera, Queen and New Orleans jazz in the cemetery - who would have thought. Set up in front of the impressive green-domed Karl Borromäus church and right next to the graves of Strauss, Brahms, Beethoven and others. What a treat! This surprise made up for missing the concert at Schönbrunn. Great things kept happening – and I was loving it. I also felt the warmth and wonder that inspired the composers and poets – 'Wien Wien nur du allein'.

Dresden - City of Emotions

It was the seventh of June, the 33rd anniversary of my brother's funeral. The brother who was born in the labour camp seventy-five kilometres away from Dresden. I hadn't consciously planned my arrival date.

I entered my room for one, I could make a racket, I could eat in bed and the wifi worked! I had arrived in Dresden and as all the hostels were booked out, I shouted myself a budget hotel right in the middle of the old town. Clean, basic and modern.

I was glad my accommodation had worked out the way it did. I needed time to myself as I suspected there would be emotional moments that could have made life in a dormitory difficult. Sometimes you just need to let the emotions flow instead of wearing the social-face all the time. Dresden would be challenging, both because of my mother's experiences in the labour camp close by in Oppach and the devastation of 1945.

I had no clue about floods in Europe until I'd booked the train from Vienna and the room in Dresden. Someone happened to say something along the lines of 'are you sure you can get through?' When you choose not to watch any TV or bother with newspapers, eventually someone will tell you what's going on. Sometimes I wish they wouldn't, like the lady in the hostel in Ljubljana who insisted on telling me all about the plane crash in England just after I'd put my son on a plane to London, even though I told her I wasn't interested and why. Some people just don't have a clue.

I decided to trust that, by the time I was due to travel, even if the lines had been cut by floods the Austrian railways would have sorted something out. People had no idea where their seats were so they took whatever was available including mine. So I scored a business class compartment all to myself and escaped the chaos in the carriage where I was supposed to sit. The conductor said I could stay as that compartment had no bookings – luxury.

The train pulled out of Vienna heading north-west for 9 exhausting hours. As we approached Prague something awakened me. I looked out the window and saw the swollen river. The Vltava was running fast and obviously much wider than normal. It was getting higher and higher and very close to the railway line. It was only the day before that the water receded enough for trains to be allowed through. Village after village was underwater, devastation everywhere. I realised that the constant showers in Vienna were the edge of the flooding rains.

As we neared Germany the situation became worse. In one place I noticed a lady looking out of the opposite-side window shaking her head and muttering. I saw that the other side of the tracks was flooded too. The entire township had water lapping at their second-storey windows. Everything except the rail tracks was under water.

We reached Dresden safely. The railway station is outstanding. The hotel turned out to be a good choice. Clean and modern, quite adequate and right on the main street in the old town so most of the points of interest were within walking distance. There is a massive shopping mall underneath, I thought I'd never find my way out of there. In fact, I don't think I ever found my way back to the same door through which I entered during my entire stay. Conveniently there is also a tram stop right out front.

After what should have been a quick visit to the mall and getting acquainted with how everything worked in my room, I went for a walk. The first amazing building I found was Frauenkirche. Just stunning! I took lots of photos, of course, and returned many times. It is a focal point of the old town.

Standing in the square in Dresden I remembered my son's words in Ljubljana 'it looks like a Hollywood set'. When exploring on my own after his departure I could see what he meant, there was a feeling of unreality and being too perfect. There was a bit of that feeling as I wandered around parts of Dresden.

I started wondering why that might be. Perhaps it's because both cities have been rebuilt after disasters. In Ljubljana, it was the 1895 earthquake, and although 'only' 10% of the 1400 buildings were destroyed, whole areas were newly designed and rebuilt. The centre of Dresden had to be almost totally reconstructed after it was razed by the bombing of 1945. Although there are charred and blackened sections of buildings where the original salvaged sandstone was used, it had a similar feel to Ljubljana. Not as strong but it was there. So hard to explain in words the feeling and aura that enveloped me in these two cities.

Back in my room, I read up on the justifications for the bombing of Dresden, and I still don't understand. Why on earth did it have to be so bad? Why destroy such beautiful old buildings? Why kill so many people? Why not just go for the strategic stuff if that is what was supposedly needed? Obviously, lives are cheap and culture dispensable when countries are at each-others' throats in the interests of 'world domination'. My mind flew back to Mum's description of her experience of the bombing of Dresden in her memoir. Before the bombing, the labour camp inmates had the feeling that Germany was losing the war. Rules at the camp had been slackened to the point where even the gates were sometimes not locked, until that memorable night. To quote from her memoir;

'On 13th February 1945, an order was given to lock our gate. We were watching how that day, from early morning to late evening, column after column was passing our camp. First came the German Army, then General Vlasow's army (Soviet Russians on the German side), civilians, concentration camp men in striped pyjamas and barefoot Jewish women. They were all going to Dresden.

The night was dark. We couldn't see the bombers, but a formation of them, like a black cloud, was passing over our heads. Squadron after squadron flew over. Then, all of a sudden a blinding light illuminated the whole town. Loud explosions followed. We held each other in a grip. Unbelievable thunder was shaking the ground. Eventually, we realised that Dresden had been bombed. From where we stood, a distance of 75kms, we saw flames rising to the sky and small objects flying around us. The Allied forces had used phosphorous bombs, with the attack continuing for some hours non-stop. At dawn, everything went quiet - only the scream of ambulances driving to Dresden could be heard. The ground around the camp was covered in ashes and fragments of torn books and lots of aluminium ribbons.

The men were picked to clean up Dresden. The horror they saw is beyond description.' (Jermolajew, Tamara 2005, It Can't Be Forever pp 44-45, Ginninderra Press, ACT)

My mother made no mention of the ongoing bombings of 15 February. Perhaps the chaos at the camp and their escape to join the March of Millions wiped it from her memory or perhaps she didn't want to go into more detail of bombings and wanted to convey what was happening at a more personal level on the march. I remember her answer when people asked her to write more; 'No', she said, 'I've had enough of memories'.

I went for a walk. Tears welled as I looked at this lovely old town. Some say that the black sandstone blocks are ones re-used from the fires. Others say that this is not the case. Whatever the reality all I can say to the citizens is good on you for the massive effort to rebuild and move on. Yes, I know there are many, many apparently senseless actions during wars, this one is just a little more personal I guess, seeing as my parents and the older of my two brothers could so easily have been caught up in it and wiped out.

I wandered to the Elbe to see the results of the flood. The sandbagging against the buildings was holding well but the river was extremely high and flowing very fast. Street signs were only just sticking up above the rushing river - they were the only indication that somewhere underneath was a road. Some boats and ferries were inundated and the water so high there was absolutely no possibility of any boat passing under the bridges.

Sunset found me joining many other tourists on the Augustus bridge. Cameras clicked madly to capture the incredible scene of a flaming red sun setting over the flooded Elbe. The approaching evening guided me back to the central square where I sat waiting till dark to get photos of Frauenkirche lit up at night. It was uplifting to people watch for a while. Such a normal sight, people leaving work, people going to restaurants for dinner, waiters preparing outside tables for the incoming crowds, tourists wandering around snapping photos and from somewhere in the square came the haunting sound of a violin. Towering above this peaceful scene were the blackened sandstone blocks.

It seemed that spending time in Austria and Germany was definitely helping to bring the language back, so I managed to order breakfast without a single English word - well done me! 'Eine Cappucino Italiano, eine kleine espresso UND einen pflaumkuchen, bitte'. Simple but better than nothing. That was followed by a walk to Zwinger Palace, famous around the world for its beautiful baroque architecture. Originally it was an open area, surrounded by wooden buildings, used by the Saxon nobility for tournaments and other courtly events. The sandstone palace was built between 1710 and 1719.

It certainly is a stunning work of architecture and a peaceful place to visit, even when it is full of tourists! The reconstruction of Zwinger was completed before the reunification of Germany. It was supported by the Soviet military administration and work began in 1945. It was largely restored to its pre-bombing splendour by 1963.

Having had my fill of walking in the footsteps of Augustus the Strong through baroque halls and nymph gardens, I needed to find which tram to catch to the main railway station, then check how to get to Oppach.

The next day I went in search of the Military Museum. The first stop was the transparent Volkswagen factory. The parking for the completed cars is in a multi-storied, round, glass parking station. Originally this factory produced the luxury VW Phaeton, now it is producing the electric model of the Golf. This is where I first heard of the Curry Wurst. The claim on the blackboard at the entrance is that it was invented in the VW factory restaurant.

I wasn't interested in giving the Curry Wurst a try as I had visions of the curried sausages we had to make in the staff canteen when I worked with my mother as her second cook. We both hated the sight of those brown sausages floating in yellow curry sauce (not the most appetising looking concoction) and my mother's description of them (in private) was also very unappetising - the customers, however, loved them. I discovered later that the Curry Wurst doesn't look like that at all.

Back on the tram and off to find the Military Museum. The museum was interesting - although the weird leaning internal walls and asymmetry did my head in. At no point did they say anything accusatory of the Allied Forces and their attack on Dresden. There were just two simple displays of flagstones from both Rotterdam in 1942 and Dresden in 1945 with the facts of both events.

It all got a bit much for me that day. After being in the military museum and walking back to the tram I so missed Mum and wanted to be able to talk to her, just wanted to hear her voice, to ask her about her life back then. I wished I had delved into her stories more when she was with us. Tears trickled down my face as I thought about the missed opportunities.

I was going to visit the Royal Palace but decided to walk over the bridge to have a look at the golden rider and the New Market instead. The golden rider is indeed VERY golden, sparkling in the sunshine. The statue, in the middle of the Market Square, is of a gilded Augustus the Strong seated on a golden horse in forcené attitude. It was created by Jean-Joseph Vinache and placed there in 1736. Luckily the statue was hidden in a cave during World War II, escaping the bombing.

I didn't stay long at the market, I wanted to find the Pfund Dairy (Pfunds Molkerei). It's in the Guinness World Book of Records as the most beautiful dairy in the world. Well, that was quite a walk. Part of my route was along the river past Kaffe Rosegarten which was partially destroyed by the flood. The garden was still underwater and the inside looked devastated. Such a sad sight. I wondered if the roses would ever recover.

I finally found my way to the dairy at 79 Bautzner Strasse. The inside is covered in elaborate hand-painted neo-Renaissance tiles produced by Villeroy and Boch. Unfortunately, photos aren't allowed, so I had to buy a couple of postcards instead. These days it is more a gift shop/milk bar making various products like milk grappa and milk soap as well as milkshakes and coffee.

Another long walk to the tram stop. Due to the road works the tram lines were also dug up and the tram stop on Bautzner Strasse was not in service so I had to walk back to Albert Platz. I was beginning to become orientated.

After a short rest back at the hotel, I decided that I should explore two churches - the Kreuzkirche and the Hofkirche. The Kreuzkirche is the Protestant cathedral, the seat of the regional bishop. The church holds close to 4000 people. Kreuzkirche was yet another building destroyed in 1945 then rebuilt and finally re-consecrated in 1955. The Hofkirche is Catholic. Also badly damaged in the bombing and although the reconstruction was begun soon after the war it wasn't fully completed until 1987.

The next plan was to go to Oppach. The 75-kilometre trip would require a train and a bus to where Mum was in the labour camp and my brother Victor was born. I awoke in the morning thinking that I shouldn't go. It wasn't laziness, just this real feeling of 'I shouldn't go'. I lay in bed and couldn't even make myself get up and get moving. Finally, I realised that this was one of those intuitive feelings to which I should pay attention.

A philosophy I had developed over many years was 'if in doubt, don't'. Whenever I've gone against that I have struggled and ended up unhappy or unsafe. So the decision was made not to go. I did find out later that it was probably a good thing, as it was rare to find English speakers out there and although that in itself is not a huge problem, there was also the possibility of no bus back and no accommodation to stay the night. I may be adventurous but taking that risk on my own wasn't a good idea. I was so glad my intuition had kicked in.

It became Royal Palace day instead. Coffee and croissant at Emil Reiman Café then across the alley to the Palace with its two treasury vaults. Spectacular works of art were collected in those days. Everything was a work of art, from paintings and statues to crockery and cutlery.

Of course, this was Dresden, and you can't avoid reminders of the destruction. This poor castle was almost totally destroyed. Miraculously some rooms and contents were untouched, mainly because of its structure and those rooms being on the outside wall. Had they been facing the internal square they would no doubt have been destroyed by the extremely high temperatures caused by the tons of incendiary bombs. Luckily so much survived for us to see, and for that which didn't survive, there were paintings, photos and descriptions so they could be replicated.

I woke out of a couple of weird dreams, one unpleasant about spiders and the other about a friend and my sons. At the same time, I was singing La vie en Rose in my head. What a strange combination.

I needed to get the image of spiders out of my head so I turned my iPod on with Pablo Neruda and others' poems for a little while. That got me back into writing mode. I ended up writing a couple of poems of my experiences;

Dresden, Germany

I walk along cobblestones
Avoiding feelings,
Looking neither right nor left,
Walking forward to yet another monument.
I don't want to feel, yet feelings come,
Tears well as I think of the past,
My past, their past,
I see pictures of shattered destruction
And I think of my mother
Interned in a labour camp nearby.
I think of losses, of love,
I think of pasts
And tears keep welling,
Amongst the rebuilding of lives,
Mine, theirs, the world's,
I'm avoiding feelings,
Yet feelings come in waves
Almost drowning me, but not quite,
I survive
And continue toward yet another monument.

Jermolajew, Helene (8 June 2013). Laughter, Tears and Coffee - Balboa Press 2017

Dresden 1945

Why? Why? Reverberates,
Bounces inside my head,
Why? As I see charred sandstone,
Why so many dead?

It makes no sense to me,
But then wars never did,
Controlling, killing, grabbing lands
Demands to do as you are bid,

Why? Why can't we live in harmony
Each free to be himself?
Why can't we just all get along
Put greed and hate upon a shelf?

Why? Why? Did anybody question?
Did anybody care?
Did anybody think about
The children who lived there?

Why? Why? Oh, Why?

Jermolajew, Helene. (8 June 2013) Laughter, Tears and Coffee - Balboa Press 2017

I have recently come across Victor Gregg a British POW and survivor of Dresden. Listening to him, he has the same questions as I do and he was there!

It was time to leave. Time to leave my tears behind. Time to farewell beautiful Dresden and time to hop on the train. Next stop Berlin.

Berlin

Ah, Berlin! What can I say about Berlin? At first, Berlin was an enigma but I sure had a great time there. Starting with bears, ending with antiquities and everything in between. The unknown reason for the bear as Berlin's heraldic animal adds to the mystery. There are many myths, which spawned the wonderful street art of Buddy Bears. You can find them everywhere - look for the bears - they lead to all sorts of discoveries and put a smile on your face.

Berlin, city of contradictions and variety. So many of my friends raved about loving Berlin when they read that I was there, but it was difficult to pin down their reasons. Luckily two friends sent lists of places that were meaningful to them. That helped to focus my attention and start getting a 'feel' for the city. I embarked on my 10-day adventure on Friday 14th of June 2013.

The first weekend was taken up with making friends with dorm mates and charging around Berlin on trains and trams tracking down the places we each wanted to experience first. Restaurants, good cafes, rocking jazz bars. Unexpectedly, we found ourselves sitting on a train in a tunnel not realising the train had terminated. The guard who knocked on the window at the end of the line had the 'oh, no, more crazy tourists' look on his face as he motioned for us to stay there and wait. The search for underground bars was fruitless so I left the young ones to their own devices at 3am.

I allocated Sunday to myself to explore the Classic Remise. On the odd Sundays of the month, it is worth rising early and taking a journey of two trains and a very long walk, (for me made longer by initially walking in the wrong direction) to this amazing place. At one point I crossed a long railway bridge, masses of steel ribbons crisscrossed beneath me. I thought of all the paths I had journeyed over my 62 years. Perhaps being lost in those thoughts was why I walked in the wrong direction at first. Is there ever a 'wrong direction'? I wonder.

The Classic Remise Berlin is a centre for vintage and classic cars, housed in a historic tram depot. Workshops, mechanics, classic cars, car parts and the Trofeo restaurant. Beautiful machines on display in the open areas and many enclosed in glass showcases on two levels. It was such a relaxing way to spend Sunday. An all-you-can-eat brunch that turned into lunch, a glass of Prosecco, a few hours of live jazz from the Sunday Stompers and lots of awesome cars to inspect – a fabulous accidental discovery.

The time arrived to use the list of interesting places received from my friends. What better way to find everything than from the top open deck of the Hop On Hop Off bus.

A young dorm mate decided to join me on the first day. It is always useful to have someone else to take photos of you. Every now and again we would part ways when one or the other wanted to hop off and then we would come across each other again on another bus. You learn a lot on the buses (mostly true, although some guides in some cities make stuff up for entertainment). I learned that the previous East Berlin has trams and the previous West Berlin mostly has trains making it reasonably easy to know which part of old Berlin you are in.

An important mission that first morning. I was determined to find a particular café one a friend back home had mentioned as being an important memory. To find it we needed to get off at the Brandenburg Gate and walk past the Memorial to the Murdered Jews of Europe to No 1 Eberstrasse. The name of the café was different to the one given to me. It had changed to Lebensart since his time there.

This little deed planted the seed of what I think I was missing. Much later I realised I didn't have a strong emotional connection. Unlike Dresden, Split, Belgrade and Slovenia I had minimal family stories to link to. The only reference to Berlin in my mother's stories was as the first stop after being taken from Belgrade. The place where they were disinfected and marched along streets to the area where various companies claimed them as their slave labour.

Starting to see the city through the eyes of another helped to begin building a connection. On the way back to the bus stop we took the opportunity to take photos at the Jewish Memorial. It is so large it would have been impossible to get a decent selfie.

It was afternoon when we got off the bus intending to go into the Reichstag building. We stood in line for ages and while chatting to other tourists found out you had to have your passport with you - this reminded me of my time in Milan in 2006 when, having found the San Siro stadium and stood in line, I discovered I needed my passport to buy tickets to the game but, as a result of that I discovered Leonardo's horse instead, the most amazing equestrian statue I have ever seen. At the Reichstag neither of us had our passports and, just as in Milan, photocopies were not accepted, so we left. I never did get there. I usually don't carry my passport with me but unfortunately, there is the odd place where it's needed.

We parted ways. I wandered off to the Tiergarten and discovered the Soviet memorial, a massive structure obviously enjoyed by young skateboarders. I found the memorial to the Sinti and Roma people who also went through a horrendous holocaust during the war. I hope the unofficial memorial, near the Brandenburg Gate, to those who died trying to escape over the Berlin wall is still there as the Council wanted it removed.

Day two of the bus tour dawned and although I think I averaged about 2 hours sleep I had to complete the tour. I was on my own this time. First stop, the Victory column with its crowning glory of a golden statue of Victoria located at the Großer Stern (Great Star) intersection of roads within the Tiergarten. Access to the column is via underground tunnels and for those who want to, there are internal stairs to the top. Opposite is the Café Viktoria. It was so pleasant chatting to the sparrows who joined me and polished off my crumbs. What a way to start a day - German breakfast, visiting sparrows, the amazing column and surrounded by the spectacular Tiergarten. I wondered what everyone else was doing at that moment.

Back on the bus to the East Gallery and Checkpoint Charlie. The first part of the old wall came into view. Stark, blackened with time and threatening, exuding a feeling of depression. I could not imagine having to live behind that wall and see it daily. The East Side Gallery (a 1.3 km long section of the Berlin Wall) is an international memorial for freedom. Artists were invited to depict their thoughts and feelings. I only saw a small section of it with various artistic expressions of feelings about Berlin, the wall and freedom. Although interesting and worth seeing I must admit that the blackened, undecorated section had a greater effect on me. On to the replica of the infamous official Berlin Wall crossing, Checkpoint Charlie.

On Wednesday 19 June 2013 President Obama was in town. A historic event it may have been but I hate large crowds so I headed off in the opposite direction. The security around the Brandenburg Gate where he was to speak was massive, I could see it building over the previous two days. Countless police cars and armoured vehicles were being parked in strategic positions and street barricades installed along Potsdamer Platz. Huge crowds were expected.

I was tired from lack of sleep and the cough that had attacked me so I thought I'd do as little as possible. I decided on Cafe Chagall for lunch in Prenzlauer Berg. This place originally started as a Russian cafe 20 years earlier, named after the famous artist and has kept some of the original menu items. Good food, terrific atmosphere and friendly staff.

The next item on the to-do list was KaDeWe (Kaufhaus des Westens). Now, another thing I hate is shopping. Spending my holidays window shopping is one of my greatest pet hates, but I just had to go and check out the hype. The second-largest department store in Europe, I was told, beaten only by Harrods. None of the clothes grabbed my attention but the shoes! And the food at the top level! Then the stuffed animals and porcelain. There was a very cool modern coffee set I was tempted by, but no, you can't carry crockery around the world and sending it home was out of the budget. Yes, KaDeWe deserves the hype, all seven storeys of it. The Sony building close by is a spectacular piece of architecture worth visiting and the giraffe out the front of the Lego building caught my eye too.

Berlin had me pondering. Apart from extending my stay and realising how much more I still needed to do, see and experience I had an insight. I think this city needs to be shared, especially if it is the first visit. I mentioned this thought to my young dorm mate and he too had come to the same conclusion, that to fully experience Berlin it would be best to share it with someone you care about or at least with someone who really loves Berlin. Why? I don't know, it's one of those feeling things, but this was the first time I had felt that in any place.

What a journey I was taken on thanks to my friends' lists. The first stop was the Pergamon Museum. I purposely didn't research, I wanted to see why this was listed. Did I have an education! I've always known I should have listened more in ancient history classes and every time I go to places like this I wish I had followed through on my interest in archaeology. I was not expecting the jaw-dropping vision I saw upon entering the museum. A complete replica of the altar of Pergamon, a white ornate edifice, then the gates of Ishtar followed by Uruk. Who knew there was such an advanced civilisation called Uruk 5000 years ago? Not I. Indescribably stunning. I definitely understood why this museum was on the list and sent a silent thank you.

To give my legs a rest I took the one-hour boat trip on the river Spree, which was included in the bus tour ticket. It was so pleasant enjoying the warmth of the summer sun while gliding past buildings old and new.

On the walk home I came across all sorts of things; shops with massive stuffed animals (bears featured a lot), bridges, passing Trabi tours, fountains and the paddling pool in the park which was fully operational that day. An exhilarating day, Berlin was beginning to hook me.

My Friday morning thought was 'I will find something easy to do'. Ha! Did I forget I was in Berlin and wherever you go will end up requiring some mega walking? Especially for me who gets distracted easily and before I know it I've gone off my planned track? And so Friday started with 'I'll just go out to Roststatte (a recommended cafe in Ackerstrasse Mitte) and then perhaps the Gallery of Modern Art. They are in opposite directions but the U-Bahn will get me there.' That would have been fine if I'd stuck to the plan. However, as I approached the art gallery I wasn't even keen on the building - it reminded me of a disused petrol station back home. I decided I wouldn't risk not being keen on the art as well, which was down at least one flight of stairs. Call me a Philistine but I have to admit to being a bit of a traditionalist in my cultural preferences. I thought some quiet time in the Tiergarten would be nicer, and it was, and it required walking and walking and then some more walking to get there. Then lots more walking through the gardens to get back to the Brandenburg Gate.

On the way, all sorts of things captured my attention; interesting doors, striking sections of the gardens, ponds, statues, flowers and a small crowd of people gathered around intriguing rocks. On closer inspection, I discovered this was the Global Stone Project, a place where people gather to celebrate the Summer Solstice on the 21st of June. I'd missed the exact time of the celebration but it was nice to discover this peaceful place and to join in the overall feeling for a little while. The rocks stand for Peace, Love, Awakening, Hope and Forgiveness and come from five different continents. The stones from Australia stand for peace. The meaning of this 'random' find was not lost on me given the purpose of my journey.

After the Stones, I discovered I was across the road from the cafe on Ebertstrasse so it was back to Number One and thinking of friends.

The next day I travelled to Potsdam, another friend's suggestion. What an education. I had no idea of the goings-on in Potsdam, my excuse is I was busy being too young to care at the time. Spies, cloak and dagger, nasty prisons, KGB, Americans, and all amongst some of the most amazing architecture and history as well as construction achievements. Apparently, the island was mostly swamp so the Dutch were called in to design and stabilise the ground before building could commence. No wonder I thought it was in Holland. So Potsdam is sitting on thousands of logs just like Venice. There wasn't enough time to cover everything, but what I did cover was wonderful.

Alexandrowka, which has many stories explaining its existence, was charming with its streets of traditional wooden Siberian houses. In the forest close by, the little candy-cake, square, pink and white Russian Orthodox church with its green cupolas enticed me. Glenicke bridge (the basis of the movie Bridge of Spies) where East and West exchanged captured spies, was a must to walk across. A convoy of military Jeeps rolled past, no doubt a tour. That brought back to my mind the fellow I saw dressed in Soviet uniform at the Brandenburg gate who, for a fee, barked orders and stamped papers for tourists, re-enacting history. He frightened the living daylights out of me as I walked past, I couldn't understand why people wanted to experience that.

My last full day in Berlin was Sunday 23rd June. I decided a quiet day in the Tiergarten and revisiting the Stones would be a good idea. First, coffee on Unter Den Linden. Having fortified myself I decided this was the day to check the information centre at the Memorial to the Murdered Jews of Europe on my way to the Stone Project. There is a museum underneath the "Field of Stelae", the above-ground area containing over 2,500 geometrically arranged concrete pillars, which I'd visited on my first day. The pillars are all at different levels and so are the paths in between. Walking through this area where some of the blocks were higher than my head and others lower, gave me a feeling I cannot describe adequately. In the underground museum, all the emotions rose up. As I read some of the names of victims and their last letters and notes my eyes misted and tears threatened to escape. The notes were scribbled on whatever materials the prisoners could find once they realised what was happening. It was so overwhelming, I couldn't stay for very long. Notes from children to parents, parents to children. Many of these are embedded in the floor under glass, a very moving experience and I just had to get out of there before I completely broke down.

Off to the Tiergarten to clear emotions. Well, that didn't quite go to plan. I was so disappointed in the condition of the beautiful area. I'm not sure who were the offenders. There had been the crowds for President Obama's visit, a concert on Friday night and the Gay Pride gathering on Saturday. Mountains of rubbish everywhere especially close to the park benches. I wish people gathering in big mobs would respect their surroundings and leave the lovely parks and gardens as beautiful and neat as they found them so others can enjoy the areas too. Rather sad that this should be my last image of the gardens. And so it was back to my hostel to pack and rest before moving on.

Only now as I write and go through each photo am I starting to put together my impressions and feelings. I wasn't 'grabbed' by Berlin immediately as I had been by some other places nor do I think I left my heart there, as I did in other places, but I do want to go back. I think I am more enthralled than 'in love' after my first visit and that fascination draws me to want to see and feel Berlin with eyes and heart that have been there and need to go again to find more understanding. So, what is it that epitomises Berlin for me? I don't think I can bring it down to just one thing; the suburban wading pool, bears, the guy in a wedding dress in Alexanderplatz, the incredible antiquities at the Pergamon, the food and coffee culture, fashion, history, spies, palaces, architecture, music and so much more all mesh together in this city of contrasts called Berlin drawing you to itself with mysterious, inexplicable energy.

Somehow, whether it was Berlin or whether it was time, I felt my heart beginning to open towards romantic possibilities, my thoughts winging towards a friend hinting that my walls were beginning to crumble. Not just yet, there was so much more to do on my alignment journey.

Poland-Wroclaw

It was a wet Berlin day and I was very glad I had made two promises to myself at the beginning of this trip;

1) Always keep my finger on the 'Don't Panic' button (after all, although not hitchhiking through the galaxy, I was travelling with very few plans) and,
2) Do not rush, allow lots of time to get places and think things through while being totally flexible.

So, when five minutes before my train was scheduled to leave Berlin it hadn't arrived yet, I didn't panic. An announcement came over saying that the train for Wroclaw (previously known as Breslau in German) at 9.41 had been cancelled - 'we apologise for any inconvenience.' I waited, they said it again. Two Polish ladies who only spoke Polish had no clue what was going on and asked me what the problem was. I don't speak Polish but I do speak Russian and English (with a smattering of a few other languages including German) so between their Polish, my Russian and a lot of body language we managed to communicate.

Eventually, I noticed an official-looking guy who was speaking in English to another traveller. I asked him about the cancellation he said, 'get that train on platform two, travel one station get off, cross the platform and your train will be there'. Ok, interesting, as it was supposedly cancelled. Anyway, it turned out it was only diverted. It would have helped if they'd said so. It would also have helped if the announcements were made in Polish as well as German and English seeing as the train was heading to Poland. Ah, the joys of international travel.

The Polish ladies decided to stick with me as they seemed to think that I knew what I was doing (if they only knew) and eventually yes, we did what the fellow said and ended up on the right train heading in the right direction. Luckily I didn't panic and leave the platform. I arrived in Wroclaw an hour late, my mother's friend Ewa had patiently waited in the wind and rain, as I had no way to let her know what had happened. I had entered the city of 100 bridges.

To welcome me to her city Ewa took me to the Four Seasons pub for dinner, a lovely little place with excellent food. The husband and wife owners love Russian music and often have live performances there. We spent a very pleasant evening listening to music, chatting with the owners and eating fantastic food prepared by the husband. I was reminded of many of our family gatherings with friends where often at least four languages were spoken around the table - here at the restaurant it was only three, Russian, Polish and English. Such a delightful evening. Ten days later we visited to say farewell.

Wroclaw is a beautiful university city steeped in history. In approximately one thousand years of existence, it has been ruled and invaded by various kingdoms, empires and dictators.

The following day Ewa surprised me with a visit to the Panorama of the Battle of Raclawice, there is only one word - Stupendous! It was painted by several artists in the 19th Century, took 9 months to complete and is massive (114 metres long by 15 metres high). A circular building was created specifically to house the panorama. Entering from the dark in silence the immediate effect is breath-taking. As you stand in the centre or move around the rotunda, the battle of Raclawice (and the ultimate victory over the Russians in 1794) seems to rage around you, such is the 3D effect. There is so much to the story of what the painting went through, how it was saved and eventually preserved for posterity in Wroclaw. The experience was incredible.

Next, we stopped at the 'oldest restaurant in Europe', Piwnica Swidnicka, dating back to 1273. It was an impressive place to visit, eat and drink beer. It is underneath the Ratusz (Town Hall), has four eating halls, most of the décor reminiscent of medieval times. A plaque at the entrance lists some of the famous people who have been there including Kaiser Sigismund of Luxemburg, Chopin and Goethe. I ordered the pork ribs which arrived on a wooden platter with a large knife and fork sticking out of them and although I'm not fond of the modern fashion of serving food on pieces of wood I had to forgive the authenticity of the medieval touch which suited the venue. The meal was luscious and the cold beer was a perfect accompaniment.

City of Gnomes

Berlin has Buddy Bears, Wroclaw has Gnomes. Hundreds of them. Whether you are young or old, a solo traveller a group or a family, going in search of these little guys is a terrific way of seeing this beautiful city. We found them in all sorts of places.

Another big day lay ahead with lots of surprises. We walked up to the river Oder near the zoo, and on the pretext of only asking about the river cruises, Ewa actually bought tickets, which happened to be for the first cruise of the 'Underwater Wroclaw' festival. The Underwater Festival constitutes over 20 cruises on the river, each has a concert, an exhibition or a performance, of some sort. Pretty cool, we were treated to a satire of what it's like to be a model surrounded by people and paparazzi - we had to participate as the crowd. Not only a lovely cruise on the sparkling river Oder but we also found a surprise gnome – the ship's captain gnome.

After the unusual cruise on the paddle wheeler, we lunched at a restaurant that serves Ukrainian, Russian and Crimean food. Early evening found us at the 'Pergola', an ivy-covered colonnade wending its way past the spectacular multi-media fountain. The light show was stunningly beautiful. Holograms appeared within the colourful water to the amazement of many. This fountain has all sorts of capabilities including pyrotechnics, so this experience is also a must for a wonderful display of light, sound, holograms and colour.

The Japanese gardens were the next day's destination. Designed according to the rules of Japanese public gardens with imported trees, plants and fish, a tea room, bridges and much more. Lunch was at the Sphinx restaurant followed by an evening of wonderful music at the Arsenal Building provided by the Wratislavia Chamber Orchestra and saxophonist Pawel Gusnar on the soprano sax. I'm not a great lover of some jazz genres and was concerned but I needn't have worried. These guys played lots of beautiful music from many genres. It's such a delight to listen to musicians who so obviously love what they do and put a whole lot of feeling into their performance. Some beautiful renditions with works from Gershwin and Chopin plus others, such a treat. The evening ended with a couple of beers with Ewa and four of her friends before heading home. Having a local to show you around has lots of advantages, you get to see things you may not find otherwise.

Relaxing day. A trip to the main bus station to get tickets and check the time for the Krakow bus followed by coffee and cake at Europejska Kawiarnia. Our drinks and cakes arrived in delicate floral china cups and plates, a little bit of elegance never goes astray. I was taken back to my childhood when Mum refused to drink tea and coffee from anything but pretty china cups. Eventually, she succumbed to mugs. We wandered through the colourful Market Hall, awash with flower, fruit and vegetable stalls. The view from the top of the stairs was a tapestry of colour. Lunch then relaxing before heading off to visit Krakow for a couple of days.

Krakow

We arrived in Krakow ready to see and experience as much as possible. Ewa chose the Klezmer-Hois Hotel, a delightful, atmospheric place located in a 16th Century building with ongoing musical and artistic connections. Often there is live Klezmer music in the evenings.

Staying in the Jewish quarter meant we were also surrounded by very tasty food. For our first lunch, we chose a restaurant with a very traditional menu. We wanted to try everything but restricted ourselves to three main dishes and a beer. When we returned for drinks and dessert that night we discovered we were the 'talk of the town' as 'the two women who ordered three dishes for lunch' - we giggled. If we were going to get a name for something, it might as well be for appreciating good food.

That first afternoon we wandered through the main square and the market hall, what a wonderfully relaxed atmosphere, you wouldn't guess the history from the current lifestyle. A band was playing in the square and a pretty young lady in a sweet purple and white floral summer frock was dancing. Was she part of the act or was she a passer-by captivated by the wonderful sounds? The band members were enthralled. The uplifting atmosphere was infectious.

My attention was caught by the produce for sale in the square. Stalls of freshly baked bread, preserved vegetables, fruit baskets so colourful they were deserving of an oil painting, delicatessen foods of all descriptions and traditional gingerbread were just a few of them. The obligatory living statues were present and bars, restaurants and cafes everywhere. One bar, in particular, is worth a mention. Piwnica Pod Baranami. This cellar with atmosphere was opened in 1956 and has been an extremely popular political and artistic cabaret since. In July each year, it becomes the home of jazz. The cabaret was so popular in the old days that when they couldn't let any more people in the door some people would slide through the window. A rather dangerous practice I would have thought as the bar is below street level, but I guess there would have been many hands ready to catch. The cabaret appears in the book A Long, Long Time Ago & Essentially True by Brigid Pasulka.

There were sculptures dotted all over the city - classical and modern, serious and funny. We walked along the walls of the city, peeked in corners and shops discovering all sorts of evidence of a city with a very interesting and diverse culture.

The next day we walked our feet off again going to, through and back from, Wawel castle. History, treasures, crazy armoury and dead kings in the cathedral. As in all castles it was fascinating to hear the history, and seeing as I knew little about Poland before WWII, I enjoyed the education.

The castle is where I discovered yet another restricting aspect of myself. In the grounds of the Wawel castle are steps that lead down to the 'Dragons Lair'. I had no idea what was down there but wanted to have a look. Well, that didn't happen as part-way down the tight spiral rock steps a panic attack struck me and I simply had to get out of there, rushing back up the steps the wrong way. I always knew I had a touch of claustrophobia but hadn't realised it had become so bad - useful to know. My huge panic attack a few months after Mum's death was still wreaking havoc. We returned to general beer tasting and searching out traditional food.

On our last day in Krakow, lots had to be achieved. Those who know about the holocaust and happenings in Poland will be aware of what went on in this city. It was an odious place for both Jews and Poles.

We had noticed an Israeli café around the corner from the hotel so we headed there for first morning coffees. I was over the moon with not only the coffee but also the presentation and surroundings. My Israeli coffee arrived in a beautiful gilded traditional pot on an equally beautiful traditionally decorated ceramic coaster. Flowers on the table added a touch more elegance.

Coffee done, we set off to Schindler's factory (yes, of the Schindler's List book and movie). There was a lot to see just in the entrance and the cafe area; hundreds of photos of most of the people Schindler helped to get out, some pieces of machinery, photos of the movie, the gate that was used in the film as the entrance to the factory, a red leather copy of the movie script and lots more.

We went back to the Square through the rectangular memorial tunnel. It was built in a place where the Jews were marched to the trains which took them to Auschwitz. In the roof of the tunnel, the word Auschwitz is carved in such a way that when the sun shines the word is reflected in the shadow of the internal wall. We tagged onto a free walking tour just at the time when the leader was answering the often asked question - why didn't the Jews fight back? I learned the process of demoralisation was brilliantly executed. By the time anyone realised what was going on it was too late. Besides, the inhabitants of the ghetto didn't believe anyone who told them that they were in danger. He quoted the movie 'The House I Live In' where apparently parallels are drawn between the way the war on drugs was being waged in the US to the system of demoralising the Jewish people. I haven't seen the documentary yet so I'm repeating the guide's words. But I do understand how people can be manipulated - it happens in every case of domestic emotional abuse where one partner demoralises the other. I've experienced that myself and it happens in every bullying case.

We also learned of the pharmacist Tadeusz Pankiewicz (a Catholic) who, like Schindler, helped out in many ways. He chose not to re-locate to a gentile area when told to do so by the Nazis and managed to get permission to stay on as the only pharmacy within the walls of the Jewish ghetto. Through his actions, many more people were saved.

In front of the pharmacy is the Ghetto Heroes Square with an art installation of giant chairs. They are a stark reminder of the transportations from that very square. It is said that the concept came from photos of children carrying chairs to the train. Some of the smaller chairs are placed at the tram stop so people waiting for the tram can use them, symbolising that anyone can be a victim.

From there we walked to the remaining piece of wall which surrounded the ghetto to prevent people from escaping. Just like the Berlin wall, stark and ominous but now softened by the greenery of mature trees.

I decided I would not go to Auschwitz. After Dresden, the Berlin holocaust museum and Krakow I couldn't handle any more - I just couldn't face any more horror. I'm an 'empath' and soak up energy like a sponge and it takes a lot to shake it off. Although people say you haven't been to Krakow unless you go to Auschwitz, I didn't need to put myself through that. My mother's stories of the labour camps and the scenes she witnessed on the day of the Dresden bombing - 'skeletons' in 'striped pyjamas' shuffling past the camp where she was interned - are enough for me. Besides, this was not only a research trip it was also my healing trip, so adding such deep emotional trauma would not have been useful.

After all the memorials of such dreadful times, it seemed incongruous to just get on with ordinary life and sightseeing. A spot of lunch then off to the main Square again to see St Mary's Basilica and explore the markets. We were side-tracked by a chocolate factory and café. It was stunning, the chocolatiers' creations were incredible – a huge chocolate replica of the old Krakow Town Hall Tower stood in the centre of the shop, all around were chocolate stiletto shoes, intricately decorated hearts, soccer boots and lots more. It was a beautiful warm evening to be out and about, with music in the square, birds going crazy at sunset and chocolate. And so ended our time in Krakow.

Back in Wroclaw, what started out as two very tired women just making their way back from Krakow on the bus and doing nothing else, turned into one heck of an awesome evening. Back to the Four seasons pub to have dinner, return the book they lent us and say goodbye. We had a beautiful dinner, then a couple of people with a guitar came in and they entertained us for ages singing Polish, Russian and English language songs (even 'Moonshadow', fancy, and they didn't even know my old nickname). Then we were introduced to a professor of something or other but as I don't speak Polish I focussed on chatting to the owner of the restaurant who speaks Russian, is an artist and is an absolute sweetheart. It was sad to say goodbye to such lovely people. He gave me a copy of his pen and ink portraits of two of their dogs, they are now in my home reminding me of good times.

To complete my visit, we were invited to a Polish farm barbecue by Ewa's friends. We hopped on a bus for a one hour ride out to the township of Sobotka, then we were picked up for a seven-kilometre drive to the property in the village of Sady. Such a charming place bordered by a National park and dotted throughout with fruit trees and a massive vegetable garden. English-speakers began gravitating to get some practice and that led to wonderful conversations. A couple who own a vineyard came along with some of their wine and a Polish concoction I'd never tried before - a tincture of pine with honey - after the initial shock it's rather nice, several shot glasses of that went down easily. Then we moved to the traditional cooking of sausages on sticks over an open fire. Farewells included some old fashioned Polish hand-kissing, nobody except Polish men does that anymore, it was really sweet. A lift home and a lovely day that reminded me so much of childhood, the farm and visiting days when people would rock up and party, was over.

As I get to the end of my Polish story I just have to make comments on Wroclaw. This is a seriously beautiful city and if you haven't been there you simply must go. Walking is, of course, always the best way to explore. I was stunned by the architecture, spaciousness, style, history and amazing sculptures. I even found my knight in shining armour. Oh, stop my fluttering heart! OK, he wasn't living and breathing, a little cold and distant but such a real looking statue I just had to cuddle up for a photo opportunity.

There was one last important act left. We needed to find a container for some of Mum's ashes. Ewa had been a very close friend to my parents, especially my mother, and had asked if she could have a little of Mum to keep. Of course she could! What we needed was to split the ashes so Ewa could keep the decorated spreading tube and I would have something smaller to carry with me. The spreading tube was quite large and difficult to carry in my cabin luggage. I visualised the nightmare of the container lid coming off and the ashes covering all my overnight possessions not to mention the plane! Even if I emptied it into a more secure container what would I do with the original with my mum's residual ashes in there? The thought of throwing it out horrified me so this was the perfect solution - the tube would stay in Poland with Mum's dear friend.

On one of our walks, we came across an antiques market. We searched the stalls for something suitable. Initially, I found a metal musical candy tin that I thought could work but no, it wouldn't have been secure enough. At another stall, I came across heavy silver-plated salt and pepper shakers. Mum had a cheeky sense of humour and as she had been a chef I thought this could be the answer. The thought brought a smile to our faces and the decision was made. Mum continued her journey with me in the salt and pepper shakers sealed in the candy tin while part of her stayed in Poland.

I moved on.

☙

CHAPTER 5

Italy

V enice, home of canals, bridges, sculptures, food, glass, masks, lace,
gondoliers and a piece of my heart.

'In Venice Tasso's echoes are no more,
And silent rows the songless gondolier;
Her palaces are crumbling to the shore,
And music meets not always now the ear:
Those days are gone, but beauty still is here.
States fall, arts fade, but Nature doth not die,
Nor yet forget how Venice once was dear,
The pleasant place of all festivity,
The revel of the earth, the masque of Italy.'
Byron, Lord (2004). Childe Harold's Pilgrimage. Urbana, Illinois: Project Gutenberg.
Retrieved September 13, 2020, with permissions from www.gutenberg.org/ebooks/5131

As I needed to get to Pisa, I discovered the easiest and cheapest way from
Wroclaw in Poland was by Ryanair to Venice, then by train to Pisa – so,
of course, I had to factor in some days of canals and vaporetti. I had fallen
in love with Venice on my very first trip there in 2006 and had sworn one
day I would return, and here I was. It was night time on Sunday 7th July
when I arrived. I had no idea where my hotel was, nor how to get there.
Luckily for me, a friendly English-speaking Italian lady on the airport bus
came to my rescue.

As I entered the vestibule of the hotel I was stunned by the ornate mirrors on every wall, each one reflecting the myriad of dazzling lights. In contrast to the sumptuous entrance, my room had the tiniest shower and bathroom space I had ever encountered.

I was still pinching myself the next morning, not quite believing that I was really in Venice, so unplanned and so exciting. I couldn't wait to explore more of the islands, passageways and canals. I thought I'd get a vaporetto to San Marco Square from Piazzale Roma - where all road traffic stops - but then I saw the sign and arrow, so I chose to walk. Pretty soon I decided that the signs pointing to San Marco and Rialto are designed to make sure you walk past every possible shop and cafe. Still, I was so glad I walked, I wouldn't have seen so many little nooks and crannies especially the countless Venetian mask shops from a boat. As in most of Europe though, there are very few places to sit and rest.

My body was complaining bitterly. For about a year after Mum died, I spent most of my time sitting on a bad office chair playing computer games, eating chocolate and drinking beer. Not to mention for the first three months I couldn't face the silence of my bedroom so I slept on the lounge with the TV on. All of this meant my back was in poor shape and I had put on lots of weight. I only found out the real cause of my increasing pain years after returning home, I need a new hip.

I reached the Rialto, coffee and the obligatory photos were a good idea. I had to mentally trick myself to take breaks otherwise I had a tendency to push myself too far. The coffee allowed me to sit down for a little while.

The Rialto was packed with tourists, it was high season, but the view was as beautiful as I remembered. The Grand Canal, boats, gondolas and the lavish palazzos rising from the water. The crowds made taking selfies difficult and then the saviour of solo travellers arrived - the random stranger. I made a deal with the kind American guy with a professional-looking camera, that if I moved so he could get his shot would he take one of me on my camera, he did. Choosing the person to take your photo is quite a game when travelling solo.

I was quickly 'peopled out' by the crowds at the Rialto and decided to go to the, hopefully, less populated island of Burano. In July Venice is packed, it's impossible to get a photo of anything without crowds. It was a fair walk to find a jetty where I could catch the correct vaporetto. I must have misheard the man when I checked that the boat was going to Burano - because after travelling right around Murano I had a look at the map and figured I'd better get off because this boat wasn't going to Burano after all.

Instead of lace, I set off looking at glass. Back in 2006, I missed the glass blowing because we arrived at the island too late, I didn't manage to see it this time either. It took me 3 hours just to check out all the galleries and shops in the area around the Colonna jetty, not realising when the factories closed. Murano glass is certainly something to behold. Some of it is garish and some spectacularly stylish and beautiful. There was a coffee and wine set in green and gold that I would have loved to see in my own home – I didn't dare look at the price.

Sculptures around the island are all made of glass, I hadn't noticed these on my first trip eight years earlier. This time, as I was on my own, it was a joy to just aimlessly wander and suddenly come upon a massive, colourful glass sculpture. The sunset boat ride back to the main island topped off a beautiful day.

I wanted to give my feet a rest, so I thought the next day it would be nice to do more tripping around on vaporetti. I was given lots of opportunities for foot resting. First, it took an hour to get to Piazzale Roma from my hotel instead of the normal 15-20 minutes thanks to an accident near the bridge and the resulting traffic jams. Then I decided I just had to get to Burano, the island of beautiful handmade lace. I didn't realise just what a long trip it was, especially when I got the slow boat to Fondamente Nove and then a very long trip via Murano on another. So my feet had heaps of rest and I revelled in lots of boat travel, such a pity it was all inside the boat, I would have liked to be outside with the wind and the waves. I reached Burano just after 3pm. It was worth the effort. I found myself thinking I could rent a place for a couple of months and get my books written. Beautiful lace everywhere, with ladies sitting in shops merrily tatting. The canals are lined with colourful houses and crossed by bridges, lots and lots of bridges.

Although I hate window shopping, Venice is different. Every store has stunning creations to enjoy. On Burano it was so tempting to buy more than necessary, however, good sense prevailed and I only succumbed to a few souvenirs to send home to friends. Then, back to the main island and the Jewish ghetto.

Ah, learning after learning. The previous day I learned (luckily by observation, not experience) that it's not a good idea to sit in the back of a vaporetto - a group of people was drenched by a rogue wake from a passing boat. The next day I learned that the word 'ghetto' used to mean 'foundry' in Venetian and took on the new meaning after the Jews were confined on the island where foundry slag was stored, forming the first-ever ghetto in 1516. Interesting how meanings change.

I'd vaguely remembered reading about the ghetto ages ago and looked it up. The Old Ghetto was the setting for Shakespeare's 'The Merchant of Venice' (I probably should have paid more attention seeing as we did it three years in a row in High School). The ghetto is in the Canareggio region and is divided into the Ghetto Nuovo (new) and Ghetto Vecchio (old). The two areas are separated by a narrow canal. Memorial wreaths with explanatory plaques are attached to many buildings commemorating previous inhabitants who perished there. There are many kosher stores and restaurants as well as synagogues scattered throughout the area.

Of course, I had to investigate at least one Kosher restaurant as I love the food. I came across Gam Gam. The name fascinated me. The menu was extensive and so, of course, I ate too much. How could I not when the flavours were so wonderful and the 'red' Israeli beer was really good.

I managed to get some thinking time while relaxing over dinner next to a Venetian canal. My thoughts took me to another learning. I noticed people thinking I was doing something amazing in my life. The lovely owner at the

Four Seasons in Wroclaw thought it incredible that I spoke fluent Russian although born in Australia. The very helpful Italian lady on the bus from Treviso who helped me find my hotel in Venice, couldn't believe that I was travelling alone and kept congratulating me. The waiter at Gam Gam was equally amazed. I guess I should pay attention and give myself some recognition for the things I take for granted about myself. Travelling solo was allowing me to take time out and think through many things.

My third day in Venice was a day of saying farewell and isn't it ridiculous but it actually brought tears to my eyes. There must have been a reason for this but I didn't know what it was - somewhere, some time I may work it out. Anyway, as it was my last day there I thought I'd better do some of the things I hadn't yet done, so... off to the Bridge of Sighs, from the outside as I had no intention of standing in line for hours. The line stretched a very, very long way. One day I will return, perhaps one October again when the crowds are gone, and go inside the bridge which connects the Doges Palace to the prison. Descriptions I've read of the inside of the bridge are very interesting. One can only imagine the devastation felt by prisoners being led from the court to the prison, especially if they really were innocent. Poor old Casanova (the only prisoner to ever escape) must have had some interesting thoughts go through his head.

'I stood in Venice, on the Bridge of Sighs;
A palace and a prison on each hand:
I saw from out the wave her structures rise
As from the stroke of the enchanter's wand;
A thousand years their cloudy wings expand
Around me, and a dying Glory smiles
O'er the far times, when many a subject land
Looked to the wingéd Lion's marble piles,
Where Venice sate in state, throned on her hundred isles!
Byron, Lord (2004). *Childe Harold's Pilgrimage*. Urbana, Illinois: Project Gutenberg.
Retrieved September 13, 2020, from *www.gutenberg.org/ebooks/5131*

In my wanderings I discovered the royal gardens, an area with trees and flowers and seats. The majority of tourists obviously weren't interested in this lovely space so it was very relaxing to sit and dream amongst the greenery and quietude.

I walked the arcades of St Mark's Square wanting to have coffee at the Florian Café. It was lunchtime and much too busy, so I went back to the Guglie area, planning to get some good, healthy, sweet-smelling strawberries and nectarines for lunch. I started well with a cup of watermelon but ended up at 3pm with an espresso, a mini pizza and a Sicilian cannolo. Then, a brief re-visit to Murano and Burano. All this in the interest of some decent sunset photo chasing. Unfortunately, that time of year didn't seem to lend itself to great sunsets in Venice - or maybe it was just the three days of my visit there. They were so much more spectacular in October 2006. Still, I had a ball just riding around on boats and enjoying the views. I miss the creak of the boats at their moorings, the smell of the diesel when you stick your head out of a vaporetto to take a photo, the rush onto the boat to try and get an outside seat (even though you risk getting drenched). Eventually, I wrote a short poem of my impressions.

Venice

The vaporetto chugs across the lagoon
Belching diesel fumes as it passes bricole and statues,
Palazzos are left behind to the tourists
Who, now, in the distance are swarming like ants before rain;

A launch speeds past, its young passengers smile and wave,
In its sparkling wake the vaporetto chugs on,
Towards distant islands
Of coloured glass and snowy lace.

Jermolajew, Helene. *Laughter, Tears and Coffee* - Balboa Press 2017

And so it was farewell Venice, with a promise to return and who knows, maybe I'll find a way to spend a few months there writing. After all, miracles do happen.

Pisa

A smooth train ride from Venice via Padova, Bologna and Firenze and there I was in Pisa. Why? When I could have stayed in Venice which I love so much? Well.... it was all because of Andrea Bocelli.

While still at home I came across information that made my eyes pop. Andrea Bocelli has an open-air theatre in his home village of Lajatico, about 45kms out of Pisa. He only performs there once a year and it was at a time when I would be in Europe. I bought a ticket and was ready for the excitement. Travel to other countries was guided by this event. It was time to slow down a bit, have a look around Pisa, go to the concert and perhaps catch up on some writing.

I had my wish - a real, proper bathroom with a proper shower where I could stand up, have lots of beautiful hot water flowing over me and have both hands free. A real shower recess with a door. Sometimes it's the small things that get me excited. Whoever thought it was comfortable and convenient to sit in a bath with a hand-held shower, or to have no rim around the shower so water flowed into the bedroom area, or to stand holding the shower in one hand was oh, so wrong.

The first success of this trip was finding my way through the Pisan postal system. I did ask for clues at the hotel reception (which they happily provided and listened while I practised). The take-a-ticket system was familiar and the lovely lady behind the counter spoke reasonable English - after she let me test my limited Italian. I was rather proud of myself.

The centre of Pisa is much like many European towns with a central pedestrian shopping plaza (Corso Italia) which you walk along to get to almost anywhere. It stretches from the Railway station to the river Arno with shops on both sides and streets leading off it. On the way to the Post Office, I came across an interesting sight, two men in orange robes obviously meditating and doing something that appeared to be impossible. How does one person hold a pole in one hand with another man sitting on top of it?

Then, I was off on the first leg of my Pisan Hop On Hop Off experience in the heat of the Tuscan summer sun. Yes, the bell tower leans. I think it wanted to have a better look at the beautiful Baptistry and couldn't straighten up again. Seriously though, there are all sorts of explanations about the lean. In all of them, only the Tower is mentioned. On the bus, the guide said that many buildings in Pisa lean a little, even the Baptistry in the Campo dei Miracolo, but not as much as the Tower. It has something to do with the amount of water in the soil. The Tower had the worst lean and they have now straightened it a little, after all, you can't straighten it completely - nobody would come to visit the 'Previously Leaning Tower of Pisa'.

I was quite surprised by the open green area where the Tower leans. As well as the famous tower there is the Duomo (cathedral) the Baptistry and the Camposanto (cemetery). All the buildings are stunningly beautiful and the surrounding bright green grass of the 'field' accentuates their whiteness. The surrounding ancient wall adds a feeling of security.

There is so much more to Pisa than the Leaning Tower, one example is the ancient university. It is a public research university founded in 1343 by an edict of Pope Clement VI. It is the tenth oldest in Italy. Not only is it one of the top universities in Italy but it also houses Europe's oldest academic botanical garden, founded in 1544. By the end of the tour I was beginning to feel heat affected. Prevention of my possible reaction to being overheated was needed - one salt tablet, then 2 litres of water. I've lived in this body a long time and know exactly what would happen if I didn't pay attention.

The day of the concert dawned (13 July 2013) and I was feeling much better. Successfully negotiating the buying of a rail ticket to Rome in Italian at the station felt wonderful. The next challenge was to walk to the supermarket for supplies for the concert and some lunch. The supermarket yielded two very healthy and tasty peaches. And a block of Milka chocolate. A little lie down as I knew it would be a long night and I thought I was organised.

Then panic! I received an email that my booking for the coach was too late and there were no seats. What to do? I had visions of missing the concert, the whole reason for being there. Ok, think! And Don't Panic! As the reception staff were very helpful and fun, I rushed to the front desk to see what their advice might be. Yes, they had a solution and yes, it would cost megabucks but there was nothing for it, it was either take the cab they could arrange or miss the concert. They did say that if they could find more passengers, the fare would be cheaper. We did find more passengers but it didn't make the fare very much cheaper.

The cab turned up and off we went, we were just getting to the edge of town when a call came through that there were more passengers so back to town to pick them up. The passengers turned out to be a father and son from California, the father having given this trip to his son as a 50th birthday present. What a fantastic gift.

To get to the concert you drive 45 kilometres out of Pisa. No public transport, hence the cab (or a coach if you remember to book one in time). You are dropped off about 500 metres away from the entrance at the bottom of a Tuscan knoll. Then a walk up the hill and down the other side. Going up the hill was fine but then we came to a complete stop and stood around waiting for an hour. To this day I don't know exactly why, they never explained, but there were rumours about security not being sure whether to check bags or not. Finally, they started letting us in and it was a shuffle for the last 100 metres until we got through the entrance and into the field of the theatre. The view when we reached there was tremendous, the beautiful golden rolling knolls of Tuscany all around with the higher green-blue hills in the distance.

The stage was set with massive statues of two naked men, one crouching at the front to maintain his decency, the other a torso looking like he was about to hop over a wall. During the concert, they were lit in various coloured lights and became very effective. There was a massive amount of equipment and structures that later became stages for dancers and singers.

My seat was next to a young Indonesian guy who had lived in Switzerland for 12 months and is a mad Bocelli fan. We had some nice conversations and laughed that two people from a similar area of the world would end up sitting next to each other in Tuscany.

As the sun set over those golden knolls and the crescent moon rose, the music started. The atmosphere was electric, sometimes a hush and other times the applause was deafening. The music was stupendous and of course, it wasn't just Andrea Bocelli, it was his friends as well. The first half began with a reading of Andrea Bocelli's poem Borgo Natio (My Native Village) read by the Italian actor Giorgio Albertazzi. The first musical half was classical, mainly Verdi, and the second half lighter music. So everyone got a bit of everything. The second half started with a reading of another Bocelli poem, Al Crepuscolo un Angelo Mi Parla (An Angel Spoke to Me at Sunset).

The program included Anema e Core, Love me Tender, My Way, La Vie en Rose (they very cleverly inserted a film clip of Edith Piaf) and so much more. The guest musicians, singers and dancers provided terrific entertainment. There were names like Lindsay Kemp, Francesca Malacarne, Ricardo Cocciante, Simona Molinari amongst many others and of course the choir of the Theatre of Silence. The choir's rendition of O Fortuna was incredible. The dancers, the choir, all the soloists were amazing and then, of course, Bocelli himself. What can I say other than WOW! and BRAVO! Even now as I write this, many years later, and look through my photos and souvenir program my spine tingles and eyes mist.

Every now and again it would hit me 'I am in Lajatico, under the Tuscan sky listening and watching Andrea Bocelli live!' I mean really, how mind-blowing is that? The whole concert was brilliant and of course, the encores brought the invisible house down. Time to Say Goodbye and Nessun Dorma accompanied by a mass of fireworks ended the evening under the Tuscan moon. What a breathtaking experience, I just wished that my mother could have been there, her eyes would have sparkled.

And now, the evening over, the crowd started walking back to the coaches and cabs. At one point I could see the lights of the traffic as it wound its way back towards Pisa. I found the cab and my fellow passengers and off we went, joining the snaking line of red tail lights.

After that spectacular night, there was only one day left to finish exploring Pisa. I would have liked to see more of Tuscany and the coast but I wasn't prepared to risk driving on the wrong side of the road, so I had to be content with seeing what I could locally. Had I been staying longer I would have discovered how to get to places by bus or train.

The orange guys were still there, one still sitting on a stick. I wondered if they ever went home because, no matter when I walked past they were there day and night. If I hadn't seen some very slight movement once I'd have believed they were statues.

The visit to the supermarket this time yielded the best find yet – coffee yoghurt. My coffee fetish was definitely a theme on this grand tour, manifesting itself daily, in many forms.

There are lovely artworks, statues and buildings in Pisa. I came across Keith Harings Tuttomondo, an acrylic created in 1989. The statue of Vittorio Emanuelle, the first president of unified Italy, stands just before the entrance to the Corso. The paving around the railway station is a work of art on its own and the airport building is quite different to other airports with all its greenery. The river Arno and bridges, separating the two sides of the town, is beautiful and the ancient city wall is one of the most complete surviving walls in Europe.

Time to say Goodbye

Finally it was farewell to Pisa, to Bocelli and the Tower. While trying to decide where to go next to catch up on some writing, I realised Belgrade was calling.

Why is it that the night before travelling I don't sleep very well, leaving me tired and having to think harder to make sure I don't mess anything up? I caught the train to Rome then a flight to Belgrade. I could not find any way to check my luggage in on-line, the website said I had to check luggage at the airport. Well, that cost a small fortune. Luckily the considerate guard on the train to Rome didn't fine me for forgetting to validate my ticket, so that money went towards the luggage instead. Always remember to validate your train ticket, it can get expensive if you don't.

I'd been to Belgrade with Ginski in May, tracking down my mother's schools. So why go back? I needed a rest from sightseeing and I had more research to do on my parents. I needed to get additional chapters to Mum's memoir done. I thought perhaps the place where she lived for a while and spent a year in University studying medicine - before she got married and the war broke out (no, her marriage didn't cause the war) - might give me some inspiration. I'd been avoiding re-reading her book but I knew I had to, to be able to fill in a few gaps, as well as take it up to the end of her life.

CHAPTER 6

Serbia Take Two

M y nice, calm and very expensive flight from Rome arrived in Belgrade. The welcome back from the staff at the Hedonist Hostel was jubilant, hugs all around. It felt like a real homecoming, these guys start feeling like family the minute you step through their door. A big thank you to everyone who worked there. You made me feel very welcome.

After my visit in May, the Hedonist became the hostel I judged all others by. They set the bar very high knowing exactly how to make their guests feel at home and providing all the right information and entertainment. Both the weekly crepe nights and regular barbecue nights meant that we could all meet each other in very social gatherings. To think I almost ignored it when researching hostels in Belgrade.

This time there were heaps of Aussies. The Exit Festival had just finished in Novi Sad so Belgrade was full of young tourists. The hostel was bursting at the seams with fascinating travellers. It was Palacinke (crepe) night.

There are three reasons I prefer to stay in good hostels, the fascinating people you meet, the social events the staff put on and, of course, the affordability. In great hostels, they know exactly how to balance the in-house entertainment with peace and quiet and advice for outside recreation. Hotels mostly tend to leave you to your own devices so I only stay in them when I either need a break from socialising or there is no alternative.

Although the most important part of this world trip was my healing, that couldn't happen without researching my parents' early lives. As they spent most of their youth in Serbia, it was logical to return and continue my research. My plan for the first night back was to hop into bed, get some writing done and get a good night's sleep.

Well, as Robbie Burns said 'The best-laid schemes o' mice an' men/ Gang aft agley' (translates to 'often go awry'), no writing was done. My Norwegian room-mate and I sat up chatting late into the night sharing travel stories. Luckily we were the only two people in the dorm that night.

As a result of the late night my day started much later than planned so top gear was needed to achieve my goals. To get to the closest markets it is easiest to walk down Skadarlija street - it used to be known as the Montmartre of Serbia where the Bohemian life was led by poets, writers, singers and artists in the cafes and restaurants. In the early 20th century Olga Janceveckaya, one of my favourite Russian Gypsy songstresses, performed there. There were rumours she was a spy (not sure for which side), true or not it adds colour to this place. Skadarlija is very much a tourist area but maintains its old-world feel with cobblestones, masses of flowers in window boxes, restaurants serving wonderful food and al fresco dining bringing a buzz to the street.

Tenuous connections kept appearing as I continued to research my parents' lives in their favourite city. Quite possibly one or both of them frequented this street in their youth and now, here I was walking along the same cobblestones. That thought kept amazing me.

I went back to the bakery that Ginski and I discovered when we were there in May, for some local 'street food'. It was so nice to be back albeit, sadly, on my own this time.

I hadn't realised how close the markets were to the hostel. Down Simina, turn left on Skadarlija, through the Bohemian Quarter of cobblestones and charming restaurants, past the murals, across the major thoroughfare of Cara Dusan and there it was. Not immediately obvious but I eventually found the entrance. Hidden behind the buildings was a huge market. I loved those markets - cheap, colourful, full of vibrancy and wonderful fresh produce.

I walked back to the Hedonist along different streets and dropped into Jevrem restaurant for lunch. The external rustic décor was inviting and the inside didn't disappoint. My lunch was delicious and huge. Just as the description 'restaurant of home-cooking' suggested. I discovered that on a Friday night a pianist played at dinner time so I booked.

Back at the hostel, I was thrilled to see that people I'd met on my first visit just happened to be there again. It seems to be a place to which people keep returning. There were lots of chats with the two Russian girls with whom I still communicate over social media.

Now here's another thing I love about hostels, when you find a really good one set up perfectly for socialising, you end up sitting around chatting and meeting other travellers, you hear their stories, get invited to their countries, you learn more and sometimes make life-long friends. That night was one of those times and low and behold a friendship began with Natalie, an absolutely delightful and interesting young lady from Australia, lured by the aroma of my rissoles sizzling in the frying pan. We had a lot in common and she asked to borrow Mum's book. We have stayed in touch ever since and have managed to meet up back home several times. Our conversations are always as fascinating as they were in Belgrade. A beautiful old soul.

It was becoming obvious that my original reason for returning to Belgrade (thinking I would find time and quiet space to start some serious writing) just wasn't going to happen, although I did manage to at least write up each day's events in between the fun. Apparently meeting people and creating memories was much more important.

It seemed that word was spreading that I write – not surprising I guess seeing as I was sitting at the computer in the lounge area a lot. People kept asking me what I was doing so the story of my parents' lives and my research was repeated many times. A young fellow came up one night and the first thing he said was 'I've been told you write and I need to talk to someone who might understand'. So that took us into a lengthy conversation about muses, people thinking he's crazy and so on. All he really needed was confirmation that other people also have words forming themselves into creative expressions at weird times. Poor guy had obviously been put down by both family and friends when he shared his thoughts. I enjoyed chatting and supporting him in actually writing his thoughts down instead of just letting them become lost out of his head. I hope he is writing.

Only in Belgrade! I went for an innocent walk, popped into an antique shop for a quick look and ended up joining the owner and a customer in rakija, white wine, cevapcici, loud music and dancing. I could not believe the other two when they both got on the furniture to dance. It was difficult extracting myself from the clutches of the antique store – which was taking on a surreal atmosphere and I thought that at any moment a piece of furniture would drag me into some parallel universe. I finally made my excuses, left the other two to their dancing and drinking and continued exploring Knez Mihailova.

You'll find all sorts of things along that amazing street; fountains, sculptures, cafes, restaurants, hotels, shops, people selling weird stuff on the pavement and lots more. You could easily spend an entire day there. Knez Mihailova is protected by law as one of the oldest and most valuable landmarks of the city. It is named after the Prince of Serbia Mihailo Obrenovic III. Its one-kilometre length takes you from around the University Department of Philosophy to the entrance of Kalemagdan Park and was the main street when Belgrade was the Roman city of Singidunum.

It was time to get organised for dinner and live music at Jevrem. Self-imposed time out from re-reading Mum's book and researching was called for. As if I hadn't challenged myself enough, now it was dinner by myself in an atmospheric restaurant - worth a pat on the back.

The night turned out to be interesting. I sat down and while the waitress was chatting to me I noticed an elderly man and lady looking at me and smiling, I began to feel a little awkward. Then the sweet gentleman came over, it turned out that he was the pianist and wanted to ask what sort of music I liked so he could play it for me, so gracious. No sooner had he left to go to the piano than a lady came and sat at my table and proceeded to give me a Serbian history lesson, in Serbian. Luckily I understand enough to make some sense of it. The waitress couldn't stop apologising, but it was really sweet although I would have preferred to just listen to the music. Anyway, she stayed for a drink and left after giving me several hundred years of history, she must be very lonely.

A lovely dinner, strange talks, enchanting music and then back to the hostel. I walked into a party in the common room, the obligatory vodka before going clubbing. Soon they were all jolly enough and it was late enough for the young ones to go out and although I was invited to go along I had to say no. I'm still 'old school', going out at midnight just doesn't fit my reality. So there was some quiet time for me, at least until everyone came back, much worse for wear.

I'd had a flash of inspiration the previous day. Who could point me in the right direction for information on the period when Mum and Dad were there? Maybe if there was a Russian church they might know. A bit of research and, yes, a church in Belgrade (The Church of the Holy Trinity), within walking distance according to the map. After a night of deep emotion reading some of the saddest chapters of Mum's book to get my questions organised, I was off to church in the morning. A very long walk followed by two hours of standing and a long walk home took its toll, but I was glad I went, although as usual there were more questions than answers.

On that day a Serbian priest was leading the service as the Russian priest, who could have possibly given me answers, was in Moscow and wouldn't be back for more than a week. The churchwarden took my email address and questions promising to pass both on to the priest upon his return.

The absence of the priest caused some re-organisation. I wasn't planning to stay that long, what to do? It seemed, though, that he may have been able to help me out, as this is the church where General Wrangel, leader of the white Russian Army is interred. I had heard many a story from Mum about the General and the evacuation of the army to Yugoslavia. Mum's uncle was in that army. There were also the stories from Mr K on our amazing discovery trip to Bela Crkva. Although no research could be done that day, once the choir started singing I just had to stay on. A very small choir but what beautiful voices!

On the way out of the church, I ran straight into a Serbian wedding going to St Mark's next door, complete with 'lumpovanje'. This is a traditional musical accompaniment for the bride and groom. A very loud brass band with accordions and drums accompany the wedding party through the streets playing a very loud style of traditional music. Again I remembered my mother's stories of weddings in various towns and villages. I wondered, were these the churches of her Easter stories of leaving the Russian church at the end of the midnight service just as the Serbs were going to theirs?

The next few days were taken up with exploring museums and the fortress, a fascinating rambling place built at the confluence of the Sava and Danube rivers. An interesting visit to the National Museum on the main city square, Trg Republike. I hadn't even thought about this area being part of the Roman Empire, but there it is, lots of relics and ruins. I hadn't known about the Milan Edict either, perhaps in our current times, we need to be more aware of what it says and perhaps expand it. The Edict of Milan was a proclamation granting all persons freedom to worship whatever deity they pleased, effectively establishing religious tolerance.

Next was a visit to Tito's Mausoleum (also known as The House of Flowers) and the two museums next to it. A Finnish lady who was also staying at the hostel accompanied me. I found both the mausoleum and museums interesting and important because of my parents' story.

There are times when the leader of a country can fundamentally change your life. Hitler changed the world for everybody and touched my mother's life directly. She refused to clean snow from the streets of Belgrade and was taken away on a truck to work in a labour camp in Germany. She spent most of the war in slave labour.

Stalin, Roosevelt and Churchill affected the lives of millions of Russians with the Yalta agreement. My parents, while getting out of Germany once it capitulated, had to avoid the Soviets at all costs or they would be sent to the USSR most likely to certain death. Then there was Tito. My parents dreamed of returning to their beloved homeland but on discovering that Yugoslavia was now communist and Tito was at the time friendly with Stalin, their plans had to change.

Five leaders affected my family's life. My parents ended up crossing countries, continents and seas so I could be born in a free, wonderful country. Of course, I had to visit the mausoleum of the man who, without even knowing who they were, changed my parents' destiny. Real history.

Not only is Tito's white marble grave in the mausoleum (although supposedly he is actually buried outside amongst the flowers) but there are displays of all the gifts he received. One of the displays fascinated me in particular. This was the exhibit of batons brought to him each birthday on 25th May. It all started in 1945 when the youth of the country organised mass baton relays throughout Yugoslavia. The batons conveyed birthday wishes for long life and good health to Tito. There are apparently 22,000 of them in the museum, many very elaborately decorated. Eventually, the 25th of May became known as Youth Day.

Sometimes hostel life can be awesome as it was that evening, with crepe night, a birthday watermelon (spiked with vodka) for one of the girls and live entertainment by a bunch of Swedes and a saxophonist from somewhere else. At other times it can be very annoying as was the next night when I was awoken at some horrific hour of the morning by the Brazilian boys who had been out all night and for some reason needed to have a conversation in the dorm.

31 degrees in Belgrade felt so much 'hotter' than 31 at home, maybe it's the humidity. Due to the heat and lack of sleep a walk to the post office, the gelato place and the supermarket were enough for one day! The afternoon was spent lounging around drinking local beer and chatting to a young lady from Chile about Mum's book, my research and her amazing search for family - now that's the way to spend a hot languid afternoon on holidays.

There is an unwritten set of hostel manners that the decent travellers adhere to. It was quiet until 5am, then shattered silence! Alarm goes off, the girl finally gets up looking for the phone. Is it in the locker? No, maybe in the luggage? Yes! Alarm gets louder, hmmm, can't see in the dark, light goes on, finally, alarm stops. She visits the bathroom, back in bed, silence again, till 5.45 when the same person decides it's time to get up, bed light goes on, lots of rustling, zippers opening and closing. She leaves, the light stays on. Within 30 minutes she broke just about every one of those unwritten manners.

Even though it was 33 degrees I decided to go to Zemun. It was once a separate city on the Danube. I managed to walk a little distance along the decorated riverside paving but the heat got the better of me and I left.

From the bus to Zemun I had noticed a massive market with a very Ottoman looking roof so on the way back I hopped off to explore. Located across the road from the central transportation hub, Zeleni Venac is massive. It was exciting scouring rows upon rows of everything you can think of, not just food products.

Due to the absence of the Russian priest, I decided to go to Hungary for a week. Time for the next adventure. It is much cheaper and more convenient to go by minibus. The Hedonist books the bus, you leave at a civilised hour of the day, it is safe and the driver looks after the border crossing by collecting all the passports. The border guards have a good look at you before handing back your passport, but we didn't have to get out of the bus, so that was good, we must not have looked like a bunch of smugglers. It was a temporary farewell to Belgrade.

Budapest

I checked the weather report, they were predicting anything from 39° - 45° for Belgrade, luckily I was travelling to Budapest where the prediction was only 38°! If only that were true.

There I was, sitting on the top deck of my boat hotel on the Danube, watching the sun as it set behind the trees on Margit island. The minibus from Belgrade had arrived a few hours earlier. The temperature at the time was 43° Centigrade.

Finding my boat was a problem. The bus driver thought he knew where the boat was and dropped me as close to Parliament House as he could, telling me that the boat was behind the building. After half an hour of walking in massive heat, I discovered that there were no boat hotels behind Parliament House, they were all further along the river in the opposite direction. It was seriously hot! I was dripping wet from both sweat and pouring water on myself - I couldn't drink it as it was now very warm from the high air temperature. My salt tablets were buried deep in my luggage. I could see large boats berthed along the river bank and felt that one of them had to be mine, but which one? The path gave way to cobblestones and as my suitcase bumped along the stones my mind floated back to two events separated by 5 years.

It was 1967, I was 16. We had moved to the north side of Sydney Harbour and I was missing the country. Mum and Dad had split up and to make ends meet my mother was working two jobs. During the day she was cleaning houses and at night she was cooking in a large restaurant. That summer day was very hot, her cleaning was mainly in the living rooms of a large house with huge windows. At night the air conditioning in the restaurant kitchen had broken down and again she was working in high heat. By the time she came home, my mother was vomiting. She went to bed, I called the doctor. In those days, luckily, the family doctors still made house calls at night.

Mum's doctor sat with her all night. I later found out that he was very worried she wouldn't make to morning. I can't remember what happened the next day – I assume I went to school. Mum wouldn't have let me stay at home. My mind has a very efficient system of not remembering details of family traumas. I may remember an event from early childhood but the details blur. I do remember that a little later the doctor told us to always carry salt tablets as both Mum and I had a propensity towards dehydrating very quickly due to our bodies' inability to store fluid efficiently. Well, that explained a lot about the water-in-water-out problem I had.

Five years later I had moved to my boyfriend's house and was working in a retail lighting store in Parramatta. It was a very hot summer day. The store had no air conditioning and no fans. There was no direct line between the front and back door for a breeze to blow through (had there been a breeze that day) and the display lights were on. After lunch I succumbed to the dreaded heat, collapsing on the floor under my desk. I was working on my own but luckily one of the lighting representatives came in and found me. Then the part-time afternoon colleague came in. I have no memory of how I got home. If I caught the usual public transport it would have meant a bus, a train and a lengthy walk to get home – could I have done that in my condition? Did someone give me a lift? I have no idea. What I know is it took several showers and a long bath in Epsom salts to start feeling normal. The next day the weather broke and the temperature dropped.

As my mind wandered through those memories and my energy was flagging, I saw the name of my boat. Such blessed relief that I would soon be able to get some cold water and hopefully a shower. I had made it!

Budapest was amazing already and I had only seen a little through the bus window and on my walk. I knew I was going to love that week. First things first. My room organised and the bar and grill found. My room on the boat was a little hot and smelled of something unidentifiable, the air conditioning wasn't very efficient so I had a feeling it would be a hot box, but I DIDN'T CARE. I sat on the deck wishing all my dear friends were there to share the beautiful sight of the Margit bridge all lit up, with Parliament behind it, and the Danube a rippling river of gold. There was a storm brewing, the temperature dropped a little and the breeze picked up. I was so glad I had chosen that place. I decided to have lemonade to celebrate - I was all beered out.

I awoke to a cool gentle wind carrying the music from the fountain on Margit Island over to me. I couldn't remember the name of the first (classical) piece but it was followed by 'Cecilia, you're breaking my heart'. The land of contrasts.

It was Budapest orientation day, two lines of the Hop On Hop Off. The city is incredible, there are so many places to hop off that I began thinking that a week wasn't going to be enough. Budapest is often called the Paris of Hungary but I think it's more like Rome, Vienna and Paris all rolled into one. I could easily photograph every building and every corner of every building, just as I did in Rome in '06, stroll down boulevards and the river bank as in Paris and ogle the amazing architecture just like Vienna. The plan for the next day was to find out if the Budapest castle is equal to Schönbrunn, after all, Sissy had a strong connection to Hungary, and there is the Elizabeth bridge named after her.

I had a big day planned. I managed the Castle, Heroes Square, the outside of the Synagogue and the multimedia fountain. The Buda castle has a long history dating from 1265. There has been destruction, invasions, take-overs, political decisions, re-building and on goes the turbulent history. Next to the castle is the area called the Fisherman's Bastion, which catches the eye immediately. You would swear it was a Disney building but no, it was built between 1895 and 1902. It is a neo-Gothic and neo-Romanesque style terrace with stunning views of the Danube and the Pest side of the city. It has seven towers which represent the seven Magyar tribes that settled in the Carpathian valley in 895. A fairy-tale structure.

Halfway through the bus tour I hopped off to find lunch and came across the Wreck pub. Old tyres, motorbikes, posters of the Ratpack and Miles Davis, old LP records for decoration and 44-gallon drums as tables. So that's where I had lunch. Cappuccino and 2 slices of Hawaiian pizza. The equivalent of $3.70 Australian.

Evening was upon me. I had been hearing the music from the multi-media fountain as I sat on deck. After a day of exploration and the excitement of the castle, I went to find the source. To get there I needed to walk along the river then cross Margit Bridge. On the way, an old biplane buzzed the island. Somebody said it was an old Soviet machine and it happened every day at dusk. Yet another re-enactment of Soviet days.

Finally, I reached the fountain. The water sways and dances in perfect harmony to the music and the colours explode with passion. The Margit island fountain is absolutely on par with the spectacular one in Wroclaw. This one plays two tunes on the hour during the day and then at 9pm every night it has a half-hour of the whole repertoire, just gorgeous. By then it's dark and the colours are vibrant. I sat amongst all the other visitors, enthralled. People treat it as an outdoor theatre and bring their picnic dinner with them.

Religious tourism was called for the next day, but first some decadent food. I went in search of somewhere spectacular for morning tea hoping to find some local Dobos torte. My choice was the ultimate cafe poets' venue. The New York Café. What a history, a place where poets and literary people met, conversed and created.

If you open the New York Café's website you will read 'There is no literature without a Café – stated Sándor Márai (1900-1989), a Hungarian writer, who himself frequently visited the historical building of New York Café to get inspiration.'

Surrounded by Versailles-worthy opulence I felt very special as I munched my way through a degustation of assorted desserts, but no Dobos. On the ceiling, Sistine Chapel-worthy art framed with stuccoed angels, gilt and marble columns looked down on me. I thought of the cafes where we meet back home and wonder what our writing would be like if we had such history and glamour surrounding us.

I visited the Great Synagogue (Dohany) I'd seen from the outside. I had never heard of this branch of Jewish religion, it is only found in

Hungary. Called Neolog, not as conservative as Orthodox Jews and not as modern as Reformed Judaism. The ghetto was next to the Synagogue. Built between 1854 and 1859 it has elements of several architectural styles including Moorish and Byzantine. After wandering through, amazed by its stunning interior with its decorated ceiling, stained glass windows, polished wood and decorative lighting, I entered the courtyard. There before me was the most incredible silver tree. The Emmanuel tree. Fine threads were appearing again connecting to my youth.

Tony Curtis was one of my favourite actors in the 1960s. Of Hungarian-Jewish heritage, his real name was Bernard Schwartz. I discovered that he set up the Emmanuel Foundation to help raise money for the restoration of this synagogue and to sponsor the creation of the Tree of Life in the Memorial Garden. The stunning tree is a memorial to all who perished and in memory of his parents. It is a beautiful work of art created by Imre Varga and a must-see.

I moved on to visit the neo-classical St Stephens Catholic Basilica designed by Miklos Ybl. On the way, I came across market stalls neatly lining the wide footpath. There was everything there from hats and bags to pottery, jewellery and alcohol.

St Stephens Basilica proved to be another huge and ornate church, 96 metres high. Apparently, regulations prohibit any building to be taller than 96 metres. Perhaps this is why the vista of Budapest from high points is so charming and emotive – no skyscrapers.

Having had my fill of religious architecture and art I was off to conquer Vaci Utca (the 1.3 km pedestrian street). Shops come and go but if you don't go to Vaci Utca you will miss out on an amazing street. Go there, have fun.

And so, two glasses of Szent Istvan Korona Cabernet Sauvignon (those who know me and wine will at this point be saying 'Whaaaaat'?) Yes, a red I could drink - I hoped it would help me get to sleep so I could get up in 6 1/2 short hours to go on my next tour.

Breakfast included learning my first words of Hungarian, 'Jo regelt' – 'good morning'. Tour day. It was fun. A Japanese mother and daughter were already on the bus when I boarded. The mother started chatting to me before I'd even sat down. We three hit it off really well and spent a lot of time together. I'm glad we did because I got this niggling feeling that most people were steering away from these two lovely ladies. We all oohed and aahed at the size and ornateness of the cathedral in the original Hungarian capital Ersztergom, what a history this country has. But that's Europe - invasion after invasion, each conqueror destroying the past and the next one rebuilding. Lots of Roman ruins all over the place but the guide said there is no money to even start reconstruction.

We stopped at a wonderful restaurant perched on a hill. Massive windows framed with ivy on the outside creating a checkerboard of green and glass, making the building look as if it had grown out of the surrounding greenery.

On to the Buda Castle then a brief hop over the bridge to the Slovakian side of the Danube just so we could say we had been there.

The next stop was Szentendre, the Artists Village, where artists of various media and many fashion designers are located. It was interesting and quaint although set up for tourists, with souvenir shops and restaurants. A pretty place nonetheless with wonderful stone alleyways and spectacular artworks - I was so tempted.

Soon our day was over and we had reached the last part of our tour, a boat ride back along the very pretty, but brown, Danube. The guide laughed and said Strauss must have been in love to ever think the Danube was blue. Perhaps it was blue in Vienna when Strauss composed his beautiful waltz, the memorable music to which my mother taught me to dance the Viennese waltz. My mind swept back the years and there I was dancing with my mum learning the old intricate steps. I still haven't met anyone who can do the reverse waltz or the Viennese butterfly.

It turned out that quite independently the two Japanese ladies and I booked the same tour to the Puszta (Hungarian Plains). We were excited to realise we would spend Sunday together too. I was looking forward to some open spaces and horses. For now, though, it was nearly 9pm. I was on deck with the spiders and mosquitos, Venus had risen, the horizon was a pale apricot, the boats were chugging up and down the river and I was hoping to hear some of the music from the island.

I had tracked down a friend's cousin and we arranged to meet after lunch on Saturday. I had a wonderfully crazy Hungarian friend in Canberra. I always said that Steve and his partner had a revolving door, always welcoming to all sorts of people and always ready with an ear and a 'cuppa'. All 'political correctness' would be left on the pavement, once through the door, any and all topics were discussed without judgement. How sad it is that he has also departed this Earth and that door is closed forever.

What a terrific afternoon I had with his delightful cousin Kata. We walked over to Margit Island. We talked about all sorts of subjects, had coffee, found exciting hidden places, talked some more, discussing everything from family to world politics and discovered lots of similarities. Just like her cousin, talking was easy and fun. I was slowly but surely building more wonderful friendships. My request to my angels to support me on my journey was certainly manifesting in all sorts of ways that would stretch well into the future.

Having a local person to show me around meant I saw and learned things I wouldn't have found on my own. On that island are the ruins of the Dominican Monastery of the Blessed Virgin, founded by King Bela IV of Hungary. His daughter Margaret lived in the monastery from the age of ten and became a nun there. The statue of Imre Madach, poet, writer, aristocrat, invited me to sit awhile and cuddle up.

Sunday arrived, time for the Hungarian Puszta tour. Was the history we were told true? I have no idea and I don't really care because the experience was fantastic. Sometimes when travelling keeping an open mind on the correctness of information takes a back seat to the experience. At other times I really do want to know that the stories are true. The Puszta visit was exhilarating. We were met with shots of Palinka, taken on a ride in carts and saw the amazing horsemanship, performed by incredibly good looking men in stunning blue outfits. For the first time, I met grey Hungarian cattle and dreadlocked sheep. I had already met the Hungarian dreadlocked dog (puli) as my friends back home had one, but sheep? Then there were the strange chickens with bare necks. History we can read in a book but this experience transcended words.

Lunch was wonderful, I learned that what we call goulash isn't. Goulash in Hungary is a soup, it's awesome. Again those threads appeared in my mind. Memories of Dad taking us to a motel restaurant owned by Hungarians and me sliding the whole chillies from my plate of goulash on to Mum's plate. My 16th birthday when Dad gave me a vinyl album of Hungarian Gypsy music and I wondered why. Eventually, many years later it became one of my favourites and was played many times. The traditional band at the Puszta entertained us beautifully, so much fun and terrific musicians, my Japanese friends were so excited as the daughter plays several instruments including the violin. She was enthralled. The violinist came over and played some Japanese themed tunes for her. All in all a gorgeous day.

Too soon it was farewell to beautiful Budapest, I hoped to get another glimpse on the way to Sweden in a very short while. Farewell to Kata, farewell fountains where children and adults could play in the water on hot days, stunning bridges, incredible sculptures of bronze horsemen. Farewell Heroes Square with your columns and statues of the seven chieftains of the Magyars, farewell castles, Margit Island wonderful food and the boat on the Danube - I loved every minute of it.

Return to Belgrade

My last careful climb up and down the steep stairs to breakfast on the boat and then off to Belgrade again.

I was beginning to get a little concerned waiting for the minibus to pick me up from the boat hotel. It was late and I was getting very hot. After my experience the week before, being dropped at the wrong place and having to walk a few kilometres in 43-degree heat I wondered whether the driver would find me. Eventually, an hour late, he did. So started the 380 odd kilometre trip back to Belgrade and the Hedonist Hostel.

The Hedonist felt like home the very first time I walked in there three months earlier with Ginski, on this third visit it still felt the same. The warm welcome and hugs never change.

Back to honey rakija and Serbian coffee before breakfast. I remembered many a bewildered reaction when I would take friends to visit my parents on the farm. Before breakfast dad would bring out the vodka or the slivovic and pour shots. I have always found different cultural norms fascinating and there in Serbia, I understood where my father's social habits came from.

As always the place was full of interesting people, this time mainly Swedes. Hostels are such interesting places, there will always be the odd person who is either annoying or rude or hasn't washed for several days, but mostly everyone is really great.

It was the 7th of August, not an important date in my calendar and I wasn't planning on meeting a whole bunch of new friends that day, but... there you go, I did.

Day three dawned late, perhaps it had something to do with the amount of beer consumed the previous night at the weekly hostel barbecue. I loved the barbecue nights, there is a gorgeous paved area outside with a huge brick barbecue, seats, tables and a rather large drinks fridge. Many a night was spent there laughing, chatting and meeting new people. There were many birthday celebrations with vodka watermelons, sumptuous meals, beer by the gallon, music and conversation.

Four women, three nationalities and a fortress.

Most times I found there will be at least one person to whom I relate well. This time it was several. There was a charming mother and daughter team from Sweden, they were in Belgrade for a wedding. Delightful Selin was from Turkey. We all somehow gravitated together, hit it off immediately and went on a few adventures around the city. Somehow I kept finding incredible people.

These ladies were so much fun and we still communicate through social media. Although the Swedish mother didn't speak English and I definitely don't speak Swedish we somehow managed to communicate and have a lot of laughs even when her daughter wasn't there to translate.

After a very healthy brunch on Skardalija at midday, it was exploring time. We strolled the full length of Knez Mihailova pedestrian plaza, through the beautiful Kalemegdan Park and on to the fortress on the confluence of the rivers Sava and Danube.

I find it fascinating going to the same place with different people, I always get to see things from a different perspective and through another person's eyes. We roamed the ruins, were amazed by the age of the structure and took heaps of photos.

Down a set of stone steps there is the beautiful little ivy-covered Ruzica Serbian Orthodox church (dedicated to the Nativity of the Mother of God, Crkva Ruzica or Little Rose) and the Chapel of St Petka which houses the well of healing water.

The current church was a gunpowder store in the 18th century and was converted to a military church in the mid-1800s. It is unusual and a must to visit. There was a service when we went there and then a parade to the almost adjacent St Petka chapel where you can buy bottles of holy water from the holy spring.

The rest of the afternoon was spent chilling with beers on the terrace of the Kalemegdanska Terasa restaurant. We succumbed to pizza for an early dinner and watched the sun setting over the rivers as the large fountain on the terrace gurgled and splashed next to us. Always at the back of my mind was the question, did my parents watch the sunset from the Fortress? I believe they would have and I was sharing something precious with them.

The walk home was thought-provoking. Knez Mihailovo takes on a different atmosphere after dark. It's a subtle change yet noticeable. No matter where you are in the world something changes after sunset.

Although this trip back to Belgrade was mostly about completing as much research as I could about my parents' time there, I wasn't about to pass up company on my explorations. The next day, while others were shopping and creating a very tasty barbecue for that night, my Swedish friends and I took off on a mega walk starting with the Russian church to find out if the priest was back. He was, but I would have to go to the Sunday service to be able to talk to him.

That was followed by the Serbian St Marks next door, another amazing structure which contains the tomb of Tsar Dusan (The Mighty) 1308-1355, King of Serbia and Emperor of the Serbs and Greeks. His constitution of the Serbian Empire known as Dusan's Code is said to be one of the most important literary works of mediaeval Serbia. Then on to the Nikola Tesla Museum. I knew about Tesla's alternating current invention but had no idea of the multitude of other inventions - the man was a genius.

The heat was horrendous, still in the high 30's so we three were happy to go inside to a cool museum. Poor cool-country Swedish mother was really suffering. We just sat down in the film area, watched the Serbian film and listened to a Serbian history lesson on Tesla and didn't care that there was no translation. It's amazing how much I could pick up with my less than basic knowledge of Serbian. Sometimes I wished I had continued with both languages instead of just sticking with Russian. We stayed for quite some time enjoying the coolness.

Rested and cooled down we returned to the hostel where platters of salads awaited us and the Swedish guys were busily cooking up mountains of meat. Sometimes it's marvellous being the Golden Oldie and being looked after by the young crowd. I don't allow anyone to generalise to me about young people anymore. Most of the ones I know and certainly most of the ones I met on that trip are wonderful caring people. We can all learn something from the upcoming generations. I have been learning from my own sons all of their lives and learned so much on my trip, not the least of which was how caring, respectful and delightful many young people are.

Sunday morning found me on the very long walk to the Russian Orthodox Church of the Holy Trinity. Standing in church for ages is just so bad for my back but that is tradition and stand you do. At least I did get to briefly talk to the priest who said that his uncle should be able to point me in the direction of useful information. 'Leave your email and I will pass it on' so for the third time I did just that. This time I was hopeful that I may learn something, however, sadly, that hasn't happened. I guess I was expecting too much from people who have no connection to my research. Never mind, when the time is right the information will come.

I did find little bits of interesting information in my visits (like discovering General Wrangel's tomb inside that church,) and have realised how much work history authors must go through to find information.

My walk back took me past the massive green and cream Moscow Hotel. I decided it would be nice to treat myself to another Chimney cake, the shop was almost on the way. This is an amazing pastry originating in Hungary. My son and I discovered it on our first walk up the pedestrian plaza back in May. The cake is made from strips of sweet yeast dough wound around a pipe-shaped baking spit, allowed to rise, rolled in sugar then baked in a vertical grill in front of electrical elements, a bit like a kebab grill. The original used to be baked over hot coals as you would cook meat on a spit. As the cake is baking the sugar melts, it can then be dipped in further toppings like chocolate, nuts or cinnamon – or all of them. Lovely decadence!

Oh! That Chimney Cake!
my son Ginski captured the delicious moment.

School of Medicine

After Mum completed school in 1937 she entered the University of Belgrade to study medicine. I went in search of her footsteps. I travelled on the tram assuming the line wouldn't have changed much although not knowing where my mother lived I wasn't sure which tram she would have caught. However, finding the stop where she may have got on and off the tram was more important as it featured highly in her changing fortunes.

I found the School of Medicine and the Faculty of Medicine, I suspect it was one of those buildings (or even both) where Mum began her studies with dreams of becoming a doctor. A dream that was never to be. The School of Medicine door was open so I stuck my head in and took a photo, the building old and crumbling, but renovations were underway. There were people upstairs but again, without the language I chose not to interfere.

I loved a notice on the door to the building that spelled out the dress code, basically saying that 'this is a seat of learning so no shorts, miniskirts ... those are clothes for the beach, not a university'.

Wandering further I found the chapel dedicated to the twin brother physician saints Cosmas and Damian, possibly Mum may have, on occasion, popped in there. It is there for all medical staff, students and patients, also under renovation.

A massive area is dedicated to the medical faculty, clinics, hospitals and administration - almost a small suburb. I could see why my mother would have felt quite at home in such an academic atmosphere. She loved learning, she was particularly interested in medicine and Dad's specialist used to call her his 'assistant' as she always wanted to know all the details. She remembered and did everything the specialist told her. However, she was interested in all sorts of subjects, she had what Professor Sumner Miller used to call 'an enquiring mind'. So in her late seventies and through most of her 80's she studied through the University of the Third Age (U3A) starting with Religion and Philosophy and ending with Latin and Rose propagation. My amazing Mum.

I think I found the tram stops where Mum caught her tram and where Dad, in his taxi-driving days, 'picked' her up. As it happens those stops are right in front of the St Sava Cathedral. The building of this church began in 1935 and the walls were up to about 7 metres in height when my mother started university. The inside of the church was still not fully finished when I was there although the construction was completed in 1989. It is solely funded by donations from all over the world and is one of the biggest Orthodox churches as well as one of the largest church buildings in the world. It is dedicated to the founder of the Serbian

Orthodox Church and important mediaeval figure, St Sava. The church is built on the Vracar plateau where the Saint's remains were burned by the Ottoman Grand Vizier Sinan Pasha in 1595. It is a grand and beautiful structure.

I followed the suggestion to visit Ada (Belgrade's beach), a very popular place for the locals. Serbia is landlocked, so it's a long way to the sea. Ada is an island in the river Sava which has been artificially turned into a peninsula. Although I couldn't work out an easy way to reach there on public transport, it was worth the trip. I wasn't prepared for its size or good planning. There you will find beautiful barbecue and picnic spots with lots of trees for summer shade, areas for swimming, multiple sports on both land and water (including cable water skiing), cafes, a hotel and much more. It covers an area of about 2.7 square kilometres. For golden oldies like me, there is the cute little train that drives you all the way around the lake. You can choose where to stop or just keep going as I did to get a good overview. My city council could learn a lot from there and do the same on Lake Burley Griffin.

The long farewell

Finally, the day came when I had to say goodbye. I hadn't done everything I wanted in the three trips to the land of my parents, and I hadn't found out all the information but I managed some of it, enough to keep me going and to get an understanding of their stories. Last visit to the medical precinct and St Sava - this time on the bus. The ride on the old yellow, articulated 31 bus was memorable. The bumps, jerks, rattles and rolls (not to mention a braking technique that could send you running all the way from the back down the aisle and possibly through the front window, if you weren't hanging on) will never be forgotten.

Last walk past Studenski park and the Faculty of Philosophy building to visit Knez Mihailova, on to Kalemegdan but this time along the river where I hadn't been before. I was so glad I did that because a snippet of Mum's stories came to mind about walking along the bank of the Sava and a high wall. My memory had confused that description with her university stories so I thought the university was at the top of the wall but I suddenly realised it was the Fortress. Oh, to have those conversations again. Back past the market stalls in the Fortress park, past the hotel Moscow and the chimney cake store – I discovered I had become attached to this city.

It was goodbye to the Hedonist. You guys are awesome and you will stay in my fond memories forever. Farewell Belgrade, the most chilled out city I had come across so far and Serbia, you served me well.

It was farewell to my new friends with whom I'd had so many adventures and laughs. Most of us have been in touch on social media since then so memories continue. Sadly, it was also farewell to cheap beer, brilliant honey rakija and good food.

There were other good times to be found and I was off to Uppsala in Sweden.

Checking out Vikings

Of course, the minibus driver from Belgrade dropped me at the wrong hotel at Budapest airport. OK, so both hotels start with the words Airport Hotel but the wrong one also stops with those words, the right one has several more words in the title. I had taken the precaution of giving the driver a note with the full address! At least this time it only cost 5 Euros to get the wrong hotel to take me to the right hotel.

I arrived in Sweden, land of the Vikings and crayfish, on Norwegian Air, a nice comfortable flight. Then to my friend Jen's place after the best train ride ever from the airport. A very pleasant walk, lovely home-made dinner and the Bermet spiced Serbian wine, it was time to just chill. It was also the time to meet Bosse, Jen's sister's Pomeranian. What a character! There were to be many meetings with this little fellow, but I only ever attempted to pick him up once, that event led to him spraying all of us with doggy pee.

Food shopping the next day before preparing for dinner. In the supermarket, I discovered the Swedish fetish not only for seafood but also for cheese. What an experience! Walls of cheese of all sorts and sizes. Blocks of many kilo weights and finally my search for my favourite, Jahlsberg was at an end.

And so we moved on to the evening. I knew that a Swedish crayfish party was being planned but I had no idea what one of those was... I soon found out. Crayfish decorations were hung, family and friends arrived with food and drinks, kilos of crayfish were cooked and the evening began. Crazy Swedish crayfish songs. Somewhere there is an embarrassing video of me singing a solo after someone gave me a song sheet and said 'sing this'. Now, I don't know a word of Swedish, nor do I have a good singing voice. Somehow I got through by channelling my inner Muppets Swedish Chef and at the end was greeted by looks of amazement as my friends said they even understood a few words – trust me, travellers, go to a Swedish crayfish party in summer, they are such fun.

On top of that, I found that this bunch of Swedes liked Gogol Bordello as much as I do. Who would have thought? So between the Crayfish party and Gogol Bordello songs, the Swedes were now winning the party stakes. Thanks Jen and friends, and this was only day two.

On my way to Sweden, I was reading the in-flight magazine and discovered that many Swedes are car freaks, just like family and friends back home. They own and drive American 50s and 60s cars and indulge in good old rockabilly music and clothes. Known as Raggare they organise car shows all over the country, and that's how day three was spent in Uppsala. More synchronicity. The crowd, masses of cars and a live band, made for a very pleasant afternoon - thank you Swedes for liking the right sorts of cars and music, it was just like being at the Elvis Festival in Parkes. Of course, this meant that I met a whole lot more people, Jen's mum and gorgeous grandmother and later other family members.

To quote Jen, 'So, we survived the American car show - cars, cars, cars, raggare, drunk raggare and then a quick visit to see my grandmother and my aunts. And my heart just melted when my grandmother told me to tell Helene to have a nice stay (my grandmother doesn't speak English) at the same time as she was hugging her goodbye. My grandmother is the cutest'. Yes, she is! Sadly, this golden-hearted woman has since passed.

Sunday was the day to get around to cooking my mother's rissoles and Ginski's veggies for dinner and taking life easy.

The next day Jen took me to just about every sight there is to see in Uppsala, joined by two lovely Uppsala girls I met in Belgrade. A week's walking in one day! We visited the tallest Cathedral I'd seen thus far, the twin towers of the French High Gothic Cathedral rise to 118.7 metres. If you stand in front of them and look up to the top of the twin spires there is a weird sensation of them falling towards you. Then the castle, the library, parks, Botanic gardens, relaxing by the pretty river Fyris, playing with and climbing on all sorts of statues including the Warm Man – seriously, in winter they heat the supine metal statue of a naked man so you can sit on him and warm up. Only in Sweden! All that was followed by shopping and cafes. It was lovely strolling through the town. I have no idea how many kilometres we covered on foot but it was a lot. Time and distance went by quickly with fun company, a very enjoyable way to spend a Monday.

The following day was allocated to the original capital of Sweden, Gamla Uppsala about 5 kilometres out of Uppsala city. First the museum. So much to learn, the displays were fascinating. Everything in Viking paraphernalia from costumes and jewellery, to boats and statues. There were explanations of the neighbouring royal burial mounds and so much more.

Not far away is the stone church Gamla Uppsala kyrka. It was built over the site of the pagan temple which honoured Thor, Odin and Freyr. The church dates from the early 12th century. Unfortunately, the present church is only a shadow of the original cathedral due to past fires. Inside the church are wall paintings and the tomb of Celsius, yes the thermometer man. I couldn't believe that also inside the church are original ancient bibles. One was the bible that belonged to King Gustav Vasas who was born in 1496, another belonged to Karl XII and yet another included illustrations by Rembrandt – although that one didn't look like an original. There they were just lying on a table for all to view, no glass cabinet and no-one looking over your shoulder. Near the church is its splendid red, wooden belfry.

Close by are the Royal Burial Mounds (Kungshögarna) - although they just look like any other hill. Three of the large burial mounds date from the 5th and 6th centuries AD. In both the Eastern and Western Mounds they have found evidence of people along with various grave goods including carved bronze panels, a comb, animals and luxurious weapons. I hope all the kings managed to get to Valhalla as they planned. There's also an area where they have found remnants of buildings from the Iron Age and possibly earlier.

I'd read about Vikings and their invasions and my older son loved the Asterix books, so my mind didn't connect those people with anything other than pillaging and invading. And yet, there is so much interesting ancient history to be gleaned. Thank you, my Swedish friends, for expanding my mind.

The next stop was Disagården (Disa Farm) an 1800s style working farm. Essentially it is an open-air museum where you can see a farm and village from the Uppland region. They grow grain, vegetables and fruit and tend various animals, mainly native breeds.

I was amazed at how much we covered in a short space of time. It was lunchtime so the decision was made that the most Swedish thing to do was to have meatballs at IKEA. I had never been to an IKEA store anywhere so a lunch of Swedish meatballs and mash in a giant store was an experience. Thank you, Yvonne, for driving us around and showing me places that otherwise we could not have reached easily.

I had a couple of theme songs playing their way through my head while travelling. One was Rowland Salley's Killing the Blues and the other was

'Leaving on a Jet Plane'. I'd been singing that travel theme song ever since my days of working on Lord Howe Island for a season in 1971. Again fine threads connecting back in time. The only reason I had that wonderful experience on the island was because my mother had worked there as a chef the previous year. I had been over to visit and she suggested that as I wanted to travel somewhere the island would be a good safe place. I wasn't too keen on 'safe' but didn't dare go against mum's 'suggestion', I was glad I didn't rebel that time. I was 20 years old. The song was brought back to me at the Hedonist where so many would sing it on their way out - always leaving somewhere. So, yes folks it was time to move on again. It took me a full day of trying to figure out where to go next as well as when and how. Originally I was going to go to Stockholm and then on a cruise to St Petersburg (I was told you could go there for up to 72 hours without a visa, under certain conditions) but it wasn't falling into place. Seeing as I had promised myself to follow my intuition and my motto 'if in doubt, don't' it was time for a re-think. But I couldn't decide.

One night before going to sleep, I had a word with my Universe. I said 'please guide me to my next destination, whatever place is in my mind when I wake up I will go there'. I was hoping it would be St Petersburg, but no! I woke up with Santorini on my mind. To say I was surprised would be a gross understatement. Santorini was almost 4,000 kilometres away. How was I to get there? And why?

Internet to the rescue and everything quickly fell into place. First stop Copenhagen, and although the accommodation was a little tricky in this popular city I found a hostel. So it was farewell to Uppsala. Farewell and a million thanks to Jen for looking after me (it's so good having a Swedish 'daughter'). Farewell and thank you to Therese and Yvonne for your friendship and taking me around places, introducing me to people and I can't forget Bosse (even though you barked at me), you are still so cute. Now it was 'look out Copenhagen'. I was finally going to get the chance to make a goose of myself and sing (or is that croak) 'Wonderful, Wonderful Copenhagen' somewhere in that city and scare everyone as I waltzed down the street.

Copenhagen

It is truly amazing what you can fit into three short days in a city when you have too. That's all the time I had, flights to other places were organised and so Copenhagen was a transit city. But seeing as I was there I wanted to see all I could in the time I had.

I reached the hostel rested after a relaxing journey. The train from Stockholm was fantastic, quiet, fast, comfortable, a table and power for the computer at every seat. As if such a comfortable trip wasn't enough, after Malmö (where Eurovision was held earlier that same year), there before me, appeared the most amazing sight, the double-decker Öresund Bridge over the Öresund Strait. Crossing the water was eight kilometres of white bridge which then disappears into a tunnel for another 4 kilometres. A stunning piece of engineering. The motorway is the top level and the railway is the bottom level. Such a beautiful entrance to Copenhagen.

I caught a cab from the station to the hostel, I'd had enough of dragging luggage around searching for places. The hostel was massive with its own bar and food and night-time barbecues. I had discovered that Scandinavian countries aren't cheap so hostel prices reflected that. However, Denmark is cheaper than Sweden so the Swedes pop over the border for weddings and alcohol. The piece of the city I saw out of the cab looked pretty, so after checking the map I hit the streets.

It was still the middle of summer but the temperatures were very pleasant, nothing like the 40-degree temperatures of the Balkans. The pedestrian street is gorgeous. European cities have got the concept of the central pedestrian shopping streets exactly right.

First I needed to find a spectacle shop to fix my glasses, the screw had started coming loose and a lens kept falling out, bad timing for this to start happening as I still had eight months of travel to go. However, it turned out that if this was going to happen then Copenhagen was the best place for it. I found a spectacle shop, my glasses were very kindly repaired at no charge.

Next was the Hop On Hop Off bus. Everything went well all day until one bus broke down then the replacement broke down. Instructions were confusing, people from the cruise ships were demanding their money back as they had no more time to wait for yet another bus, it was chaos for a while. Luckily it was at the very end of my tour so I didn't care but I got a lot of amusement from watching the commotion. Before all the confusion and chaos I'd had a wonderful trip. My main goals were Christiania and the Little Mermaid.

Christiania is a self-proclaimed autonomous area. There are about 850 residents. It is a controversial neighbourhood and has had many ups and downs since it started as a squat back in 1971. The cannabis trade was once again being tolerated by the Copenhagen authorities but beware, if you walk out of Christiania and have cannabis on you, you will be caught. Within the streets of Christiania there are very strict rules about photography it is NOT allowed and sneaking one in is not worth it. I saw one fellow taking a photo and out of nowhere a guy on a pushbike whizzed over and made him delete it.

The other side of Christiania has nothing to do with hash. The place is fabulous. Freetown is a good name for it. It is full of artists, jewellery makers, musicians and many other creative people. Stalls are set up all over the place so there is a roaring trade in locally made souvenirs. T-shirts and clothing of all sorts, jewellery, paintings, pretty much anything. Buildings are decorated by the resident street artists and all in all it's a very chilled out place. Definitely worth a visit, it is unique. I enjoyed my time there.

Back on the bus and off to see the Little Mermaid. Yes, she is very little but perfectly formed. She sits elegantly on a rock. The poor thing has had quite a turbulent existence, decapitated twice, painted pink, blown off her rock and removed to Beijing for an exhibition just to name a few events.

In the same area is the large and impressive Gefion fountain which depicts the mythical story of the creation of the island of Zealand on which Copenhagen is located. I had never realised that Denmark is

129

actually made up of over 100 islands, a bit like Venice except this is a whole country.

Copenhagen is full of impressive sculptures and fountains. That is where I learned about copyright laws relating to public artworks and buildings. Anyone taking photos for commercial use has to verify that the artist has been dead for 70 years before using the photos or they have to get permission from the city. Apparently, these laws exist in every city in the world and that is why there are no photos of art, buildings or tourist sites attached to this book, nobody ever seems to answer emails requesting permission, I gave up.

And so, last day in Copenhagen, I thought I was up for a lot of walking judging by the map, but many things were closer than I thought. First stop Nyhavn. You know those pretty postcards of colourful buildings in Copenhagen? Yes, it is as pretty as the postcards make it look. Like all ports, it had quite a reputation, as the commentary on the bus said 'you wouldn't tell your mother if you'd been there'. These days it's full of restaurants and expensive apartments. I had to stop for coffee. While enjoying the view, who should come along but a bunch of Morris men, yes, really, in Copenhagen.

The changing of the guard at Amalienborg palace was a must, I arrived a little early so off for some exploring close by. Not far from Amalienborg is the Rococo 'Marble Church' with its green dome, sadly, there was a wedding so I couldn't get inside.

Back to catch the changing of the guard at the Palace (the winter residence of the royal family) quite a process as there are four palaces and there is a changing ceremony at each one. This happens every day at 12 noon. There are four different versions of the watch depending on which members of the royal household are present. I experienced the smallest version, The Palace Watch performed when no royal members are in residence. However, it is still very impressive with the young men in their blue and white uniforms and bearskin hats marching in very strict patterns. I loved the scene. Marching to Sousa's The Washington Post was one of my favourite activities at school. I wanted to join the Marching Girls, but Dad would not allow it, the uniforms were too short according to him.

I'm glad I managed to see Copenhagen, it is pretty and definitely worth a visit. And now it was farewell. No, I didn't sing 'Wonderful, Wonderful Copenhagen' or waltz down the street. Packing was finalised and I was off in the middle of the night to the airport.

Finding decent coffee at 5am at Copenhagen airport proved impossible. I was totally confused when I asked a fellow at the only place open how to order a coffee and he went away and came back with a glass of liquid that looked like flat cola. After more questions, I discovered that this was my coffee and I should go over to another counter to pay and get food. I have to say that was definitely the worst coffee I had ever experienced. So off I went in search of another place. The only place opened by this time was a franchise I never use as I don't like their coffee. I should have known better than to even try, but try I did and as always was highly disappointed. Not to worry, the next stop was the land of coffee.

CHAPTER 7

Greece, Turkey and Beyond

I t's funny how things work out sometimes. This is why I find it essential to leave big spaces of unscheduled time in my travels. I found myself at Athens airport with a couple of hours to kill before next check-in and so there was time to think, wonder and be grateful for how my healing trip was working out. I had no intention, originally, to be there and yet I would find myself at Athens airport many times over the next couple of weeks. I was loving this going-with-the-flow thing. I began dreaming of some real chill-out time, sunsets, Greek coffee and ocean. No alarm clocks (unless I decided to catch a sunrise or three) and after the Copenhagen experiences definitely no drunk backpackers waking me up as they fall off the ladders to their top bunks. It was time to be alone for a little while. The thought crossed my mind 'who knows I may even find my inspiration and my poetry muse might return'. She had been absent while I was running around exploring.

I arrived in Santorini safely - it's a very sharp turn to line up for landing and a very short runway. It was after sunset when we arrived. Driving up to Oia the twinkling lights of the various villages on the way were welcoming and there was a traffic jam in Thira, to be expected given the narrow streets and the traffic shuttling new arrivals.

You can't drive within the actual village of Oia, it is all very narrow cobbled lanes winding between buildings and up and down steps. So I was taken on foot to my hotel from the tourist office. The lane leading to my hotel is the main pedestrian thoroughfare full of jewellery shops, art galleries, souvenirs and wall to wall tourists. After dumping my luggage, I was off exploring as everything is open late.

On my return from supermarket shopping and searching for a swimming costume I thought the hotel had moved - but no, it was there, I had just kept walking past the narrow lane opening. After Scandinavia, prices on Santorini appeared reasonable. I bought two whole Serbian salamis, 200g of Cretan cheese and a bottle of local wine for 14 euros – 'that will last a few days' I thought, but no, the wine was guzzled as I was arguing with the wifi late into the night.

I wondered whether it was smart drinking the whole bottle given the configuration of my room. My room number was 121, (the same as my house number back home at the time) it had a green door, and needless to say, the Green Door lyrics started 'what's behind the green door'? Well, let me tell you what was behind my green door. There were three levels. The entire floor was tiled. Both the mirror and the fridge were down 4 tiled steps with no handrail, heaven help you if your feet were wet as the bathroom was on the middle floor. The mezzanine bedroom was up six tiled semi-spiral steps with no handrail - what if you woke up disoriented and needed to go to the bathroom downstairs? It was a replica of the island caves that people used to live in, the ceiling was low and curved so even I at 5 feet 2 inches, couldn't stand up straight. The bed took up the whole width of the room. After banging my head on that very hard ceiling several times I finally remembered that I had to slide out of the foot end of the bed first then keep my head bent. As a result, I left my bag and all my clothes on the lower level. On the upside, the bed did have a railing so I was unlikely to fall out of bed onto the lower floor. And people worry about staying in hostels! I later discovered another danger, the floors were left very wet after cleaning and because of the humidity they didn't dry for hours.

My first day dawned in time to have the included breakfast. It was so pleasant sitting outside my door by the pool enjoying a leisurely breakfast in the warm morning air.

My first daylight walk and I fell in love. Yes, I know, that's very fickle of me, after all, I had loved so many places so far, but funnily enough, this country girl has an island heart and it seems that pieces of land surrounded by the ocean just carry me away. Now I was torn between Capri and Santorini as favourites, both islands are postcard-perfect, each with its own beauty and charm.

My camera was working overtime as I meandered along the cobbles and flagstones finding all sorts of gems. It is impossible to take a bad photo in Oia. The winding lanes, the stunning Cycladic white houses with their soft curves and the blue-domed churches, the bright pink and the subtler white Bougainvillea bursting with colour against the starkness of the white stone buildings. The caldera, sparkling blue in the bright Aegean sunlight, boats and yachts leaving diamond-studded wakes as they cut through the water heading towards beaches or the volcano. I have seen some stunning sights but this place took my breath away.

I wandered down to the Kastro (castle) ruins where most tourists gather to watch the sunset. Even during the day there were too many people so it would be just awful at sunset. I went off to explore alternatives.

I love how things manifest. I was passing King Neptunes restaurant on my afternoon walk, wondering where to watch the sunset when I happened to stop and look at the menu. They had lamb! I noticed a rooftop terrace, so I climbed up. There was one unreserved table facing west, needless to say, I grabbed it. And what a delight it turned out to be, the meal was scrumptious and the sunset, framed by a church on one side and a rooftop restaurant on the other, was beautiful. More synchronicity when I noticed that at the next table was a young lady I'd seen on my flight. She stood out of the crowd as we lined up to leave the plane. She wore a red and white polka dot dress and the most perfect hairstyle I had ever seen, I wondered where she had her hair cut. It turned out that she was a 21-year old Ukrainian medical student. She ended up joining me and I learned a bit more about the world. Every day I learn something new is a good day. We have remained social media friends and I've learned that not only is she a doctor but also an artist. With dinner and snippets of a spectacular sunset over, we parted ways.

Back in my room messing around on social media and writing up the events of the day I suddenly realised it was 1.30 and I should go to bed. Just then the lights went out, literally. Having conveniently forgotten about small towns and sudden blackouts I had to cast my mind to what to do. Then I remembered my Ginski's advice back at Lake Bled 'you need a headlamp Mum'. The one I bought in Ljubljana and hadn't used yet, came in handy that night, as did my phone which I needed to find the lamp. It was fun crawling up the 'steps without a bannister' to the bedroom in total darkness to find the phone. But at least I knew where it was, unlike the headlamp buried in my bag.

After realising that the whole town of Oia was blacked out, not just the hotel, I had to go and find out what Santorinians do at these times. The lamp wasn't needed outside - it was half-moon so there was plenty of light. The restaurant across the lane was lit up like a Christmas tree and I could hear the hum of a generator. Earlier in the evening, I had noticed a band playing in the church square so I headed that way. I found the band still playing, people still dancing, dogs still wandering and old men still smoking by the light of the moon. In the distance, across the midnight black of the caldera, lights from cliff-top villages twinkled their reflections. A gentle breeze played at the hem of my dress and brought just enough cool into the air. I finally decided I really ought to go to bed, I wanted to be up for sunrise and at 2.30 there was still no indication that the electricity was coming back.

Sunrise? Missed it by half an hour – I forgot that my phone wasn't set to Santorini time. Seeing as I'd missed the sunrise, day two was taken up with more exploring, more photos, more ducking in and out of art galleries and shops. Two more things needed to happen, a walk to the tourist office to book a sunset cruise and search for the post office.

This is where I discovered an interesting aspect of Greek communication. I popped into the shop, where I'd bought my swimming costume, to ask directions (it was 2.45pm). The lovely lady gave me excellent directions and off I went. I found the post office easily and entered through the wide-open door. I wasn't prepared for the tirade that greeted me. Having asked for stamps the man in there started yelling at me that I should have come earlier. Questions flew and he pointed at the door where there was a small sign which said they closed every day at 2pm. He was only there because he was running late and was sorting mail. I realised that you have to know the answers to your questions before you ask them because you may not be given the extra information needed. I struck this problem again later in my Greek travels. However, it is not just in Greece this problem arises. Back home you often seem to need to know the answer before knowing which exact question to ask as I realised given the dramas I faced with Mum's medical episodes and her will.

The manifestations and serendipities kept rolling in. I felt like I was being held up in a supportive hand and everything I wanted was happening, it was a profound feeling of safety. While waiting for the lady from the travel agency to call about the availability of the cruise minibus, I thought I'd go to the castle ruins again. As I walked out of my hotel I ran into that lady who told me that someone had cancelled out of the better sunset cruise the next day. I hot-footed it down to the agency and there was another surprise, the cruise company had decided that as there were so many requests for that cruise they would run two boats I would be on the second one - the one they normally use for private cruises. So, not only did I get to go on the cruise I wanted, but I also received the bonus of the top-notch catamaran and the minibus. I couldn't wait for day four.

Sunrise

I was determined not to miss sunrise so I set the alarm for 5am. It was the 28th of August. Showered and dressed I set off for the church square. The sea mist clung to the buildings and the yellow lights along the laneway shone on the glistening flagstones. The air was warm, the perfume of the jasmine that wound around doorways embraced me. Breathing in the scent I was immediately swept back to childhood summer evenings when the warm sunset breeze would bring aromas from anonymous cottage gardens.

I arrived at the square overlooking the caldera. I could just see the edge of the water and a few small boats at the bottom of the cliff, the mist obliterated everything else. A few orange lights shone amongst the white buildings.

The moon was still high and the eerie, warm, misty darkness surrounded me. Oia is not the best location for viewing the sunrise on Santorini, that would be at the southern end of the island, Oia was known for its sunsets. However, sunrise in Oia has its own charm and beauty.

A cat sauntered across the church square, a German Shepherd came to visit and the homeless man was still asleep on the park bench. I noticed a young man with a takeaway coffee in his hand come out of a café a few doors down. He crossed the marble-tiled church square, sat beside the homeless man, woke him and gave him the coffee. I watched in fascination the beauty of that caring touch and wondered who the homeless man could be.

As my eyes swept back towards the caldera the very first tinge of orange was appearing through the mist behind the black shapes of buildings. The grey misty sky was now dappled with lighter shades of grey. The first rays were tiptoeing towards dawn. As the fiery orange slowly crept higher the mist hiding the caldera and the opposite hills of lava began turning a dusky pink. It slowly softened to show the water beginning to sparkle.

I sensed a movement out of the corner of my eye. It was the homeless man. He walked to the low white stone wall, leant over and pulled out a broom. As the fire in the sky began spreading its aura of glowing oranges and yellows on the flagstones polished by years of footsteps, this man began sweeping the path in front of the shops and cafes. I didn't need an explanation, the actions of two men at first light said it all.

Little by little the sun rose higher, the mist disappeared, boats and ships came into view, planes flew overhead, the caldera sparkled its blue at me and Oia came to life. It was time for breakfast.

Sunset

The moment arrived to head to the tourist office and the little bus taking us to the port. I had wondered how vehicles turned at the end of the road near the jetty. I found out they didn't, they reversed all the way down the narrow, steep street to the boats. Soon we were all onboard the catamaran that was to take us around the caldera and then find an anchorage for the sunset view.

It was early afternoon and I was looking forward to several hours of cruising. It was a small group so there was plenty of space for everyone to relax, sunbake and enjoy the view. The Cat made several stops, one at the sulphur springs where those who swam could go and experience the sulphur baths. I don't swim and have terrible sensitivity to sulphur so there was no going in the water for me. There were two more stops for those who wanted to swim in the waters of the caldera, the white beach and the red beach. There is also a black beach, the colours created by the many eruptions of the volcano. The swimmers were warned that the colours won't wash out if you sit directly on the sand.

While others took advantage of the chance to swim I marvelled at the surrounding colours and textures. As fellow passengers swam out to the yellow sulphur pools the solidified ancient lava towered above them glistening in shades from pale grey to black.

The catastrophic Minoan eruptions of the Thera/Santorini volcano in 1646 BCE and the ensuing earthquakes and tsunami are enveloped by many myths, legends and stories. There is the story that Santorini was Atlantis, the eruption is apparently alluded to in Chinese chronicles as being the cause of the downfall of one dynasty and the rise of another and there is the story of a possible connection to Egypt and the Exodus.

Whatever the myths and stories those eruptions, said to have been the equivalent of 40 atomic bombs, created an incredible sea and landscape and here was I experiencing the results from a 21st-century catamaran. Underneath the glistening white of cliff-top Oia were the very obvious layers of volcanic ash from the four separate explosion phases.

Below the layers of white, grey, red and black, the blue-green of the caldera sparkled, calm and beautiful. Boats of all shapes and sizes crisscrossed. The aroma of lamb chops being barbecued on deck reached me. Finally, the music was changed from English language pop/club to Greek. I was happy.

Soon, hours had passed and we were ready for the sunset. Helios and his golden chariot were being drawn by his steeds towards the horizon where the myth says he then traverses Oceanus to return in the morning in the east. Meanwhile, we, in our modern catamaran were perfectly placed to watch the fire of the sun change from daylight yellow to afternoon orange then passionate red as the sun slowly slid into the water infusing the sea and the sky with the most amazing palette.

Before I knew it my last day arrived. A day of 'lasts' and two firsts. Last night on Santorini, last walk along the tourist lane along the edge of the caldera, last amazing gelato from Lolita's, first island gyros and first local beer and sadly my last Santorini sunset. I caught myself having conflicting thoughts on my way back to the hotel while munching happily on three awesome gelato flavours...

First thought 'I hate the farewells to places I really like', and there were many in those previous four months, but that is balanced by the excitement of what will I find next. Second thought, 'In a way this is part of what I need to really 'get' during this trip - letting go, being OK with farewells, loosening up on the need to hang on to things'. It sure isn't easy. In fact, it's almost as hard as the day I realised I had to let go of being the 'all-knowing' mother and talk with my sons as equal adults.

Nowhere near as hard as letting go of Mum.

Next thought was that once I'm off the island I may stop feeling like one of those old English ladies in a broad-brimmed hat I used to read lots about in old English novels - you know the ones where she would move to a Greek island and wander around in her hat, being eccentric and having afternoon teas?

There was a moment on that day when I thought yes, it would be nice to have someone travelling with me. Why? Two reasons, one obvious one is to share the beauty of the place and perhaps walk arm in arm under the romantic sunset. And the other? So I would dare to hire a quad bike and go hooning! Yes, sometimes I would have liked a friend with me.

Instead, as the hour of dusk approached I walked away from the town toward the port. The previous day I had noticed a building that looked like a café or restaurant. Indeed, it was. The outdoor area faced west and I thought a local beer to watch the sun set over the water would be just right. It was still daylight and as I looked across the open space where donkeys grazed on the yellow grass I saw the most 'Greek' picture I had witnessed since Lesvos in 2006. There in front of me on the dusty white track was a man riding side-saddle on his cream donkey leading a string of four saddled donkeys, taking them home after a long day of tourist rides.

Istanbul

It wasn't long after I waved goodbye to the island that I was back on another flight, heading towards Istanbul via Athens. This time I was flying business class, believe it or not, it was cheaper than economy the day I booked. So, there I was winging my way back over the gleaming blue Aegean Sea towards my new destination.

I had met Selin in the Hedonist Hostel in Belgrade, an interesting young lady from Istanbul who invited me over so she could show me her city. Once I had decided to go to Santorini I thought I would accept her invitation. I'm so glad I did.

The queue for visa purchase and passport control took one and a half hours, so after landing at 3.00pm I didn't get to my room till 6pm. Luckily I had booked the airport transfer from the hostel - it cost 25 euros but worth it seeing as I had no idea where I was going and it was getting late. I found out later the reason for the crowds was that I had arrived on the Victory day national holiday weekend.

Finally, I met up with Selin and she took me on my night-time orientation of Istanbul. By the time we'd finished dinner my sense of humour was returning. It had been a challenge hanging on to it through the airport procedures but hang on I did, just.

We had a traditional dish for dinner and then started sightseeing at the port. The deep water was shimmering with the reflections of the brightly neon-lit restaurants, cafes and bars. Along the pier, you can buy street food and tea, but we'd already eaten. From the port, we went to Istiklal Avenue, the 1.4-kilometre pedestrian street. At the southern end is the world's second-oldest subway train and the oldest in Istanbul. It began service in 1875.

The building of the train, known locally as The Tünel, meant that diplomats and businessmen could travel between their harbour-side offices in Karaköy (Galata) on the Golden Horn and their hilltop residences in Beyoğlu in one and a half minutes on steam-powered, gas-lit, cable-drawn cars. So, of course, it is a must to have a ride even though it's only one station. The number on the front carriage signifies the number of years the train has been in service.

Out of the train we headed up Istiklal Avenue towards Taksim Square past boutiques, bookstores, cafes, night clubs, street musicians and seafood sellers who would withdraw into the shadows if they saw police - they are not supposed to sell fresh seafood there.

We finally reached Taksim Square and the Monument of the Republic which commemorates the formation of the Turkish Republic in 1923. It was difficult to believe that only two months earlier this area was the place of violence and protest. Apparently, it started with protests against the proposed urban development of Gezi Park and escalated into much more. In Berlin, I had met a young backpacker who was working in a hostel at Taksim Square at the time and had a few stories to tell.

We dropped into a dimly lit club for a beer before parting ways for a good night's sleep. Another day of exploration lay ahead.

The day began with an introduction to a traditional Hammam (Turkish bath). Interesting process - sauna (which I shouldn't really do as I get badly heat affected, so only lasted 5 mins), cold pool (hate cold water so avoided that), steam room (same problem as a sauna), lots of washes of water where many other ladies were also pouring water on themselves while waiting for their turn to be scrubbed on the marble slab. The scrub is very thorough, with a loofah, and was followed by a massage and a soapy wash. I'm sure that scrub took off about 5 layers of skin. I was expecting to have lost my tan when I came out, but no, it was still there. Washed and refreshed we set off for more adventures.

There are islands to visit to get away from the city. We only went to Buyukada (the big island). I love small boat travel of any sort and being on a ferry on the Bosporus was by itself something to make me smile, but then the destination made it all the more special. The first thing to notice - there is no motorised transport there, just bicycles, horse-drawn carriages and electric golf carts. Closer to the port is where you find the majority of restaurants, shops, road-side sellers and ice cream vendors, all as colourful and interesting as any good novel would have you expect. We watched the ice cream vendors with fascination. Their antics as they served the ice cream were like watching a magician at work.

We set off exploring on foot. I was struck by the architecture of the houses, so reminiscent of a past age. The gardens shone with Bougainvillea colour and we were surrounded by blessed stillness. There are the sounds of peoples' voices and the clip-clop of horses' hooves, but that's it. No cars, no horns, no motorbikes.

A walk through the spice bazaar started our next day. The heady aroma of coffee mingling with every spice you could possibly think of was powerfully evocative.

It was Sunday, we went to church. Well, we went into a church and stayed there for quite some time but not for a normal Sunday service. Ayin Biri Greek Orthodox church in Istanbul has the reputation for granting wishes. On the first Sunday of each month, hundreds of people from all faiths flock to the church for the wish-granting service. There they buy tiny silver keys to represent their deepest wishes and attempt to unlock various icons in the two levels of the church. Meanwhile, the priest is holding a service after which he goes downstairs and sprays holy water on everyone. Then we all lined up again to get a personal blessing. It was quite an event, the most remarkable realisation was that it's all faiths all together doing and believing the same thing.

After the church service and blessings, we had morning tea at the Dolmabahce Palace followed by a tour. We were taken through the Harem area and the indescribably intricate and gorgeous grand ceremonial hall. Dolmabahce Palace was home to six Sultans from 1856 until 1924 when the caliphate was abolished. The founder and first President of the Republic of Turkey, Mustafa Kemal Ataturk used the palace as a summer residence and spent the last days of his life there in 1938. Now it is managed by the Directorate of National Palaces and the only way to see it is through guided tours.

More walking, more eating, a beer and then it was a farewell ferry ride, hugs goodbye and I went back to my hostel. I am so grateful to Selin for entertaining me and showing me Istanbul in a way that most tourists don't see.

My last day in Istanbul was spent on my own, attempting to do 'touristy' things. The day ended up quite differently to what I expected. A rather late start meant brunch at the Dervish café on my way to the attractions. I discovered that Aya Sofya is closed on Mondays so I missed out on that; every time I was near the blue mosque it was prayer time so I didn't get back there either; the crowds at Topkapi palace were beyond my capabilities of handling so I thought I'd try to conquer the Turkish postal system and send some things home - FAIL!

Not to worry, I headed off to Sirkeci railway station instead to check on a sign I had noticed the previous day about a Whirling Dervish show. While doing that I discovered the original Orient Express restaurant. Now that was fun. When I first noticed the restaurant a gentleman was sitting there just like one of Agatha Christie's characters, white suit and hat. I went back, closer to show time, to have afternoon tea and take photos. At another table were three English ladies who sounded even more excited than I about finding the place, and an Australian gentleman. They came over to say hello and ended up joining me. It seriously felt like an unfolding Agatha plot and I fully expected Poirot to appear at any moment. Do I sound a little excited about that discovery? You bet I am. All that was missing was the train - it was off being renovated.

The whirling Dervishes are truly amazing. The musicians played for half an hour first, then accompanied the meditational whirling. Even though officially whirling is still apparently banned as a religious practice, it is allowed to be performed for the tourist trade. Knowing that did not subtract from the event. As the men glide into the hall a stillness seems to enter the room. The men remove their black cloaks, bow and begin to turn slowly, then faster and faster until their tunics are billowing. They stop, bow to each other and begin again. I was enthralled.

I discovered that the Aussie I met at the restaurant was staying in a hotel not far from me so we both had someone to talk to on the way back before parting ways. And so my whirlwind visit to Istanbul drew to a close - what a weekend.

I left this incredible city thinking about the origin of the name my parents had chosen for me. St Helen, the Christian mother of Emperor Constantine. According to Orthodox belief, she found the cross upon which Christ was crucified. Constantine, her son, established Constantinople (now Istanbul) as the capital of the Roman Empire. He declared the Edict of

Milan (remember Belgrade museum and religious tolerance?) - oh, those fine threads! I flew out, grateful for following my intuition.

Kalamata and Ancient Messene

In my comfortable seat on my way to Santorini a little over a week earlier I fell to musing about how I ended up on that flight. While my mind wandered I leafed through the in-flight magazine. My eyes fell on an article about ancient Messene. It was fascinating and some vague familiar bell tinkled in my head. I just couldn't place the familiarity.

The plane banked and turned sharply ready for landing on the short island airstrip. I placed the magazine back in the seat pocket. On the flight back to Athens there was the in-flight magazine again, I re-read the article on ancient Messene, still fascinating and still vaguely familiar. What was it? Change of planes at Athens and I was winging my way back over the Aegean towards Turkey. There was the magazine again, and there was the article.

And then it struck me! I remembered. Childhood, member of the Argonauts Club on ABC radio, a writing prize and my club name. I was rower number 9 on the ship Messene in Jason's fleet. Ah, that's it! Now I have to go there. But where exactly is it? Greece is a big place!

Four days later, after my whirlwind of fun in Istanbul, I landed at Kalamata airport on the Peloponnese Peninsular.

It wasn't easy getting the information I needed about Ancient Messene, I had to remember I was in Greece, I needed to be patient. Eventually, one hotel receptionist came through with some information. There were only two buses a week to and from Ancient Messene, both leaving at 5am. One on a Monday and one on a Friday, I took Friday.

Here is where I needed all my fortitude, lateral thinking and trust in my Universe. You see, I had no idea where I was going or how long it would take, all I knew was that Ancient Messene was calling and that I would be back in Kalamata that night. So, once again I put total trust into my Universe, my guiding angels and myself. After all, this was part of my healing world journey, I was re-building myself and for whatever reason, I had to go to Messene.

5am found me at the bus station. I managed to buy a ticket. Not seeing a bus with Messene as a destination I waited. The driver found me and motioned me on board. He didn't speak English and I didn't speak Greek. I was the only passenger, so this was going to be interesting.

We left Kalamata in darkness. The hard vinyl seat was slippery, when we rounded bends I hung on. There was no way of gauging the scenery, it was dark outside, a moonless sky with a few pinpoints of stars already starting to go to bed to make space for the sunrise.

It was still dark when the headlights fell on a large brown sign, obviously something to do with archaeology. We entered a village but the bus didn't stop, so I figured that this wasn't it. As we exited the village and the bus started winding up the hill I wondered where I might end up. What if he just kept going and I ended up hundreds of miles away by the sea? Just as those thoughts were lazily meandering through my brain the driver turned around and asked whether I wanted to get off in Messene. At least that's what I understood by his body language and the word Messene in the sentence. I rather quickly decided that the sarcastic answer, 'Well, duh! Why else did I buy a ticket to Messene?', would be wasted on a man who didn't speak English, so simply nodded in response. He motioned me to stay put, that he would drive further and turn around. Many bends in the narrow uphill road later we entered another village. Parked cars blocked his turning area so I sat in the bus while he went door-knocking looking for the owners.

Eventually, we made it back to Messene. It was still dark but obviously, first light was on its way and sunrise not far off. Now, the tricky bit, how to find the ancient site. There were people with luggage waiting at the stop, luckily they spoke English and had been working on the dig. They advised that if I waited for two gentlemen to come down the hill they would probably guide me.

Soon I found myself walking down the hill with two charming English gentlemen who were working on the dig. I found out from them that Ancient Messene is a 'dig and restore' site. A massive job was being done in the reconstruction of the ancient city with original stones.

As I stood amongst the partial excavations and reconstructions of the Stadium, the Theatre, the Askleipeon, stood on the earth where ancients had walked, where Spartans, Messenians, Helots and Thebans had shed their blood below Zeus' Mt Ithome home, the first signs of morning light appeared. The kings and queens, the gods and goddesses, the violence, the history and the mythology. I couldn't believe I was to have almost a whole day exploring this incredible place and thanked my childhood club membership.

There was a very light drizzle and just enough cloud to stop the sunrise from being the spectacular colours I had hoped for. But the gentle pastels of the watered-down sky were enough. I was there, standing in the place whose name I bore as a rower on the Argonauts Club's good ship Messene. I wondered if the other 49 rowers of that ship had been here and thought, 'who knew that a children's club membership all those years ago would be such an important piece in my puzzle of healing'. I watched the sun rise and remembered our pledge;

'Before the sun and the night and the blue sea, I vow to stand faithfully by all that is brave and beautiful; to seek adventure, and having discovered aught of wonder, or delight; of merriment or loveliness, to share it freely with my comrades, the Band of Happy Rowers.' (from The ABC Weekly, *28 Dec 1940)*

The message was clear.

The trip back was equally as eventful, had I known that the answer of '2 o'clock' to my question 'what time is the bus back to Kalamata' really meant 'the bus leaves Kalamata at 2 o'clock and is in Ancient Messene at 3 o'clock or later', I could have grabbed a local cab and gone to see more sites like the Arcadian gate. Not to worry, hours of waiting at the bus stop was OK really. There was the view over the entire site of Ancient Messene, the olive groves, the sheep dotting the hills, the jeweller's shop and the museum of excavated sculptures to enjoy. I wouldn't have missed being there for anything.

On the left of my Kalamata hotel window, was the very pretty bay lined with restaurants and the Taygetos foothills beyond. As in so many parts of Europe, the beach is mostly pebbles. It's no wonder that beach lounges are needed, pebbles are impossible to lie on. One lady had solved that problem by reading a book standing ankle-deep in the water. All the restaurants looked inviting, the food on their menus sounded delicious. I chose one and ordered. Greek flavours with such pretty views.

Another day of 'lasts'. Last walk on the pebbly beach, wonderful Greek lunch by the water, a look at the bright yellow church down the street. Kalamata, for me, isn't quite the picture-postcard destination but it certainly has its own charm, great food and is saturated with history and mythology. I am so glad that those tinkling bells in my head forced me to pay attention to the magazine article.

It was the final evening. I was sitting on the balcony watching a storm roll in, the building wind was nicely cooling things down. I fully expected it would end up making a direct line for the hotel and I would have to run inside, but no it swung off to the side and I could stay and watch. Storm gone I had a farewell look at Mt Taygetos and the pink colours of the setting sun spreading across the bay.

The flight out of Kalamata started with a laugh. This place seems to be a favourite destination for British people. I entered the small air terminal and eventually found the orderly line waiting for boarding. Another person came along and randomly chose a place to stand, I heard a voice say 'well, that's not very British!' I had to laugh, something to keep in mind as I was soon to be on my way to London.

It was hello Athens, hello Attalos hotel, hello sunset from the rooftop bar, hello Acropolis and hello to €2 gyros - I hadn't seen any of those for eight years and hadn't planned to be there, but there I was. A few things had changed, the Plaka was dirtier than I remembered, graffiti everywhere, the gyros had increased by 20 euro cents in price and they had gone hot chip crazy and put them in everything including the gyros. While sitting at the rooftop bar, drink in hand, I waited for the lights at the Acropolis to come on and remembered my first trip and my unfortunate choice of a travel companion.

Yes, a full-on day. I didn't intend to do the Acropolis and the Agora in one hit, but as they lead into each other it makes sense. Amazing how much I remembered from '06 and how much I'd either forgotten or not seen that time. I was told in Kalamata that the digs are moving along so well because the European Union is involved and funding a lot of it. There are actually seats to be found in the Agora, and the places you are not allowed to go are roped off just as in Messene. I didn't hear one whistle until closing time when they blow madly to get people out. Back in 2006, that whistle was constant as people either sat or walked where they weren't allowed. A wander through the flea market and a walk to see if the famous Poet Sandalmaker was still there. I found him back in 2006 and bought a pair of hand-made sandals. What a story behind that shop, started by his Grandfather.

There I was again at Athens airport, this made it my fourth time there on this trip, officially I had now been in Athens airport more times than any other airport. I was on my way for a quick visit to a friend in Milan. Such a shame I couldn't spend longer but she had to meet her husband in southern Italy.

CHAPTER 8

England

A flight from Milan and a lengthy train ride found me, on 12th September 2013, in Liverpool England. My introduction to the city was through dragging my luggage in the rain searching for my hostel. Soaking wet and desperate I finally asked some friendly people for directions. I hadn't realised that this hostel is in the middle of the club area - ooh it was loud! There didn't appear to be much soundproofing even though it was brand new. Thank goodness I had two charming young ladies as dorm mates and surprise, surprise we hit it off and yes became social media friends. The girls next door though, were something to be dealt with, the noise from their dorm was horrific. So between the clubs and the girls next door the three of us didn't think we'd get much sleep.

I wasn't about to complain, you see, I was on Matthew Street. A bit along the road was the Cavern Club where just about everybody has performed including the Beatles. The names inscribed on the brick wall out the front list just about every rock performer I've ever heard of.

I only had a few days and I realised I had a lot of ground to cover. I had to get cracking. A partial Hop On Hop Off tour started my exploration. Then it was the Beatles story museum and on to the 'Magical Mystery Tour' bus stopping at the Strawberry Fields gates, driving past some of the Beatles' houses and ending up at the Cavern Club. A lot of fun. The Cavern Club had been filled in to make way for part of a railway that was never built, so they excavated and recreated the majority with the original bricks. The left-overs they sold for charity.

What a whirlwind of information. I really liked Liverpool, relaxed, friendly, full of places of interest including the yellow submarine, and a very cool vibe. Apart from the music scene, both the Catholic and Anglican cathedrals are sights to behold. The Catholic one was meant to be quite different to how it ended up but unfortunately, the war and costs interrupted the construction. The final completed design is stunning. Locally it bears the nickname of 'Paddy's Wigwam' because of the outside shape and the lantern tower with its stained glass and a crown of pinnacles.

The Anglican cathedral is a massive structure with stunning internal decor. Stained glass windows tower above the visitor and the ornate Lady Chapel sparkles. Funnily enough, the original Catholic cathedral was designed by a Protestant and the Anglican one was designed by a Catholic.

I hadn't realised that Elvis had had quite an influence on the Beatles and I was fortunate to be there while the Elvis and Us Exhibition was still on at The Beatles Story. A stroll along the paved and sculpture-decorated bank of the Mersey and, yes there was a ferry leaving the wharf – you guessed it, the song started spinning. It was time to move on.

I had booked a lovely old pub at the edge of the village of Standish. I loved my pub room with its feeling of serenity from the complete quiet and the view of bright green fields. What was I doing there? Well, I discovered that both my sons and friends were in the area filming for a brilliant children's show. Proud mama wasn't about to miss out on seeing her sons again, nor getting a chance to see what they were doing. After a little negotiation there I was. I caught up with the family and crew over dinner. I was so excited that I might see and hear how filming production works and gets put together.

Back in my room, late into the night, I could hear the rain lashing the window panes and I was glad to be inside my warm and cosy room. History was made on my first morning. The first time since 1967 I had tea instead of coffee for breakfast. As they say 'When in Rome...' Thank you rainy, merry England – I would have to find coffee on the road somewhere.

A rainy day meant that I could spend time on the set, that was so much fun. On the way I found coffee but it was pretty awful even adding the espresso to the cappuccino didn't help, but I was finding that the wonderful country air and the slow lifestyle were doing me the world of good.

I discovered food and coffee were a challenge. My search for coffee continued with no real success and my first foray into mushy peas didn't turn me into a fan. However, there was fun ahead. The crew's antics and the fabulous costumes were hilarious. I was even given the job of clapper lady, everyone was working hard. I was so impressed. I ended up back there many times.

Road Trip

The rain stopped and it was time for exploration. First, a visit to an art gallery/shop/tea room in the village of Chipping before going on to Skipton castle. After many, many miles of little country lanes, I arrived at John Brabin's house and shop. It was charming and loaded with history. Then back up the narrow country lanes on to Skipton. Along the way, I had a moment when I wondered whether I would get to my destination by nightfall. There in front of me was a massive piece of machinery that looked like a combine harvester, travelling very slowly. It was the machine that trims those lovely tall English hedges. It seemed to take up the entire width of the road and I was a bit concerned for my hire car. I took myself in hand, decided I had seen enough Midsomer Murders episodes of policemen whizzing past farm machinery on English country lanes and got past. Every day I learned something that answered a question I'd had – now I knew how those hedges were kept so tidy.

Arriving in Skipton the first thing I found was the Russian Tea Room. It's a gorgeous place and finally, I had found great coffee. Lots of people said not to bother with the castle because it was empty, and yes it is empty, and it's not one of the beautiful ornate European palaces, but I found it interesting. It has had quite a history, not the least of which was to withstand the three-year Civil War Siege of 1642 to 1645 against the Roundheads. Stark, very well preserved, 900 years old, 4-metre thick stone walls. One of the first to have round watchtowers in England. I liked it. I went up and down stairs and in and out of massive rooms wondering who had walked these floors over the centuries.

As I wandered through the 'empty' castle I loved that no barriers or ropes were keeping you to a central walkway. I touched walls, walls that held the memories of 900 years of conversation, war, breath, love, hate and probably a little debauchery. You can stand on the ledges at the arrow slits and look out over the landscape from where the invaders would come. In the curing room, I could almost smell the bacon.

I loved the emptiness and the freedom of being able to touch and imagine. I remembered how, on the farm, Mum would throw everything out the window, after getting nowhere with telling me to clean my room. I loved those days, loved the emptiness of my room and loved spending hours sorting through things I hadn't seen in a long time. Then I remembered how one of my favourite things was an empty, clean exercise book. My birthday is in February and we were poor so my birthday presents were mostly things for school; pencils, exercise books, erasers. I loved opening the book and seeing the blank pages waiting for me to give them a meaning. I lovingly covered them in brown paper with Mum's help and wrote my name on the cover. Once school started I couldn't wait to fill up the book so I could get a new one and feel that delight of the empty pages again - it was a long wait.

Is that why I loved wandering through the castle? Empty, waiting for visitors to imagine stories that could have happened there, empty of furnishings yet full of history.

The drive home took me past lots of dry stone walls, fields and pretty scenery. So few places to stop and take photos because of the narrow roads. I managed to pull over in one place and a lady stopped and told me that the hill I was photographing in the distance was Pendle Hill, where George Fox had his vision that started the Quaker movement and where 19 women were supposedly burned for being 'witches' in the 17th century. Well, that did it, I now had to go there didn't I?

In the meantime, I spent my evenings listening to BBC4 in my room – one night I learned all about the Antikythera mechanism. I had never heard of it before but just think, Archimedes developed the first mechanical computer 2000 years ago, so the Greeks were on the verge of technology as we know it and if the Greek civilisation hadn't collapsed, we may very well have been 2000 years ahead now. The mind boggles.

On my son's recommendation, I spent one morning wandering around pretty Parbold Village. Walking along the river complete with ducks and narrowboats and under the stone bridge reminded me of so many English TV shows I enjoy. I even found more good coffee.

On the Road Again

It was time for another road trip, I was loving being able to drive again after all those months. This time to Blackpool. An interesting place. My hotel was a challenge, in fact, I had to get them to change my room as it was a massively long walk from the lift, down a few steps even though on the same floor, and the hallway was getting narrower and narrower. Apart from an uncomfortable claustrophobic feeling, I refuse to carry luggage up and down stairs. The place was way too big, old and very tired. Having the water of the Irish Sea across the road, however, meant that it was a lovely area for walks. There was a brand new tram system that travels the whole seven miles or so from Fleetwood Ferry to Starr Gate so you can easily get to all the touristy spots.

I didn't get far on my daytime walk as I ran into a lady walking her granddaughter's Shi Tzu and we started chatting. I found out heaps of information from her that saved me a lot of time and meant that I managed to see most things all in one day. She told me about the Illuminations. They are like Christmas lights on steroids every night. Really wonderful creations and of course cars and buses cruise up and down the road rubber-necking. Lots of people on the trams hop on and off then walk. I have since found out that the design of the illuminations changes every year. What a job, creating all those installations. Then there is the home of Fishermans Friends, I'd never thought about where they might be made, but here they are, a family business that went global.

What a night. After a day of doing pretty much nothing, other than catching the tram to check out Cleveleys, having more fish and chips by the water and then battling with more online accommodation bookings, I took myself off to dinner and then to the stunningly beautiful historic Grand Theatre. 'Dream Boats and Petticoats', the show was so inspiring and fun with all the whooping and hollering, clapping and singing. That was the audience - we knew all the words! On stage it was fantastic. Terrific performances from every cast member. A night of quality pop music from my era and the beauty was that all except two cast members were young. Mark Wynter, an English teen idol from the 1960s whose greatest success was a cover version of Venus in Blue Jeans, was in the show. In his 70's, still performing and wowing the crowds. What a joy!

On to another unplanned road trip. Given that the nice lady had stopped to tell me about Pendle Hill and the witches when I was on my way back from Skipton, I had to go there. From Blackpool to Wigan through lots more narrow country lanes and I was in the Ribble Valley. The Heritage information centre told me about a lady in Newchurch who knows all the history of the witches. And indeed she was very knowledgeable. I spent a lot of time in her witch shop chatting and choosing a witch to send home to my friend Magda. Then on to nearby St Mary's 16th Century church with the all-seeing 'Eye of God' in its west tower. Some quiet reflection time and a stroll amongst the Autumn leaves in the back lane and it was time to move on.

Luckily I didn't stay any longer because as it happened the satnav had no idea where my Wigan hotel was. I had moved there for my final night in the area. I drove around in circles as it tried to find the place, got me close but not close enough. I rang the hotel, that didn't help. Not to worry I asked a guy who was getting into his car and I finally made it to my destination, somewhat exhausted and stressed. Then it was my last supper with my son and my life was about to take yet another turn. I wondered what else I would discover and where else I would end up.

As someone said in one of the hostels, 'it's the goodbyes that are the most challenging in this travel thing', which they are. But I guess that makes the 'hellos' all the sweeter until there is another goodbye.

London

I arrived at my hotel at Heathrow airport. A good rest was warranted after six hours of bus travel and before the long trip across the Atlantic on Monday. So what exciting things happened on the way? Lunch was an eye-opener and a taste sensation, and the massive cup for the espresso a bit of a worry but OK in the end. I discovered that French toast at Manchester airport is called 'eggy bread' - it needed a tad more soaking in the egg. The basic version comes with honey, anything extra you order comes on top of the honey. So...my bacon French toast was eggy bread, honey and bacon. Actually, it wasn't bad. It reminded me a little of the Canadian pancakes I had in Queensland, a 3 stack complete with cream, maple syrup and bacon. Come to think of it, it also reminded me of my teenage midnight Dagwood sandwiches that included anything I could find in the fridge - both sweet and savoury.

The bus trip was in two sections - Manchester to Birmingham, change coaches, then Birmingham to Heathrow.

A whirlwind weekend in London meant two days of Hop On Hop Off buses. There was no other way of covering much ground. I saw lots of tourist spots, walked on London Bridge and found great places for food and coffee in and around Leicester Square. I met up with one of the Wigan crew and had a proper catch-up and chat. I saw the 25,359[th] performance of Agatha Christie's Mousetrap and chatted to a lovely elderly fellow from New York who was sitting next to me. Such excitement to be seeing a play in the West End.

And just like that, part one of my healing trip was over. Thirteen countries, 22 cities, 3 islands, and an uncountable number of villages in 153 days. I stayed with old friends who took me in and showed me a wonderful time in their cities and homes. I met an incredible number of amazing people, many of whom are now friends. Some have shown me their own cities.

I thank you all for your friendship, help, advice, exuberance and acceptance. We succeeded in our purpose of taking some of Mum's ashes home and partially walking in her and Dad's footsteps. I spent time with my family members. That was such a buzz, you guys don't know how much that meant to me.

With some sadness, it was farewell to Europe with a huge thank you to my friends at home, who were following me and supporting me - especially in those moments when I got a little maudlin. Thanks for holding on and allowing me the space to express my sadness.

The next day I was to be in New York, staying with one of my best school friends whom I had seen only once since 1967. If it wasn't for Alice, I don't think I would have survived those school years of 1966/67. She was the only one who realised I was going through periods of depression, although I didn't have a name for it at the time.

She would sit quietly with me on the school verandah, so this reunion was going to be a tremendous celebration.

Part Two

The Other Side of the World

᭙
CHAPTER 9

USA

My introduction to the USA was less than spectacular. The airport computers crashed so that held us up. We spent two hours inside the immigration room at the airport while they tried to figure out what to do with us. My friend who was waiting at the barrier was becoming anxious as there was no information given to those waiting. Well, what's two hours, I was to have six weeks of catching up with one of my dearest friends from high school.

My time in New York was split between staying at the apartment in Queens and the house by the beach on Long Island - a lovely mix of city, country and beach.

Alice proved to be a great tour guide, so I didn't miss out on much in either place. I thought I'd never walk again after day two. Walking through towns and villages in Europe was massive, for five months. It turned out to be nothing compared to the walking we did in New York.

My initiation to New York was a walk from 42nd Street through Central Park to the East Side and back with the obligatory photos with Elmo and Mickey, through Times Square, past Radio City and Trump Tower patting a police horse on the way. I was ready for a rest. Luckily the next day was the beginning of a leisurely couple of days by the beach.

We spent three wonderful weekends in the less populated areas of Long Island, such fun and respite from the hustle and bustle of the city. I never realised that most of Long Island is actually the 'country'. There were drives to Port Jefferson where we lunched on clam chowder and calamari. We visited pumpkin farms where huge orange pumpkins were almost ready for Halloween. We stopped and talked to the bison at the bison farms and visited the Hamptons. I also didn't realise that the Hamptons were so far away from New York City, blame it on all those TV shows.

We stopped at Montauk Harbour. The roads wound through pretty autumn colours and the beautiful blue ocean greeted us at the end. I learned about endangered species at Oyster Pond and the filming of Jaws at Montauk Point where Long Island Sound meets the Atlantic Ocean. We enjoyed an Italian concert at the Suffolk Theatre Riverhead while sipping imported beers. An afternoon of reminiscences through the wonderful voice of Micheal Castaldo was so very refreshing. So many memories came flooding back - some great, some not so great - spanning my entire lifetime. My departed accordionist brother had played many of these tunes with his dance band. The music was wonderful, the voice was beautiful and a few Peronis went down smoothly.

We had lunches and breakfasts with lots of Alice's friends and barbecues watching the sunset from her deck overlooking the Sound. There used to be steps leading down to a private beach but sadly Hurricane Sandy destroyed part of the cliff and the access so we had to walk down the road and then via the public beach.

Our weekdays were mostly spent in New York sight-seeing. We covered so much in those three weeks. Grand Central Station - I wasn't keen on how far underground the station was and what a rabbit warren it is. There are 100 tracks! The concourse, the passages and the markets were much easier to handle at ground level, although they became hot and stuffy. I had to get out, breathe cool air and have a coffee before plunging back into the station. It certainly is grand. We followed up with a stroll down the streets of diamonds. My goodness, nothing but gold and diamonds for blocks. A walk up Broadway and I was getting a hint of what people rave about.

Some of our sight-seeing was, of course, from the Hop On Hop Off buses. We covered so much ground and water. The 9/11 memorial – its beautiful reflection pool with such an aura of sadness. The NASA and air force displays on the Intrepid. I loved the tour through the Intrepid and the shuttle. It took me back to the days when Mum and I, and later a school friend and I, used to tour the visiting aircraft carriers in Sydney Harbour. I suspect that I may even have been on the Intrepid as I think they said that she visited Sydney in 1967. Whatever, it was exciting and brought back memories of visiting the ships and of course sneakily checking out the cute sailors when I thought Mum wouldn't notice. They showed a movie of the Intrepid being hit by kamikaze planes, the smoke machine and surround sound bombing noise was making it seem real. The movie was shown in the hangar deck where they received their first direct hit.

We caught a ferry to see Manhattan from the water and as the country was in the middle of the United States federal government shutdown of 2013, the Statue of Liberty was closed, but I did get to see her from the ferry. We visited Strawberry Fields in Central Park and the John Lennon memorial mosaic a link to my time in Liverpool. I just happened to be wearing the jacket I'd bought at the Beatles museum. Sadness descended as we later stood in front of the Dakota building where John Lennon was killed.

There were days we mostly focussed on food. Coffee, of course, played a major role in my explorations. We did the New York pizza, Bubba Gumps for dinner overlooking Times Square, Hard Rock, coffee and cakes in Greenwich village and the M&M shop. Ellen's Stardust was such fun - all the staff sing hoping to be seen by Broadway talent scouts, a must to visit. There were many other places Alice took me for lunches and dinners, along with some of her friends. It was so nice to meet such amiable people.

Musical Road Trip

Before we knew it, my month in New York was over and it was time for us to start the musical road trip.

25th of October, 8am, we took off from Laguardia for Springfield, Missouri via a brief stopover in Chicago. Little did I know, new fine threads beginning back in January were being woven into the future.

A rental car from Springfield and there we were in Branson. For those who may be a little jittery about travelling solo, but who want to find somewhere where they can feel completely safe, where no-one tells you not to go to certain areas, where the people are all friendly and helpful, where you can go out at night and there is a lot of fun to be found – I FOUND IT! I was asked on my return where was the safest place I visited in the USA and I could honestly answer Branson.

Branson was my kind of town. We met a lovely couple from Illinois at breakfast who convinced us to go to Silver Dollar City. I hadn't planned on that place as I had made a very incorrect assumption that the name suggested gambling and poker machines – not so. I'd forgotten lesson number 2 of train the trainer courses 'never assume, it makes an ass out of u and me'. We took the couple's advice and thoroughly enjoyed ourselves. I'm not normally into theme parks but this one is different. Its origins stem from so many people visiting the caverns that the locals began providing entertainment. It has become a colossal place of colonial craftsmanship, theatres and rides for kids of all ages. Three episodes of the Beverley Hillbillies were filmed there and apparently, Buddy Ebsen learned lumber skills to help build one of the log cabins.

An awe-inspiring day was followed by an equally awe-inspiring evening. Yakov Smirnoff is a fantastic comedian, artist, professor of art as well as having a Master's degree in psychology. You'd never believe that he arrived in the USA from The Soviet Union not knowing a word of English and there he was with his own theatre, has entertained Presidents, been in movies and seven episodes of Night Court. The seats in his theatre have retractable tables, they served dinner and the show continued with Yakov sitting in a similar seat on stage with his meal having a conversation with the audience and answering questions - Dinner with Yakov was different, very funny and psychologically deep.

While exploring Branson we came across a Gospel show by the Bacon Family - what lovely voices. Four generations of the family performed in that show, 94-year-old Granny was an amazing pianist. We loved the whole two hours. That was followed by the Dolly Parton Dixie Stampede. Another brilliant show in a huge arena, terrific horsemanship, parades, stunts, races and a lot of audience participation. During the show, we were served a spectacular four-course feast which included a whole rotisserie chicken. Branson just kept getting better and better.

We woke to a very foggy morning so, sadly, we didn't get to see much as we drove around. We had planned to drive through the mountains for the beautiful autumn colours. Instead of colourful trees, we explored Downtown which is the older part of the town by Lake Taneycomo. It has an old-world feel with beautiful shops. We came across Waxy O'Shea's Irish pub - wonderful food and huge servings. The softest calamari for lunch and later terrific nachos for dinner. By the time we'd had lunch the fog had cleared, the sun was shining happily and it was time for our two-hour cruise on the Lake Queen. The colours were stunning and I saw my first bald eagle. At first, I thought he was a statue in the tree, he was so still.

Branson Bald Eagle

165

Music, music, music and more music, which is what I had planned for this trip and music is what we got. Breakfast at the Uptown Diner. We walked in, paid our money and found they have live performers at breakfast time! How unexpected! Georgina Holiday, what a talented country singer, on the first morning. Breakfast in these parts is 'interesting' to say the least - I drew the line at grits and a few other things after tasting them. We discovered there was a George Strait tribute in the evening, met the performers and bought the tickets. So lucky, last tickets but one of the best tables.

After breakfast, to fill in time, we went to the wax museum, what fun taking photos with a few Hollywood legends. The morning sped by, the whole reason for coming to Branson was upon us - Legends in Concert with DeanZ (2013 Ultimate Elvis and Heart of the King winner). I had met Dean in Parkes (Australia) in January at the Elvis festival. He talked about Branson during his spectacular performance. When I spoke to him afterwards he suggested I should include Branson in my trip through the USA so there I was, having a wonderful time - oh, those fine threads. I had no idea that a chance meeting with DeanZ in Parkes, which led me to see him in Branson would play a role four years later in meeting a new friend and writing colleague whose home town was Springfield, Missouri where we had landed and hired our car. Some things are just meant to be.

Back to the Uptown Diner for the terrific George Strait show. Gordy and Debbie are fantastic. I have almost worn out the CDs I bought that night. Dinner was included, the diner was packed and we had a lot of fun.

Our last breakfast at the diner in Branson was accompanied by the lovely Georgina and her mellow voice again. She asked for requests, I requested Connie Francis and the cheeky lady came over and made me sing, oh dear! I'm surprised that nobody left the building. And then, it was all over, I bought Georgina's CD and it was time to move on.

A couple of hundred miles later, mostly travelling through stunning tapestries of autumn colour, we arrived at the Heartbreak Hotel, Memphis. I couldn't believe it. I was in Memphis. We had catfish and ribs dinner at the Blues City Cafe and discovered the local brew, a really nice dark sparkling lager. A brief walk down Beale Street and then a rest. Poor Alice must have been exhausted as she was doing all the driving, but she never complained.

Next day was Elvis day. We bought the VIP tickets. We were the only people on the shuttle, no standing in line, and could go through as many times as we liked. What an experience to walk through Graceland, the adjacent buildings and the resting place of Elvis, his parents and paternal grandmother. It's a real time capsule, nothing has changed since Elvis lived there. The pièce de resistance was finding out that our shuttle driver Tommy went to school with Elvis, was friends with him and even got to go on some concert road trips with him. What a delight, I wish I could have spent more time with him. The Meditation Garden (the family resting place) is beautiful and serene and at 7.30 every morning for an hour you can go in there for free before the tourists start rolling in.

After dinner at a Chinese/American buffet, we went back to the Rock N Roll cafe near our hotel to see the entertainment and have a drink. I was only expecting a Buddy Holly tribute, and yes the guy sang Buddy Holly numbers up until his break, then he came back and changed it up to a whole lot of other Rock N Roll numbers and a few fabulous blues songs. Another eventful and amazing day on our musical road trip.

We started the first day of November by catching the shuttle from Heartbreak Hotel to Sun studios. We were shown around what is still a live studio, stood where Elvis and his contemporaries stood and recorded. Where the Million Dollar Quartet spent that amazing day and we were allowed to pose with THE microphone. We went through the Rock N Soul Museum, so much to see that the mind explodes. In the evening we took ourselves off to the Jerry Lee Lewis Honky Tonk and cafe. Incredible. The band playing that night was Jason James and the Jerry Lee Lewis Tribute Band. Ray, the bass player was from Jerry's band, the drummer was simply amazing and Jason was indescribable. What a night. We rocked on with these guys for hours and met a few really nice people in the process. Seriously, the current generation thinks it has the creative, weird, 'out there' music cornered, but honestly without the 50's none of this would have been possible. The 50's started the musical revolution and watching the replicated antics of the era proved it. What amazing musical ability to create what became the cornerstone of modern music for generations to come. I loved every single minute of that day.

And the beat goes on and on. There we were in the land of John Lee Hooker, Robert Johnston, Muddy Waters, Howlin' Wolf and so many more. Yes, it was Clarksdale, Mississippi. Located at the famous crossing of highways 61 and 49 - The Devil's Crossroads. In its heyday, in the 1920s the town was full of millionaires, their money coming from cotton. Of course, to support the millionaires was the other side of town, where the depths of poverty reigned for the slave workers. This is where the Mississippi blues were born, thanks to those suffering, poverty-stricken people. And the music continues. Delta blues are alive and well. It was Hambone festival that weekend so we were lucky. We popped into a few arty shops, went to the Delta Blues Museum, had lunch at the Yazoo Place - real espresso and great burgers. Dinner at the Ground Zero Blues Club co-owned by Morgan Freeman. It wasn't easy to find because we first didn't think that the run-down looking building was it. But it was! And what a place it is! Housed in an un-renovated building which was once used by the Delta Grocery and Cotton Co. and had stood empty for thirty years. Cool place, basic good Southern food, the decor is indescribable. Every inch of surface is covered in graffiti and signatures of visitors. It wasn't planned that way apparently, but the story goes that one day someone gave someone else a marker. True or not it is an amazing sight. The dim, moody interior is accentuated only by a ceiling full of Christmas lights. The music is first-rate. The band that night (Stan Street and the Hambone Blues Band) was exceptional. It was a pity we were still exhausted from our previous night's partying in Memphis and then the drive down, so only stayed for a couple of hours.

Sunday is quiet in Clarksdale, so we had to go searching for things to do. We found the Blues and Rock Museum, owned by a Dutch guy. All of the contents are from his own amazing personal collection. Then it was off to have a look at the Shackup Inn, where I originally wanted to stay but it was booked out - a bunch of plantation shacks that have been renovated on the inside. Then to the Riverside Hotel which used to be the hospital for African Americans where Bessie Smith died after a car accident. I sensed such sadness in that place. I can only imagine the misery in those rooms. The room where Bessie died is there with her portrait lying on the bed. On the other side of the spectrum, there is Cutrer Mansion built in the Italian Renaissance style by the daughter of John Clark, founder of the town. What a division there must have been in those days. Today the town is trying to maintain the historical aspect, especially of the suffering, poverty-stricken workers' areas. I remember my mother once saying that the best music comes from poor and oppressed people, I believe she was right.

We found Red's Blues Club 'Backed by the river, fronted by the grave'. Another ramshackle building, the inside dimly lit with red lights. Big A (Anthony Sherrod) was playing that night, what a wonderful musician. It turned out there was a group of visiting Aussie blues musicians from Melbourne there and as often happens they joined in and we had a whole lot more music. What an incredible world we live in.

The adventures of Clarksdale over we moved on to New Orleans, the final stage of our musical road trip. New Orleans grabbed me immediately. There is a vibe I hadn't experienced anywhere else.

To get a feel for the town and to see some of the places we wouldn't get to on our own we joined a bus tour. It's not recommended to go to the cemeteries alone so a tour with a guide is best. New Orleans cemeteries are reminiscent of the Italian style but for a different reason. The French settlers discovered that it was not possible to bury coffins in a settlement that was below sea level. The solution was ornate above-ground chambers.

I learned more about Hurricane Katrina and the devastation it caused. There was still about 40% of the city not liveable. The 9th ward was the worst hit and so many houses were just left empty and broken. It was heart-breaking. We learned about 'shotgun' houses, an interesting architectural style that helped keep some coolness indoors.

We spent our evenings mostly on Bourbon Street exploring bars and music, a box of CDs was winging its way home as a result. My teenage years in Sydney were spent in restaurants and cafes with live music and dance floors. Over the years this has vanished and has been taken over with DJs and recorded music. So walking into each bar in New Orleans and finding live bands and singers was wonderful. I loved every minute of it. At the Tropical Isles, I was introduced to French Cajun music. I already loved Zydeco but this was a little different. That is where I discovered Hand Grenades – oh, beware the Hand Grenades! They go down easy and then they reach the brain! Then there was the standing ovation. The band was asking where people came from and when I, buoyed by hand grenades, called out 'Australia' everyone stood up and applauded – so why wouldn't I love that town? We discovered the Funky Pirate too and thoroughly enjoyed listening to Big Al Carson while sipping on Pirate's blood ale. Sadly, I have found out that the big man recently passed away.

Night times get a little crazy in this amazing town. Unlike any other place, most clubs don't have a cover charge but you are expected to buy a drink every set and also to leave a tip for the band (mostly that's all the band is paid). Also, all drinks are served in plastic as, unlike any other place I've been, you are allowed to drink in the streets as long as the drink is in plastic. So, there is constant movement as people wander, drinks in hand, from club to club. I thought Friday night was crazy but then along came Saturday. Not only did people start their drinking by lunchtime and the tourist numbers just kept building but at night there is dancing, music, performers, buskers, people on balconies throwing mardi gras beads at the people on the ground, the odd parade goes by and all the souvenir shops are open. Then we noticed the most wonderful sight. A wedding party walking from the church service to their venue, police motorcycles in front clearing the path followed by the bride and groom then all the guests twirling white handkerchiefs in the air - such a memorable scene.

Our days were spent exploring as much as we could. There was Oak Alley that used to be a Creole sugar plantation. It is named after the twenty-eight, 300-year-old immense oaks that form the alley leading up to the house. It's not Gone with the Wind though, apparently, the Creoles didn't go in for that style of ostentation although they did live the high life. The house is beautiful but not immense. It is filled with as much original furniture as they have been able to find. The place fell apart as the original family lost it after the Civil War and was only restored in the 1920s. We had a very tasty lunch in their restaurant and I sampled all three juleps.

We then did the swamp tour. It was exciting cruising down the swamp and meeting wild pigs, raccoons and an ibis. No alligators, unfortunately, it was too cold for them, but I did get to hold a baby alligator back in the office. We were taken past the homes of the locals built right on the water's edge, I giggled at the swamp humour on many signs. There are no roads, boats are the only form of transport. We travelled through the swamp grasses and duckweed into the forest where baldy cypress trees cloaked in Spanish moss stood sentinel before us. As we ventured further the eerie garlands of swaying moss evoked a ghostly atmosphere. I could see how stories were created by fertile imaginations.

Frenchman Street was exciting to explore - the markets, cafes and blues houses. The riverside was a place to stop, reflect and enjoy the vast expanse of water knowing it wasn't so long ago that this beautiful river had caused such devastation.

Before I knew it our trip was over. Sixteen days of experiencing the most amazing places and music had come to an end. Our bags were packed, including the 12 pieces of lye soap bought at Silver Dollar City and dried in the back of the car. We dropped the car off and parted ways, Alice flying home to New York while I was on my way to Miami.

Miami

I was on my own again and back to staying in hostels. There aren't many hostels in the USA, luckily I found one in Miami. I was reminded of the Hedonist - nice people, relaxed atmosphere, fun common rooms, a bar, a kitchen with everything you could possibly need. There weren't many guests but enough around to have some good conversations. Mostly Spanish speakers but also a couple of Greek girls and two American guys.

The first thing I really wanted to experience was some quiet time on the beach at sunrise. This wasn't as successful as I would have liked. First, there was the typical young fellow you find all over the world trying to chat up middle-aged women. It took me some time before he finally shut up and left me alone. Then it was quite cloudy so the sun struggled to show its face over the Atlantic. Although the sunrise wasn't quite what I wanted it was certainly very beautiful. The ship on the horizon twinkled as the dark clouds began to be rimmed with gold. Where there was clear sky the reflection of the rays formed a golden sea path towards the beach. The birds came out for breakfast, some scavenging along the waterline in the sand, others hovering in the dawn sky in search of food in the water creating a sense of peace. Photographers, with expensive equipment and tripods, began arriving as dawn broke.

With the sun now high in the sky I joined a bus trip around Miami. It's an interesting city. Although it has 5 million people it didn't feel that way. There are 23 islands, mostly populated by famous people of various sorts, stars of stage and screen, musical performers and in the past some of the more shady characters.

Just about every second hotel and street has featured in movies and TV shows, it's almost like living in a movie with the stories of murders and mayhem, stars and their businesses. I discovered that the 43rd Miami International Auto Show was on. So many beautiful cars from all over the world, acres of luxury all under one roof. I think I left a lot of drool behind. I stopped in Little Havana to try some Cuban coffee and food. Cuban coffee is interesting, very strong with lots of sugar, somewhere between espresso and Turkish. I watched the Cuban men in Maximo Gomez Park aka Domino Park, playing dominoes at lightning speed. From the top of the bus I suddenly noticed a familiar aroma – eucalyptus trees, how strange I thought, to smell home on the other side of the world.

A 4-hour ride from Miami Beach on a coach brought me to Key West. My main wish was to see Ernest Hemingway's house and the Southernmost Point of the USA. I chose Amigos for lunch, the hugest plate of nachos appeared before me, I had no hope of getting through that but I did my best!

Fortified with food I felt able to explore. It was very special being in the place where Hemingway wrote. His studio was complete including the original typewriter. The whole place is a time capsule. Then, there are the polydactyl cats, they were everywhere. Anything up to 50 offspring of the original 'Snow White' were sleeping on beds and bookshelves or wandering the grounds.

The trolley tour took me to the southernmost point. People milled around waiting to get a photo with the sign '90 miles from Cuba'. I walked back to the coach stop. I found Key West to be a fascinating blend of cultures, foods and languages. There were clothes shops, key lime pie, and streetscapes to enjoy. Along the way, I bought Zombie T-shirts for my son in honour of the short film, Zombies in Utila, that he and his friend had created.

Reflection

In amongst the sight-seeing around the city of Miami, I had plenty of time for reflection. Time to think about my reasons for travelling and time to consider how I was progressing. When I left Australia I was on the edge of some sort of breakdown. Luckily, in the year after Mum's passing thanks to my wonderful grief counsellor and my girlfriends who travelled with me on several short trips I hadn't fallen over the edge but... the effects of the previous years were still well and truly entrenched. Watching Mum suffer before passing on, the guilt for not being in the house when she had her stroke, the legal actions and various accusations of things I never did, or even contemplated doing, kept me awake at night for many years. The patch of grey that appeared overnight in my blonde hair reminded me every time I looked in the mirror of the deep effects. It is still there, staring at me every time I brush my hair, but now the balance has swung more to the side of remembering that I found my way through the emotional mess I was in and the fortitude it took to get here.

I also realised in my ponderings that quite possibly there was another layer I was dealing with. The residual effects of relationships that needed more work and the effects of how I was treated in my workplace the year Mum died. I had done a lot of work clearing the deep emotional effects of past relationships, but I was sure there was some debris hiding in corners of my emotional filing cabinet that had avoided being dealt with. They threw themselves into the compost heap of thoughts at night and wriggled, intertwining themselves like a pit of adders.

I took stock of what I had achieved since leaving home.

Before leaving I had organised the round the world ticket and a few of the stops I was to make visiting friends. Out of the previous 26 weeks, I had spent 12 weeks with people I knew; One month with sons and daughter-in-law, a week at my Polish friend's place, a week at my Swedish friend's place and six weeks with Alice in the USA. The rest of the time I was on my own, filling in the blank spots, randomly deciding where to go next, how to travel and where to stay, making many friends along the way. I had been through many emotional ups and downs while trying not to focus too much on the 'downs'. I intuitively knew, by travelling, some magic would happen to clear the 'adders' and help me heal.

In one respect I realised that not paying too much attention to the 'downs' is a pattern and one that possibly helped those bits hiding to stay hidden. During the long years after the soul-destroying collapse of my second marriage I developed a system that often worked in getting me through in the moment. When things were really bad and I felt like I was falling into a deep dark hole I would let myself hit bottom, then I would drag out all the Italian records and play them to death until I would slowly start feeling better and a ladder would appear to help me out of the pit. Why Italian records? Well, in my teenage years while all my friends were listening to Elvis and other rock and rollers I was mostly listening to late-night Italian programs. I was brought up on European music and I found the Italian music of the 1960s, in particular very romantic, very danceable and soothing. And so, it was that music I would turn to in my darkest moments. However, that was not the music that helped me after the horrendous eight years of a relationship with a narcissistic Italian. When he finally left it was rocking dance music that I played.

In childhood it was different, no-one would believe it but I was painfully shy. I also had a very high dislike of injustice. My mother used to tell me how when I was young (I'm guessing somewhere between 6-8) my brother accused me of buckling his bike wheel, Dad spanked me with what he had in his hand at the time which happened to be a wooden tomato box lid that he was about to nail onto a box of packed tomatoes. Mum described my reaction - 'I had never seen anything like it' she said 'you looked at your father, turned on your heel and walked away, not a tear was shed'. Up until that time apparently, I used to follow Dad everywhere. As an adult, I realised that that is the way I deal with high levels of injustice. If I am accused or abused unjustly I may try to sort it out initially and put up with it but, eventually, the shutters slam down and that relationship changes forever.

The other coping mechanism I developed was the persona of an extrovert. I noticed people liked me more when I was smiling and chattering. I couldn't allow the deep shyness and low confidence to take over, I still remember that terrible feeling. My mother needed me to translate when dealing with vegetable market agents, writing letters or talking on the phone. She did pretty well herself but of course, there were times when she needed more English than she had. So I created the extroverted layer. Mum's insecurity about her English language ability began creeping back as she headed towards her 80s and 90s.

What am I now?

The Myers-Briggs test that labelled me as an off-the-scale extrovert never totally fitted me. I knew on the inside that the extrovert persona was initially a construct, even though by adulthood it had become 'me'. Inside was the child who liked reading, writing poetry, listening to music and was very shy and insecure. I discovered Jung's word 'ambivert' and that fits much better.

This was how I was travelling. When with people there was the extrovert partying with the best of them, when on my own, travelling or in a hotel, I thoroughly enjoyed the alone time and the silence. I was very proud of myself when I realised how far I had come.

The massive task of organising each leg of travel sounds daunting to many people, but I loved it. Deciding where to go next and how to get there kept my mind busy and added one more notch of achievement to my belt. Along with that the people I met proved to be amazing. Many have remained friends and I must thank them all for the part they played in my healing. None of them would have realised that they were so important to me. In fact, I didn't realise it at the time, only after coming home and reflecting some more did I understand the power of all those I met along the way and how grateful I was for their acceptance. After all, it's not often that a 60 something can end up with so very many friends who are at least half her age.

So, while I was thoroughly delighting in seeing so many places I had wanted to see for so long, my deep grief was slowly being healed by re-building confidence and trust in myself, by amazing people I met, by learning more about the wonders of the world and the support I was receiving from some dear understanding friends back home. There was so much more to come.

CHAPTER 10

Central America

Farewell to Miami and hello to Antigua, Guatemala. Being greeted by a traditional band at the airport was fun, customs didn't give a hoot about the form I had meticulously filled in and after 48 slightly crazy kilometres on the road, I arrived in the town of cobbled streets.

I had no plans for my stay as I fully expected to be in Guatemala a few weeks then move on to other Central or South American countries. Little did I know I would become captivated. Each day of three months was spent experiencing and learning about the beautiful city of Antigua and the country. And more about myself.

I checked into the quaint hotel and decided that the best thing to do was to find the Ocelot Bar, track down my son's friend Shaun, the owner, and have some late lunch. Success all round. I met some of Ginski's friends almost immediately. The looks were priceless when I introduced myself, he had obviously made his mark. Three of us went off for dinner and sat around a courtyard fire pit. On our walk back Piano Mike showed his friend and me the Cafe No Se - I remembered seeing part of a travel program at home, not long before leaving on this trip, about this very place not realising where it was. The café is dark and cave-like and if you duck through a very low door you end up in the Mezcal Bar which has a bookshop called Dyslexia attached to the front, a unique place. My new friends were wonderful when it was time to leave, they put me in a tuk-tuk, told the driver exactly where to take me and let him know that I should get there safely.

There is only one way of exploring a new place and that is to plunge right in. So here I was on day two, a Saturday, armed with minimal information setting off along these charismatic streets. Of course the first was to find good coffee. The map of the city clutched in my hand I started down 6a Calle Poniente (6th Street West). Antigua turned out to be quite easy to explore given the way the streets are named with the points of the compass. Guatemala grows some of the best coffee so there is a huge coffee culture. I discovered many cafes with excellent coffee right from day one. It seemed I was definitely being guided well. I didn't find the café suggested to me but walked into another only to find out it was celebrating its 21st birthday so my second coffee was free and it came with a slice of free birthday cake. I was won over. Fortified with great coffee and cake I decided to explore the market.

I thought that Las Ramblas in Barcelona back in 2006 was a labyrinth and that Zeleni Venac in Belgrade was huge but both are almost easy compared to this crazy place of narrow passageways both outdoors and undercover. The paths between stalls are crowded and yet somehow the Mayan women weave their way through carrying produce on their heads. You can buy almost anything there from clothes, hardware, food, flowers, meat, and I'm sure that if I'd looked hard enough I could have found a zebra. You must be able to see this place from the moon.

Oh my gosh! What had I done? Last time I did something like this I was 29, a single mother of an almost-two-year-old Ginski and looking for something to learn to keep my brain active - something ordinary and casual like a DIY woodworking course or a welding course. Instead, I found myself signing up for a full-blown BA in Modern Languages. Well, that had mixed results. On Monday 18th November 2013, only my third day in Antigua, at 62 and 3/4 I signed up for a 3-month Spanish language course with an exam at the end and including 60 hours of Salsa lessons. Exams? with my rebellious nature? Salsa? with my back? How I would have loved to learn to dance to those Salsa rhythms. My body was telling me my dancing days are over.

I always said that I wanted to immerse myself in at least one of the languages I learned in my younger days, so here it was. Careful what you wish for eh? I started with a different school for a week then switched to the long course.

I found new accommodation, I needed somewhere cheaper with hot water in the shower and preferably a kitchen as well as wifi. I found all of that just down the road from my first hotel in a hostel run by locals. I chose a single room and everything I wanted was there, as well as an incredible view from the rooftop lounge area. At the beginning of my trip as I was hopping from place to place, a friend back home had asked me if I was ever going to settle anywhere for a reasonable amount of time - well Antigua, Guatemala was it. Who knew.

Up until then, I had no idea where I would be for the three of what used to be my most loved celebrations, Christmas, New Year and my birthday. I had explored all sorts of possibilities and it looked like with the stroke of a pen I had unconsciously made the decision. Since returning home I've found cause to let go of all those celebrations, for various reasons the sparkle vanished and there was no point in hanging on.

I was in this town mainly because of my son Ginski. He had been there a year or so earlier and raved about it, so I decided to visit. This is where he learned Spanish, met heaps of friends and made several videos especially the four-part 'How many People Can You Fit Into a Chicken Bus World Record' - youtube.com MartyandGinski. Their hilarious videos are worth watching.

In my first week, I became friends with my first Spanish teacher and on our final day, we jumped on a chicken bus for a trip to the neighbouring area of Jocotenango where the 'Chicken Bus' video was filmed. We tried to see the Mayor involved in the video but sadly he was too busy that day. However, I did get to ride on chicken buses there and back, quite the experience. We wandered around town and my teacher took me to a marvellous wood carving shop full of all sorts of items ranging from Christian religious to Mayan and food. The carved fruit and vegetables were so lifelike.

In my first week, I endured three days of cold water in the shower before the hotel moved me to another room closer to a bathroom that had hot water. I completed my first week of Spanish and found all sorts of places of interest. In my second week, I moved to the hostel and there I stayed for the majority of my three months, although I did change rooms to one with an ensuite.

In that hostel, I met so many wonderful fun travellers and made some really good friends. I was reminded again of Belgrade, the constant stream of interesting people to talk to. I felt a little like 'mother hen' to all those incredible young people helping some of them orientate themselves. Antigua is on what is colloquially called the 'gringo' trail. Young travellers tend to visit the same places and are either progressing clockwise or anti-clockwise through those countries so are often crossing paths, I was the only one who was staying in one place for an extended time. We had parties on the roof, many conversations, cooked in the kitchen and most of my Spanish lessons with my new teacher were held up there.

Preparing for Christmas

One particularly memorable evening was the night of the Burning of the Devil. Someone decided we should celebrate by getting a whole lot of pizzas for dinner before heading out for the night. So there we were, a table full of pizzas and beer. One fellow had brought a bottle of Mezcal from Mexico (complete with the grub) and our evening of celebrations began. Dinner over we headed off for the burning. One of the most amazingly wacky events I have ever experienced. The seventh of December is the eve of the Festival of the Immaculate Conception in Catholic countries and there in Guatemala they have a festival of burning the devil so that Mary may enter into a cleared space.

It is believed the burning of the devil (La Quema del Diablo) started in colonial times. The belief is that the devil lives in rubbish, behind furniture and under beds. The tradition of each household burning piles of collected rubbish with an effigy of the devil on top began. Eventually, the powers-that-be recognised the hazards of this practice, and a central festival was created.

A massive devil is made of papier maché. The year I witnessed this event the devil was enormous - tall, red, with huge wings. He (one year it was a she) is placed in Barrio La Conception and tempts fate by being between two petrol stations. Yes, TWO petrol stations! The question 'why there?' has been asked many times and the answer is always 'it's tradition, the devil was burned here before the petrol stations were installed'.

My new Spanish teacher was petrified that I would get hurt and urged me to watch from a restaurant balcony about a kilometre away. No way! If I was going to witness something this amazing, I was going to be right in the action.

The effigy of the devil, made by local artists, is packed full of firecrackers and doused with petrol. Crowds gather for the event, many jostling to be at the front. Food stalls are set up and sellers of all manner of toys and devil paraphernalia abound. Glowing devil horns are popular with both adults and children.

I was there in time for the warm-up which included a brass band, and a guy in a devil suit pouncing on unsuspecting people. The town crier read out the devil's dreams (often political) just like the sign at the effigy's feet, and a fellow in a death suit helps the town crier. While all of this was going on two men on tall ladders hung strings of firecrackers all over the devil. They poured several gallons of petrol on the effigy and on the dot of 6pm after the countdown he was set on fire. Smoke, sparks, flames and massive amounts of firecrackers entertained us all, it was exciting. Firecrackers exploded in all directions so you had to be careful, bits of devil fell off and burned on the ground and everyone was covered in ash. A roar went up as the last bit of the devil burnt away and all the negative feelings and bad experiences of the year were reduced to ashes. Somehow with the fire, the crackers and the falling ash, part of my anguish was also burnt up.

The fire brigade stepped in to douse the embers. The crowd moved on, the music on the stage started up and the street food vendors were doing a roaring trade.

As we dispersed a shadow was cast on our group, it seemed not all negativity had been burned away. We were heading towards a bar for some musical entertainment and one young lady discovered her flimsy cotton bag had been sliced and her wallet was missing. Which meant going through the excruciating process of police reports for her. One of the young fellows volunteered to stay with her and help. No matter where you are in the world you need to be very careful with your belongings. My son had his phone stolen from his pocket in Italy, this young lady had her wallet taken in Guatemala. Back in 2006 on my first European trip, I had my entire bag stolen in Spain and I have heard many stories from various places. On this 12-month trip, I had no problems. I had learned from my first experience, and of course, I had my angels with me.

The rest of us went on and had a lovely time listening to some amazing blues from Jackson and Joe - it was the first time I had seen a guitarist use a shot glass on the left hand for the slide guitar sound. And so the evening was over.

Christmas season had started, along with its many religious processions. Religious parades in Antigua are like nothing else I had ever seen. For each festival there are floats adorned with life-size statues, flowers and all manner of decorations. By floats I don't mean those on wheels, these are very heavy objects that require many people to carry them.

One day I was up on the rooftop of the hostel when I heard a huge explosion. I looked over the edge and couldn't see a cause for this. A little later there was another one. Well, curiosity got the better of me, off I went to find out what was going on. What I found after winding through a couple of streets following the sound was the most colourful, incredible sight.

Overnight alfombras (carpets) of flowers had appeared in the middle of the streets, people were out in their colourful best clothes and traditional costumes. Priests, assistants, town criers, Mayan women in traditional garb, a band and so many others. Drums were beaten and horns played. Food stalls were everywhere and all the people selling colourful toys and decorations walked through the crowd. As I made my way to the front of the procession I saw a massive float being carried by about 30 people - huge statues of the three wise men and an enormous float of Mary and angels. These things are so heavy I was told that the people carrying them change approximately every city block. During Semana Santa (Holy Week) the floats are bigger needing about 80 people to carry each one and the carpets are made of coloured sawdust.

In front of the float walked the town crier. The smell of church incense hung in the air and at regular intervals, the big crackers would be set off from what looked like a mini rocket launcher (a piece of metal pipe on legs to stabilise the mini bomb) followed by two lots of strings of crackers which a fellow would light and throw on the footpath. At one point they were exploding so close to motorbikes I thought they would catch on fire but all was OK, except every time these things were lit they would set off the car alarms nearby. The people of Antigua know about life on the edge, I wondered if this could be partly because of living so close to an active volcano.

I followed this procession for three hours up and down streets, past the markets and churches and through the famous arch to the Cathedral. I discovered that they would be going through the other half of Antigua, I couldn't do that much walking. I watched the procession continue on from the Parque Central as the volcano (El Fuego) decided to add his little bit to the action. Eventually, I gave up and went for a beer at the Ocelot. It seems every celebration in Antigua, including birthdays, is accompanied by fireworks.

I was invited to spend Christmas Eve with my teacher's family. The house was full of people of all ages. It was a fun night. The table was laden. Just like all cultures I have been with, no matter the level of poverty or wealth, the Christmas table is always abundant with whatever the family can afford. I couldn't stay too late as the home was in an outer area and I had to take a tuk-tuk back. I was told there is a curfew on tuk-tuks entering the central tourist area of Antigua.

I was back home in time for the midnight fireworks. I watched from the hostel roof. Christmas Eve is the big celebration, Christmas Day everyone sleeps and then it's back to work. I was told that the Christmas fireworks are minor compared to New Year's Eve in Central Park. Of course, those who went to Guatemala City for Christmas Eve were getting a spectacular show. I thought what I was seeing was lightning until someone said it was the fireworks from the city.

I realised that if I could see the effects of fireworks some 40 kilometres away then my mother's experience of the bombing of Dresden from the labour camp 75 kilometres away must have been fearful. The sight of 2,700 tons of bombs and the resultant firestorm must have been horrendous.

New Year's Eve

The fireworks at 10pm and midnight were amazing. I hadn't been excited by fireworks for a long time, perhaps because they promise a lot yet for me don't really deliver or perhaps I had simply lost my childhood wonderment. New Year's Eve in Antigua was back to basics, no music just heaps of people, some blowing party horns, and lots of fireworks set off by hand. The Ocelot was pumping by 10pm and was still going when I left at 6.15am. I can say that I entered 2014 in style. It had been a long time since I had stayed up all night to catch a sunrise. In fact, it was that epic time when Mum and I drove 70 kilometres of dirt roads singing our entire repertoire of Russian songs all the way, to Mt Franklin then hiked to the 1646 metre summit to greet the new century's sunrise. 2000 was greeted by the sun struggling through mountain mists, my mother and I drinking champagne and eating chicken and croissants. 2014 was heralded in with pretty orange clouds, flaming Lamborghinis and new friends. I wondered if Mum was watching from one of those orange clouds.

I convinced my Spanish teacher to go to a coffee plantation one morning, so no grammar, and lots of bad verbal practice, but gee, the plantation was interesting. As a mad coffee drinker (none of you noticed that right?) this was a terrific experience, seeing how my favourite beverage is created from start to finish. Then it was a visit to my new hairdresser at Golden Studio for a tidy-up, and finally an evening at the opening of SNUG, an Irish themed tiny bar next door to Travel Menu. It was packed. The drinks were free from 8 - 9pm. Shaun did a great job of being barman for the night. So yet another place to keep an eye on - a person could get spread very thin with all these ex-pat bars in town.

Lake Atitlan

Came the time I realised I really should go further afield and explore. My choice was Lake Atitlan. It is described as the most beautiful lake in the world. I haven't seen enough lakes to compare but it certainly is beautiful. Lake Atitlan is a caldera completely surrounded by volcanoes, so there is no inflow or outflow of water. As the bottom of the lake silts up with various weeds the water level rises and many homes have been inundated over the years.

My first weekend was in the village of San Pedro de Laguna. Getting to the villages is an interesting process. I chose to go on a tour bus as the stories about the chicken buses were a bit concerning. I was very glad of my decision, the shuttle was crazy enough, but watching those chicken buses fly past us made me thankful for my safer ride. At the lake, however, I took the public boat (the boating equivalent of a chicken bus) rather than one of the super expensive privately owned boats. The public boat is cheap and you need to be prepared for rustic conditions. I'd been warned that the best place to sit was in the middle because if you are in the front you can get saturated. So, there is a mad rush for the back and middle seating. The boats are small. Only the centre has a cover and the seats are just wooden planks stretching the full width of the boat so getting to a spot isn't easy. The ride was exhilarating, no life jackets, the boat's engine stopped several times on the way but we finally made it.

I'd been told that San Pedro was the party village, and so it was. However, exploring the village and surrounds on the edge of the lake ringed with volcanic hills was engaging. Its cobbled streets, ramshackle buildings and colourful people endeared me.

What a weekend it turned out to be, just what I needed. Two of the young people staying at my hostel in Antigua were also at San Pedro. It was great catching up with them again sharing some of their travel movies and photos and having the Friday Shabat dinner at their Israeli hotel. The beauty of travel did not escape me as I thought 'here are an Australian/ Russian and two Germans sharing a Shabat meal with a group of Israeli tourists'.

No sleep until after 1.30 when the bar closed and the noise stopped. Then awoken at some unspeakably dark hour by a very over-enthusiastic rooster. I was seriously contemplating going and finding him and eating him for breakfast. In a way I didn't really care, I was prepared for the partying noise and I did choose to stay in a hostel by the lake with a bar downstairs. I'm sure it's quieter away from the lake's edge. However, I don't really operate well on sleep deprivation. When I took my phone off charge I saw a message so hopped onto Facebook and found the most delightful link sent by a dear friend which reminded me of why I was there and my travels, exactly the right thing at exactly the right moment ('How to Be an Explorer of the World' - an enlightening read) that improved my morning tremendously.

At breakfast in the bar I met a lovely young Kiwi lady, we got to chatting, she was fascinated in my stories, I was fascinated in hers, and we ended up going for coffee at an Italian restaurant she and her partner found the previous day and continued so many conversations until after lunch. I cannot believe she was only 22, such an intelligent and wise young woman. I then climbed the ruin of what looked like a mini Mayan pyramid. On that walk, I kept looking for the mountain formation called the Indian Nose. I couldn't see it anywhere. When I downloaded my photos there it was, I'd been looking at it all along. Suddenly it seemed to be in every photo. Surely there was a message in that.

On the return journey, I found myself stuck in the bow of the boat. As we pulled away from the jetty we were given a very large tarpaulin. The lake was choppy and the waves were threatening to drench us. The system is that all the front seat passengers hold the tarpaulin up and hide underneath it. Well, that was different.

A few weeks back in Antigua and it was time for another trip. This time San Marcos at Lake Atitlan for the weekend with hopefully, some blissful tranquillity and a few massages.

San Marcos La Laguna was different. It is full of signs for natural healers and yet it's actually hard to find anyone. The guys whom I met at San Pedro who advertised themselves so well, weren't here - one was in the city, the other was 'places unknown'. I managed to have one fantastic massage with one lady, booked another time and, yes, you guessed it, she wasn't there. I hung around for ages but there was no sign of her. Oh well, I saved some money and decided to just enjoy the tranquillity. Did I just say tranquillity? Dogs! A lot of dogs! Somewhere in the distance, I must admit, but every time I woke up I could hear them, lots and lots of dogs barking into the wee hours of the morning. In San Pedro it was that darned rooster, here it was dogs.

I found a blues/jazz venue, Blind Lemon's, so I decided that would be my evening's entertainment. What a guitarist Carlos was. Even with the very loud Evangelical music from next door, we had a great time listening to him. I had cause to thank my son again for his advice about a headlamp. Not only was it necessary for reading in bed but it also lit my way along the dark village paths - which had very deep, uncovered gutters alongside them.

Costa Rica

Back in Antigua, I settled in for a while and then my feet became really itchy. One of my fervent dreams before leaving home was to meet sloths. I had even toyed with the idea of going to a sanctuary to volunteer. My travels didn't work out in a way that I could do that and anyway the body was saying that it wouldn't cope. So, after some negotiations with my Spanish teacher for time off, I booked a one week trip to Costa Rica.

I arrived in Puerto Viejo after quite some ride over the mountain in the shuttle bus. We started out in full sun from San Jose airport and by the time we reached the top of the mountain, it was fog, mist, low cloud and rain. Well, I guess we were driving through one of the National Park rain forests, so one would expect rain right? Double yellow lines meant nothing. Imagine driving down a mountain in top gear with a massive amount of trucks and other vehicles and everyone overtaking whenever they feel like it, double lines or not! Surprisingly I saw only one accident on the way. After about four and a half hours, we arrived in this crazy place. It smelled a little like Christiania, it was Saturday night so the streets were full, all eating places were packed, all the Reggae/Rasta souvenir shops were open. I was looking forward to exploring and getting down to the beaches and definitely finding those sloths.

I had found that little touch of paradise I was looking for. I went in search of my breakfast coffee and found so much more on the way. Great coffee in two places, a beach to drink one of them by, complete with fascinating leaf cutter ants, and a cute little cafe for the second coffee. The owner of the hostel had told me there was a resident sloth in the tree next to the stairs, 'look up next time you go downstairs' she said, 'he might be there'. There he was, just hanging around in the tree waiting for me to take photos. Indescribable excitement.

The smiling sloth

Feeling all warm and fuzzy having had that smiling face looking at me for so long I set off to find Cocles beach. I needed to know how far away it was, to time my pre-sunrise walk. That beach really is lovely and popular with both surfers and swimmers. I was wishing I hadn't signed up for three months in Antigua as I would have loved to stay on in Puerto Viejo. But everything has a reason, there are no accidents. Possibly because, if I hadn't signed up for that length of time, I wouldn't be there when my son returned for a visit. To see my kids, I would probably walk to the ends of the earth, not only stay a few months in one place.

After a noiseless sleep, my second day began with birdsong. Bliss. I ran into a Canadian lady I'd met the previous night at Paya Pan, a breakfast place by the water. Her story of overnight events in the very dodgy sounding hotel was hilarious. This included moisture coming through the ceiling fan onto her bed, realising it wasn't water but that the girl upstairs was sick and wet on the floor... How gross. Taking said girl to the medical clinic at 2am because no-one else would, and yet the lady was still smiling. Needless to say, she moved hotels.

I arrived at the Jaguar sanctuary, called that because the very first injured animal brought there was a jaguar. The sanctuary started by accident, two biologists built a house and just wanted to live there, then the locals found out and started to bring injured wildlife to them, and from there they turned the place into a rescue centre for all wild animals. They nurse animals back to health and if it is viable, set them free. Some choose to stay like Toucy Toucy the toucan who couldn't be bothered leaving even though he could. The deer won't be set free because she is too tame and would walk straight up to a hunter and hand herself over. The majority of the others have their cages left open when they are well enough or taken into the jungle once they are retrained to care for themselves. The margay was a challenge as it had been set free twice. The second time it ate all the neighbour's chickens. So now they have to find an enclosure deeper in the jungle and large enough to retrain him to hunt out there and not find his way back. Then I had monkeys climbing and sleeping on me. No photos of the occasion as we couldn't take cameras into the enclosure. The monkeys are really good at stealing things and pulling them apart, so we had to be 'monkey proofed'. No touching the sloths either. Their skin is very susceptible to problems from humans, as they have a delicate ecosystem in their fur. Research is being conducted on the fungi, algae and moths in the fur of three-toed sloths from Panama on possible use against some parasites, cancers, and bacteria.

I had discovered a bar called Lazy Mon with live music. Thanks to one of the fellows at my table I learned that Austin, Texas has a terrific music scene. While researching that I discovered they also have an international poetry festival. With a little reorganisation, I could be there.

It was almost time to farewell Puerto Viejo. I didn't want to leave. I was going to miss the easy Caribbean lifestyle. A leisurely walk through the lush greenery took me back to Cocles beach then returning to the Lazy Mon for music and cocktails. I was going to miss the sunrises and sunsets, the palms, beaches, roadside stalls of colourful Rasta paraphernalia and even the interesting man on a pushbike with a small carved boat on his head. I would miss those wonderful, captivating sloths.

I felt very annoyed with myself and quite foolish when I realised I had arrived in San Jose a day early. There are no accidents. Had what happened next happened on the correct day I would not have been able to fly out.

I was staying at a very expensive international airport hotel paying megabucks for the room, thinking this place would have to be safe in terms of food and drink - how wrong I was. A whole different type of stomach ailment attacked me in the middle of the night. I couldn't even get out of bed the next day and I sure couldn't eat. For the first time, I was really concerned. The medication my doctor had insisted I have with me was not as effective as I had hoped. However, the following day, fortunately, I was able to get out of bed so I decided I could fly out later in the day after all. I'd spent close on 40 hours without food and thought perhaps I should have something. A factory packaged chocolate bar seemed to be a good idea. I crossed my fingers for luck and slowly munched on it. Back in Antigua I still wasn't perfectly well but a few home remedies and I was back. My teacher was very impressed at how much my spoken Spanish had improved in a week and finally agreed with me that speaking to people was just as important as copying out pages of grammar.

Puerto Viejo sunset

Flores

You can't be in Guatemala and not visit the pyramids in Tikal. The trip started with a shuttle to Guatemala City to pick up the overnight bus to Flores.

We left Antigua for the 9.30 pm coach from Guatemala City. I didn't bother showering beforehand because I could freshen up when I got to my hotel in Flores. The bit I saw of Guatemala City was terrible. But then, most transport hubs in most cities are pretty awful. The shuttle pulled up at a bus station and we all had to get out, still not sure why, no parking spot there so the shuttle parked around the corner and we followed on foot, immediately surrounded by a group of men all demanding money. Our driver shepherded us around the bus to get away from these guys. Luckily he checked my paperwork quickly and I was back on the bus as this wasn't my terminal. The rest were stuck out on the street trying to sort out their tickets. There were so many mistakes, phone calls to booking agents, one young couple had not been told their bus had been changed. Finally, everyone was organised and I was on my way.

After being scanned and our bags searched for firearms I was finally on the coach for a 10-hour trip to Flores. Broken sleep, iPod required to dull all the other noises, like the banging bathroom door. We arrived in Flores. A fellow told me my hotel was within walking distance, he seemed OK so off we went, yes the hotel was close by so I gave him a tip, nice man. Then the challenges set in, they said there was no reservation, so no room, no shower. Lots of phone calls later things were going to be sorted but no room till after my tour of Tikal. That would mean that my face was going to feel like it was falling off with the grease, grime and lack of sleep.

Eventually, the tour was organised and a shuttle turned up. We had an English speaking guide for this ancient Mayan site. The theory is that the Mayans came overland from Mongolia. The temples are incredible buildings, I was in awe to stand before them. There are so many more uncovered mounds hiding who-knows-what sorts of treasures. After four hours of walking, I was hardly able to move so chose to rest at the café while waiting for the others to return. I was fascinated to see a parade of Coatimundi wander past, tails in the air, looking like a single file of striped chimneys. By the time I returned to the hotel my room issues had been solved. A lovely hot shower - after 34 hours!

After breakfast the next day I met a lady from the capital who also wanted to take the boat trip to the museum island. We teamed up and she had another friend join us. Neither lady spoke English so my Spanish got another good workout. The museum was a strange place and the fellow running it was very knowledgeable and unusual. He verified the Mongolian theory and also answered the question the guide at Tikal couldn't; the belief that there was contact between the Egyptians or Phoenicians and the Mayans, artefacts have been found that could not have been accessed by the Mayans in any other way. When that contact was made is unknown - whether before the Mayans arrived in Central America or after. So many mysteries yet to be solved.

The bus back to Antigua overnight was fine, except that we were stuck in traffic for two hours in Guatemala City which made us two hours late. I had to wait for the 10.30pm shuttle and was back at my hostel at midnight.

The first two and a half months sped by. Five mornings a week my day would start with Spanish lessons. Then it was time for exploration. Every day there was something to find, wonder at and experience. There was market shopping in that expanse of winding tracks or at the Bodegona supermarket where you would never know what unrelated items they would sticky tape together as sale items, like a toothbrush attached to a jar of pasta sauce. Wandering through various other shops of knick-knacks, clothes and artwork was always exciting. Ruins of churches were a major attraction. Cafes, restaurants and bars. Some became my favourites. As is the case, once you make a few friends you gravitate to where they are. Luckily the first friends I made were a bar/restaurant owner and a couple of fantastic musicians. Thanks to them I discovered the incredible music and art layer of Antigua and met even more people.

One of my musician friends was also a poet and had a book launch at the artists' farm, a very interesting evening of art, music and fun. I still wish I could have bought a spectacular 3D artwork of the most stunning jaguar I had ever seen. His eyes spoke to me and I would have loved to bring him home. Unfortunately carrying him in my luggage just wasn't possible.

One day a lady stopped me in the street. I had noticed her watching me from across the road so I was on alert. However, there was no need to worry, she was an American who had lived in Antigua for 15 years volunteering. She had created a space for women travellers to get together for dinner. Every Sunday evening we would dine in an affordable restaurant and share stories. I met one of the most inspiring women aged 91, travelling on her own and very independent. She related her story that she and her late husband loved travelling and when he was dying he asked her to keep travelling and go to all the places they didn't get to together. That's exactly what she was doing. I looked forward to those Sunday dinners. Travellers came and went so no Sunday was exactly the same.

Farewell Guatemala

Here I was, having celebrated Christmas and New Year with amazing strangers and new friends getting ready for my sixty-third birthday. With great excitement, I was waiting for Ginski to arrive. He had suggested he swing by Antigua on his way back to Utila from the UK, catch up with friends, spend my birthday with me and then we could travel together to the island.

On a whim, as I was passing a newly opened hostel I popped in to have a look and decided I would move there so he and I could have better accommodation. It was a very comfortable place and surprisingly quiet. A full 10 hours of much-needed sleep made me so glad I had moved. I was nearing some serious party time.

When I booked the hostel for Ginski's visit I was told that they were booked out on the actual night of my birthday. Not a problem, I thought it would be sensible to spend that night in a hotel within crawling distance of the Ocelot, where I intended to celebrate - a great move!

My night started brilliantly. As I walked through the gate into the inner garden of the Ocelot there were all the staff members holding balloons, flowers and the blackboard with not only all the usual Happy Hour information but a happy birthday note for me as well. This was going to be a great night. And so it was. We danced, sang and drank almost every cocktail available. In the days leading up to this event, I had written a couple of poems about the decision to spend my birthday in Antigua. Ginski read one of them out. Oh, what a night! The Ocelot guys were just wonderful, made me cry with their attention. Two bunches of beautiful roses, a massive cake and the sign. The Fabulous Bobby Darling and Amazing Grace outdid themselves in a wonderful evening of music and most of my friends were there. The Ocelot rocked! Unfortunately, the moment came when I reached my point of no return and there was no way I could continue on to the 'after bar'. I have to say that I think it will be very difficult to ever top that birthday celebration – 63 will always stay in my heart.

I don't advocate partying and drinking as a way to heal from grief and trauma. However, I needed to remember what happiness and joy felt like, and remind myself that I was in charge of me and now that I had nobody left to care about me, I needed to take care of myself. I needed to experience freedom, to just party sometimes without anyone looking over my shoulder. You see, I was a 'miss goody two shoes' most of my young life. While my friends were out having a good time and learning how to cope with life I lived in fear of stepping over the line and upsetting my mother. As a young girl of 10, one day I became very involved in my piano lesson I was late coming home. I got a belting I have never forgotten. At 16 I was late coming home after a ballroom dance lesson when a girlfriend and I went for coffee. No belting this time, just my mother dragging me out of the café in front of everyone. Understandably Mum was very protective of her only girl and had me on some pedestal that I had no hope of living up to. This, of course, caused quite a bit of friction and I suspect was one of the many reasons I was susceptible to partners who weren't there for my best interests. I had a lot of life lessons to learn. It all evened out eventually and Mum and I became even closer.

I was prepared to follow whichever path lay ahead to get myself to a place of balance and true happiness again. That is why my birthday was so important. It was my mother who always organised my birthday parties from ages 13 to 21, as well as my first wedding. I learned from her how to throw a good party, how to cook and how to be that proverbial duck - calm above water while paddling madly underneath. From 21 until 60 (except for my fortieth which was very well organised by my second husband) I threw my own parties, and I was tired of having to do that and tired of not trusting that anyone else would do it for me. So 63 became so very important because I knew I would never organise another party for myself, and there was no Mum to fall back on.

My only effort was to ask permission of Shaun to invite all my friends to his bar for my birthday and like magic, everyone created the most wonderful night for me.

The days in between my party and leaving were filled with meeting some of Ginski's friends, saying final farewells to my friends and visiting the various haunts I had come to love. Sitting on the roof of the hostel on those last mornings watching El Fuego puffing madly into the sky is indelibly etched in my mind. The final night was, of course, spent at the Ocelot amongst friends old and new and a final Flaming Lamborghini, I just loved the theatre of that cocktail performed by Luis. A good night's sleep and we were headed to Utila.

Antigua Guatemala

Where full moons shine on cobblestones
And sunshine bleaches Mayan bones
Volcanos stand so strong and tall
And often Fuego makes a call
With smoky signals from his crown

Or is that a Vulcan frown
To let all those way down below
See his force and let them know
Just how temporary life can be
While he stands tall for all to see?

Antigua, where bougainvillea flowers
And Jacarandas send purple showers
Where Mayans walk with grace and sway
Bearing baskets on heads all day,
Where churches fell so long ago
From Hade's quakes so far below,
The ruins stand in memory
Reminders for all here to see
That any day or night or year
It could repeat and end right here,

Antigua could become Pompeii
With no-one left to clearly say
What really happened in this town
When lava flowed the whole way down,
But meanwhile, midst tectonic plates
People live, still tempting fate,
Mayans walk on cobblestones
And sunshine bleaches their old bones.

Jermolajew, Helene February 2014.
Laughter, Tears and Coffee - Balboa Press 2017

(Note: on 3 June 2018, five years after I'd written this poem, Volcán de Fuego began erupting, thousands unable to escape the ongoing eruptions and pyroclastic flows vanished, an ash column rose to about 15 kilometres in height.)

Volcan de Fuego from the roof of my hostel

Utila

All the travellers I met in Antigua had either been to or were going there. There were varying degrees of liking or disliking the place. Had I not had my wonderful son with me I probably wouldn't have chosen to go, it sounded so much like a young person's island and it's not an easy place to get to unless you know your way. So there we were sitting in the bus owner's office (a friend of Ginski's) waiting for the next bus to La Ceiba then the ferry to Utila. I had no voice and my throat felt like razor blades, so I was very glad to be on my way to a Caribbean island.

On the wharf the next day I noticed a young couple with an Australian Blue Heeler cattle dog. As travellers do, we started up a conversation and through them, I met my new friend Rose. We would bump into each other in cafes, share breakfasts and conversations - it was rather wonderful knowing a local who was closer to my own age group.

After 16 hours on buses, meeting the owner of the bus line in what some people call the 'murder capital' of the world, San Pedro Sula, a night in a hotel in La Ceiba and a three-hour ferry ride we arrived. Utila is an island that belongs to Honduras and we had to travel through some of the poorest and most dangerous areas of the mainland to get there.

And so, two weeks in this crazy place began. It was so very nice to be on an island and near water again. Our first dinner at RJs was such a surprise. We found lamb AND coleslaw with dill - oh my goodness I think mother and son were in Heaven at that point. My voice was very slowly getting better and I hoped that the massive coughing attacks would stop soon - they were driving me crazy. At least the razor blades had gone and I could eat.

I very quickly learned that the video song ('If You Come to Utila') created by Marty and Ginski is very real and true to the island. It is a destination for those who want to learn to dive and those who want to party. I don't swim so diving was out for me but I did get to spend a magic afternoon on a dive boat while Ginski was off leading a group. What a beautiful afternoon that was, out on the clear open water with nothing to do but relax.

Although the island has become known as a backpacker party place, there is a serious ecological side. The diving schools have grown out of the fact that Utila is at the south end of the Mesoamerican Barrier Reef System, the second-largest in the world. It has amazing marine life including the elusive whale shark. There are more than 80 diving sites around the island. It also has a history that dates back to pre-Columbian habitation as do the other Bay Islands. Utila also has the Whale Shark and Oceanic Research Centre and the Iguana Research and Breeding Station.

Most of my time was spent exploring on my own. The eastern side of the island is where the action is so I was busy visiting beaches and restaurants on the days my son was diving. The private beach was a respite. It was beautiful and quiet. White wooden beach chairs dot the sand, a restaurant and bar serve nice food and drinks and you can explore the mangroves or swim out to the sand bar. The beach is protected by the reef so the water is still and clear. The owner/manager has a pair of stunning macaws that flew freely and he let me feed one of them as it sat in a tree - a colourful way to spend the day.

The public beach at the other end of the town was similar but no macaws and no white wooden chairs to sit on. It did, however, have the Rehab Bar with its '12 steps' to the bar and restaurant. My soul was at peace sitting on a bar stool, my feet dangling over the clear, turquoise waters of the Caribbean, sipping on a beer, surrounded by stunning silence.

One of the many things I loved about the places I visited in Central America was the freedom of design and location. Admittedly many places would never pass our building codes but over there it was charming. One such place was Treetanic – owned by an artist. Over the years the whole place has been turned into a mosaic wonderland. There is accommodation, a restaurant, bar, and almost every surface inside and out is decorated with found objects. Everywhere I went in the town there was evidence of peoples' creativity in their decoration of buildings. My camera went mad!

Getting around was reasonably easy, although I only Walked the full length of the eastern area once. My worsening chronic pain was making walking rather difficult, but it wasn't going to get the better of me. Often I chose to use the tuk-tuks or went café/bar/restaurant hopping. Towards the end of my stay, Ginski acquired a scooter so I had a few lifts.

Evenings were mostly spent with my son and his friends, invariably at various bars and restaurants and a few private meals. We were invited to a couple of Shabat meals by a group of Israeli tourists, flavourful food and nice traditions. The last thing I would have ever expected was to be on a Pre-Columbian island in the Caribbean with a rich British, Spanish, Dutch and African history enjoying a Shabat meal with Israeli style food. The world is one.

The time to leave was approaching - the last opportunity to spend time with Ginski for I don't know how long. I was about to enter the last leg of my journey and he was staying. So I spent every minute I could with him. One of those evenings was at the Skidrow Bar. The Utila song was playing and we all sang along, a few people asked to be introduced to me because they wanted to know who I was and how did I know all the words to the song!

The Marty and Ginski shirts had arrived and that required celebrations during signing and sale time. I was going to stick to vodka tonics but, of course, there was no avoiding testing the local Giffidy drink. It is a potent, diabolical Utila version of rum with a massive amount of local herbs, one was more than enough.

It had been one of those crazy tropical rainstorm days, so it was nice to get out of the apartment to have dinner. I was sitting at Rehab with my son overlooking the water waiting for our order of 'world-famous' wings. The sky and sea were ablaze with the colours of the setting sun. My heart was sad. I couldn't believe it was my last night there. Where did those two weeks go? I was off to San Diego the next day via Roatan - a full day of travel leaving Utila on a boat at 7am.

My last morning dawned and it was time to leave. Ginski had organised my travel by motorboat to Roatan. There used to be a regular ferry but the captain had been killed and there was no way I was going to get on one of those tiny puddle-hopper aeroplanes. I hugged my son goodbye and climbed on the boat with the rest of the passengers. We pulled away from the jetty and I waved to the lone figure. He stood there in his familiar stance hands on hips, watching the boat leave. As he became smaller and smaller, the lump in my throat was getting bigger and bigger and my heart was sad at yet another parting. My heart always breaks when I wave goodbye to my children, not knowing when I'll see them again.

With this son, it is always a particular sadness. Is it because he was only eight months old when I had to escape from the car when both our lives were threatened? Is it because after escaping and running up a dark suburban street on Christmas night, dodging into driveways hoping someone would be at home and praying that the baby wouldn't cry that he had the sense to be very quiet as I clutched him in my arms? I don't know, but as I write this I feel the lump in my throat rising and tears prickling my eyes. Ever since Mum died I find I cry a lot more and much more easily. Making-up for all those years of stoic not crying?

Like most parents, I'd had a lot of practice saying goodbye to my children. The first day at school, first holiday away from home, scout camps, school trips, first road trip when they got their licences, my heart gripped with terror. And that horrible empty-nesting night. The second marriage had long been over, older son was out for the night and younger son was off to his year 10 formal. After all the excitement of getting him to his formal and taking photos, I came home to an empty house. I had never felt such emptiness before, I had never felt so alone. I put music on to fill the dark silence and the old Santana songs only made me feel worse. I rang a friend and went to stay the night there, finally understanding what other parents meant when they talked about 'empty nesting'. This was only a practice run, a one-night event, but I had a sense of what to expect when the real thing came around some years later.

I wondered, are all these mini farewells throughout life a way for us to start building some strength for when we have to say our final farewells to loved ones? To let us know that we can make it, no matter how sad and broken we feel? I didn't know then and I don't know now. Many thoughts and memories climbed over each other as the boat moved forward. Soon my son, the jetty, the bay, the houses and the whole island were distant specks and we were in open water. Time to shake my head and clear the brain as the next leg of my journey started.

Farewell to Ginski and Utila

CHAPTER 11

Back to the USA

A fter the three-hour boat crossing, I was in Roatan. A short taxi-ride to the airport and a three-hour wait for my flight. It was an exhausting day. The airline did a great job of getting me to San Diego via Houston. I still couldn't believe that I had just spent two weeks with my son on Utila and the time was gone already!

As I lay my head down for the night the memory of how this part of the trip happened caused me to think about all the roads and tracks that had led me here. I wondered whether all this had been put in play somewhere amongst the stars. Some years before, as my third serious relationship had come to a dramatic end, I started playing games on Facebook and connected with a few others who also played the same game. One of those people lived in the USA and after some months she asked if I'd like to be a Facebook friend, not just a game friend and so we connected. When I was planning my trip I asked her if she would like to meet up for coffee and where did she live. The answer came back 'yes' and San Diego.

Long before this trip, I had become fascinated by 'The Secret' DVD and the Law of Attraction. I saw Esther Hicks in Sydney on one of her visits. Then I discovered Mike Dooley's 'The Universe' messages and signed up. Those messages were so helpful and I read them daily. Before leaving home on this epic journey I had asked my angels to help me find something that would help heal my body, mind and spirit and make me whole again before returning home.

So, when back in January, in my Guatemalan hostel room, I read one of those messages from 'The Universe' and between the first part and last sentence the words London or San Diego jumped out at me, I paid attention. It was almost like neon lit up the words. 'Ooh,' I thought 'what's Mike doing in those places? I'd love to go back to London, but then, I'm going to San Diego soon'. Given that quite obviously this was meant to be I immediately signed up for Mike Dooley's Infinite Possibilities weekend.

Day one in San Diego was coffee with Abbie, her husband and daughter - what beautiful people they are - I thoroughly enjoyed those few hours together connecting with someone I had known for years but never met. After that, I walked down to the Marina, I couldn't figure out how to board the inclined elevator so walked up the mountain of stairs, my body paid for that later of course. Lunch was at Tin Fish followed by a walk along 5th Ave and the Gas Lamp area, a place of old-world charm. The previous night it was like flying over a giant Christmas tree as we flew in - it was equally pretty on the ground in daylight.

San Diego had caught me. It was only day one and I was raving. I went in search of dinner, decided to head to the waterfront to find the Greek Island Cafe, having little confidence that it would be open or even real Greek - wrong on both counts. Not only was it open, but it is also as Greek as it gets. Real lamb, real Tzatziki, real Greek salad, although I wasn't sure about the addition of whole jalapeños. All that and a lovely sunset. Unfortunately, I allowed my excitement to take over and overdid the walking. Not to worry, all that meant was the next day would be done on the Old Town Trolley. Something about San Diego reminded me of Sydney, with added character. Perhaps it was its position on the edge of the bay.

My day started with the zoo, I just had to see the pandas. The place is massive. I bought the pass which included bus rides around the zoo and even then I couldn't get to a lot of exhibits because of the amount of walking required. But four hours got me to a lot and even a whole colony of koalas. It was so exciting to get to see mama koala with joey on her back running around and climbing – I had not had that opportunity at home. It was hard to separate which animals were the most stunning and I thought I was over zoos.

I met all sorts of people in the hostel and learned about important places to visit. One such place was Balboa Park. Truly stunning. Museums of all sorts, space travel, cars, cafes, gardens, wonderful architecture, greenhouses full of orchids and masses of tropical plants, statues, art and a green train to take you around this vast expanse.

My initial exploration of San Diego was over and the time arrived to move to the conference accommodation. More serendipity was to follow. Within the conference information, Mike Dooley had created an opportunity to find a room buddy for those who wanted to share the cost but were travelling alone. I signed up for a shared room. In no time I had a response from a lady from the Philippines. We emailed and chatted and decided we would get on well so agreed to share. On meeting Bethh I realised that this was another one of those 'meant to be' situations - I couldn't have had a better room-mate. It turned out that Bethh is a top iridologist and owner of PINS (Philippines Institute of Natural Therapies) in Manila. How meaningful this meeting was going to be was not evident until I'd been home for two years. We got on very well, spending most of our time in laughter, a wonderful start to what was to be a mind-blowing weekend. I was looking forward to sharing four days with like-minded people.

'Infinite Possibilities: The Art of Changing your Life and Living Your Dreams' had begun, as did the answer to my request from my angels for something to re-align my body, mind and spirit. Right from the very entertaining opening speeches, I could see that I was right in choosing to attend.

We spent the weekend learning through laughter and challenging ourselves. Each of us met people with whom we developed friendships.

At one point I was reminded how much I had enjoyed my one semester of Improv theatre some years earlier and how much I missed it.

I walked away from that weekend with four close friends: Val who invited me to visit her in the Californian wine country; Bethh the iridologist, Nikki, a psychologist and Rona psychic and empath. I will never forget that weekend and all the amazing people. I left on Sunday evening knowing I would be OK. These four women were going to be important to me over the ensuing years, but I didn't know that yet. Infinite Possibilities conference had ended but the ripples of joy and learning keep on rippling.

Thank you to my Universe for providing this amazing opportunity for learning and healing, for fun, for new international friends and the possibility of sharing with others.

Nashville

My last full day in San Diego was spent exploring. Hotel Del Coronado was a must, this historic resort dates back to 1888 and is a stunning wooden structure. I could feel the history oozing through the walls. A walk along the beach and a quick visit to Dublin pub for a St Patrick's Day beer with lunch. Green was, of course, the colour of the day. The time had come to say farewell to this beautiful city but not to the memories.

Before leaving New York for Guatemala Alice had suggested I leave all my winter clothes at her house then I could return to pick them up. I had also decided to leave my mother's ashes there as I didn't want to risk losing her in Central America. I thought she would enjoy being in a house overlooking Long Island Sound. Mum loved the ocean and Alice had expressed her deep love and respect for my mother, who had taken Alice under her wing when we were teenagers.

And so it was back to New York for a week. The time was spent in lunches and dinners at wonderful restaurants, visits to the huge Russian delicatessen and grocery store - I think I could live inside that place and just eat all day. We went to Long Island for the weekend and it was rounds of saying goodbye to the lovely people I had met the previous year. Annoyingly, I started feeling unwell. I had no idea what the problem was but I just couldn't eat. There were no specific symptoms, no nausea, no pain, no headaches – just could not put food in my mouth. The weather predictions weren't great either but Alice and I were committed to our trip.

We arrived in Nashville safe but for me not entirely sound. I had been sick with that weird no eating thing for nearly a week and had lost 7 pounds, I guess that was an upside. We flew in on some gusty winds (a bit of a bumpy landing) and light snow. It was COLD! Given my level of health, I stayed indoors the next morning catching up on sleep while Alice went exploring on her morning walk. I hoped that by the time she returned with a report on what she had found I would be feeling better and in a better frame of mind.

We did some exploring. Alice became very concerned for me as I was getting weaker and weaker and starting to wobble. I really needed to find some electrolytes and vitamins otherwise I was going to dehydrate severely. Alice had a brilliant idea, remembering that the hunting shops usually have all sorts of drinks. She popped into one and hey presto, Vitamin water, just what I needed. I didn't go with her, I couldn't wrap my head around hunting shops. We went into one during our previous road trip and I was stunned by the beautiful murals of wilderness scenes complete with stunning sculptures of wildlife and underneath was all the equipment for killing those very animals.

Finally, we were off exploring properly the next day. We started with the Grand Ole Opry backstage tour, having decided to do both the Grand Ole Opry and the Ryman Auditorium (Mother Church of Country Music). Along the way, we decided to go to the Opry Country Classics that night. Have I mentioned that I love my Universe? Not only did I get to go to a live recording of the Grand Ole Opry at the Ryman, but we were at the very first show of that season. Funny too, there were two guys from Brisbane sitting in front of us. It was raining when we came out so that meant no wandering around checking out the parties and the music.

Another full day began with a beautiful cruise on the Cumberland River aboard the paddle wheeler General Jackson Showboat. What fun we had. First, we joined the Captain's tour. We were told that if the flood, four years earlier, had risen 26 inches higher they would have lost the boat, the pier - everything. As it was everything on land was devastated, the mall was flooded and the Grand Ole Opry was under 4 feet of water - that building is quite some distance from the river. The captain was a pleasure to talk to and let me wear his captain's hat for a photo.

The show was highly entertaining and when my table neighbours reported me as being from Australia, yes, of course, I had to do the 'shrimp on the barbie' and the 'that's not a knife... 'quotes. All good fun. Tasty lunch, although my ability to eat was still reduced. Then up on deck for more music on the trip back to the landing. Such a pleasant afternoon.

On the way back to our car we popped in at the Rainforest Cafe for a look. The place is set up like a rainforest and they have a ranger who takes children on tours around the café and explains about the plants and animals.

Back in town we roamed a few more music venues. My question was, what happened to country music? For me, it seems to have been over-modernised. Some of the locals agreed with me that the heartfelt country feel seems to be missing. Much of it doesn't twang my heartstrings. Is it the new style of voice? The music itself? The modern intonations? But, I guess that is progress and part of progress is change. Ah, yes, change, I used to create and present courses on the subject. In 1789 Benjamin Franklin wrote a much-used quote about '...nothing being certain except death and taxes.' I add the word 'change'. Minute to minute, day to day, year to year change happens whether we like it or not. It is inevitable. As our ever-expanding Universe changes so all else follows. We change, grow and expand. And so it is with music, some of those changes we like others we don't, but luckily within that expansion, we can find that which still resonates with us and pleases us.

The next day started with the Country Music Hall of Fame and Museum. Along the way, there are little theatres with lots of seats showing videos of various histories of Country music. Then to Ernest Tubb's record shop, where his tour bus is on display, some people may remember Ernest Tubb and the Troubadors. I relished the hour and a half we spent listening to Leon Rhodes from the original Troubadors and his famous guitar beautifully accompanying Annita Stapleton. I am so glad I had that opportunity as Leon passed away in 2017.

We found the Music City Bar and Grill and thoroughly enjoyed an hour there listening to a terrific band doing great covers of Merle Haggard, Johnny Cash, George Strait, Buck Owens and a few others. People-watching was fabulous fun, most of the crowd was the usual motley crew in jeans, but then a group came in, possibly a wedding party, the young handsome men in tuxedos, the beautiful girls elegantly dressed, a lovely sight. Then we were off to see what that night's Jamboree was about. Bluegrass and gospel - I was thrilled. The host band (the Farmhands) are all excellent bluegrass musicians, the guy on dobro was dobro player of the year. Then the 'New Coon Creek Girls' arrived, they too were great - the two fiddlers were wonderful. And so one hour, two bands, gospel and bluegrass and a bit of comedy, some radio commercials and we were done for the night.

We took it easy the next day, nothing too strenuous after the midnight jaunt. I really wanted some photos of 'Musica', a massive bronze of naked dancers that towers over the street. Brilliantly done but rather controversial given that it is in an area where much of gospel music started. After another visit to Opryland we stopped at the piano sculpture, I took some photos, took one step up, tripped and broke my camera. I knew I was going to have to replace it soon, but I didn't want it to be right at that time. I was very grateful that it was my small camera and not the big expensive one - or an essential body part.

My amazing Universe just kept making things better and better. Before leaving New York for Nashville I sat down and explored concerts. Of course, the mind was mainly on country music, so several shows were booked. I also found that Cher was performing. We thought about it and almost decided not to, but then I thought to myself 'am I crazy? Prepared to pass up Cher just because the seats weren't super cheap? Not on your life.' I found seats and paid before I could think for too long. So there we were at Bridgestone Arena Nashville Tennessee for Cher's Dressed to Kill Tour. We found our seats, six rows up from the floor, just about eye level with performers and so close to the stage! How were these fabulous seats still available when I booked?

I had no clue who the support act was, didn't think about it in fact. I noticed there was a massive flag on the curtain on stage and paid no attention assuming it was for Cher. Then a voice came on the microphone, I thought, 'hmmm, that voice sounds familiar' then I thought 'that woman looks familiar' then I read the curtain, it said '35th Anniversary 1979 - 2014 Benatar Giraldo' Oh my goodness! We had Pat Benatar and Neil Giraldo, right there in front of us. What a fantastic surprise bonus. A whole hour of those two. That was followed by two hours of spectacular Cher, what can I say, she excels herself every time. Those costumes, the scenery, dancers, songs. She even did a duet with Sonny of I Got You Babe (Sonny on video of course). We were so close that when she came to our end of the stage I felt that I could almost reach out and touch her. What a spectacular night!

Austin and San Francisco

And, before I knew it, our time in Nashville was over. Alice and I parted ways again, she home to New York and I, on to Austin, Texas.

Thanks to that random conversation in the Lazy Mon bar in Puerto Viejo three months earlier I now found myself in Austin, Texas. I also discovered that Jesse Wadeson, a fantastic singer whom I had met in Antigua, Guatemala, was in town and would be doing some gigs. The soft Texan spring evening settled around me. I caught up with Jesse at Whistler, not far from my accommodation, and spent an hour or so listening to some great blues and soul under the stars.

I was staying in my first and only Airbnb. Hostels are few and far between in the USA. I loved where I was staying, my room was great and my hostess was fun.

I found the Strange Brew Cafe for the first day of the Austin International Poetry Festival. 'Cafe' doesn't sound very 'international', but it is only one of the venues and actually has several dedicated rooms for entertainment. There I was listening to all those talented poets and they opened up the mic to the public. What an honour, I read four of my poems to an audience of fantastic poets. I can now honestly say I have presented my work at an international level.

The next day I met Aussie Thom, the world poet. What a gorgeous character, he invited me to read that afternoon at the Full English cafe and at the following night's midnight to dawn open mic at Strange Brew. There was a wonderful morning session on the Beauty of Language where poems were read by their writers in French, Spanish, Russian, Hindi and Punjabi then translated into English. Later in the day, a very expressive Italian poet performed all his poetry in Italian then handed out English translations.

The previous night's cab ride home was funny and entertaining. I hopped in the cab and noticed the driver was playing Italian music. We had a chat about the singer, it was Milva whom I remembered from my youth when I used to listen to those late-night Italian radio programs in Sydney. Then another song I used to love in the '60s (Casa Bianca) came on and I was thrown back to being 16 again. I assumed the driver was originally Italian given the music but no, he was a 62-year-old South Korean. Apparently, South Koreans love European music.

Researching Austin I had discovered, not only a poetry festival but also the Lonestar Rod and Kustom Roundup. Yes, a lot of cars. Acres of them. It was interesting to see the difference to what I'm used to back home. A lot of Rat Rods while most of the fully restored ones were classics. I did enjoy the slightly strange juxtaposition of rust against shine.

The rest of my time in Austin was taken up with more poetry, finally finding the new Johnny Cash release, local food and visiting every western store in town searching for a shirt for my Hungarian friend. He had asked for one to match the boots he had requested to have made in Guatemala.

My next stop was San Francisco. As my new friend Valerie from the Infinite Possibilities conference had invited me to her place in wine country I simply had to go. I flew in via Salt Lake City which was surrounded by snow-covered hills and wrinkled land formations.

The Hop On Hop Off bus took me to all the essential places. The morning fog that comes off the Pacific Ocean hides the Golden Gate Bridge creating an eery sight. I hopped off only once to explore Haight Ashbury, the birthplace of the San Francisco Hippie era. It was fun browsing through all the strange shops, the smell of weed was rather noticeable, smoking in the street seemed quite OK. There were heaps of vintage clothing shops, a music store as big as a bowling alley and great food and coffee. I spent hours there, even had a hair trim. I met a lovely lady from Bristol at the bus stop, also travelling on her own but doing a cruise from LA to San Francisco and spending the day on the bus too. Traditional Ukrainian Borscht for dinner from a local restaurant brought up wonderful memories of my mother's food.

Valerie picked me up from Fishermans Wharf, drove me around all the sights of Sausalito and Tiburon. A late lunch at Pizza Antica in Strawberry Marin County and a wonderful evening at her place, savouring port. The next day was equally as enjoyable. A wine country visit to Imagery winery, lots of Californian poppies along the way, lunch at Red Grape Sonoma Plaza with more wine and massive burgers.

Over the next two days, we did some very pleasurable touring. Santa Rosa, where Charles Schultz lived, had many sculptures of Peanuts characters. Fine threads led me to an antique store with many Russian items from the Russian River community. There I bought an icon for my son's wedding. Giant redwoods in the Armstrong woods were next. Redwoods are such beautiful trees and the incredible silence, aroma and feeling of tranquillity encased me. Sadly, it wasn't long before noisy people turned up having loud conversations instead of enjoying the magic and majesty of such a stunning place. The annoyance of similar events in the Schönbrunn palace forest returned briefly. At least I had a few moments of the redwood magic.

At 3am I got up for a drink of water. I thought I had the layout of the lounge sorted so didn't turn the light on. What I hadn't realised was that the lounge was solid wood and I had misjudged. Smash! Many a silent expletive went through my head and only after hopping back into bed, something didn't feel right. Yes, I had done enough damage to significantly move the nail in its nail bed and make my big toe bleed. Luckily it didn't feel broken, so I could continue my journey as planned with only a slight limp and very bruised toe.

Valerie drove me to the Larkspur ferry terminal on my last day. The trip to San Francisco on the Bay proved interesting, passing San Quentin, Alcatraz and the Golden Gate Bridge. A seven-hour bus trip from San Fran to LA took me through some very interesting landscapes. I stayed at Podshare, a whole different concept in hostels, totally open space with 'pods' built into the walls. Each pod had plenty of space to store all your luggage and had a privacy curtain. The staff were friendly and made sure everyone met everyone, nice atmosphere. We all went off to get take away Indian food for dinner three blocks away.

The walk to the tour bus the next day took me past the gold stars on Hollywood Boulevard and then the Chinese Theatre with all the signatures in the cement paving. I hopped off for a stroll along part of the Santa Monica Boardwalk and took in the Skate bowl and graffiti artists' structures. I ate the best fish and chips on this entire trip at Danny's Santa Monica and great gelato at Venice Beach. I was tired but still had to do the tour of stars' homes and up to the Hollywood sign. Had I not listened to the friend who had said not to bother spending too much time in LA, I wouldn't have had to rush that visit. There is a lot to experience for a first-timer. Before I knew it my visit was done. Time to get to the airport and fly home.

Sydney

What would home mean when I got there? Would anything have changed? How would people be? It wouldn't be long before I found out.

I landed on Aussie soil on Wednesday sixteenth of April 2014. I had a few days scheduled in Sydney staying with friends then it would be back to good old Canberra. Where the heck did those 12 months go?

First I had a little ceremony to perform seeing as I was in Sydney at the right time. I bought a pink rose and headed to Darling Harbour. Why a pink rose? My parents and brothers arrived in this wonderful country on the seventeenth of April 1950 on the refugee ship General Stewart. As they approached Sydney they couldn't see a thing, the city was fogged in. Mum being her usual self, had befriended and helped a lot of people on the journey (she was the only one who wasn't seasick). One particular lady was standing next to her and was terribly afraid of where they had arrived. Mum was looking down at the water and saw a pink rose, she turned to the lady and said 'look, roses grow here, it must be a good country'. That calmed her friend down a bit. The ship docked at Darling Harbour. That lady visited us on the farm some years later and joined us on a trip to the Jenolan Caves. In 1965 I stayed with her in Melbourne for school holidays, she was a sweetheart.

In no time I was home, in my own place. I was astounded when I thought about where I had been, what I had done and that I was back. Even though I wasn't sure how I would settle into daily life again, there was more excitement to come while reconnecting with all the beautiful people who had been following me around the world via my social media ravings.

And so within a month of returning, I had been graciously given accommodation by my dear friend Magda while I sorted myself out. In that month I bought a car, reconnected with my son, daughter-in-law, friends and kept a promise I'd made before leaving these shores to have coffee with the two loveliest gentlemen I was honoured to call friends.

I was home.

Part Three

CHAPTER 12

What now?

S lowly but surely grief begins to loosen its grip on our hearts and minds creating a space to begin paying attention to other aspects of ourselves. Aspects also begging to be healed. Results of pasts, scars from traumas, habits and beliefs that once were friends protecting us from the big bad world but now look more like enemies stopping us from living life to the fullest. It wasn't long before I realised that something still wasn't quite right. Emotionally I had improved dramatically. I hadn't gone over the edge, I was much happier, I wasn't spending night after night with adders in my head. I spent 12 months back home and noticed that one thing had not changed - I was still sitting around waiting for someone to be available to go out for coffee or lunch. The words of friends who had been away on postings for years came back to me. When I asked them why they often immediately re-applied for another posting they would say that while they were away they had changed but 'home' hadn't, and they didn't feel like they fitted in any more.

I understood that my experiences were mine alone. After the initial slight interest in seeing a few photos and hearing a few stories, peoples' interest waned. After all, they had their own lives and families. I wasn't really needed by anyone. I felt like I had more work to do. I rented out my unit and moved to the coast two hours' drive away.

I ended up spending two years by the beach completing the work I had started on my grand world tour. In those two years, the fine threads that had begun during my trip started to weave their story. I joined a writing class and Judy, my tutor, became a close friend and editor of my poetry book. I started writing this travel memoir but ended up publishing my poetry collection as it demanded to be first. I joined both Italian and French language classes and spent part of almost every day on the beach. I watched sunrises and sunsets. I walked beneath full moons and wrote more poetry. I cried, I dreamed, I laughed. I wasn't sitting around waiting.

I went to Melbourne to be a contestant on Millionaire Hotseat, sadly I didn't win but it was fun. I travelled to the Philippines to join my two friends from The Infinite Possibilities conference for some stem cell therapy and trips to the beach and volcanoes. Another friend recommended a fantastic chiropractor at the coast who finally tracked down the cause of my pain, it turned out I had used up all the cartilage in my hip.

And then, one day, there it was, an inkling of the next huge lesson I needed to learn. I needed to learn the art of letting go of expectations. Over my lifetime I became very tired of disappointments, some caused by broken promises and toxic people, others caused by me having expectations that no-one was ever going to meet.

It was a long hard road. I began achieving my goal one Mothers' Day when the only person to congratulate me and give me a kiss on the cheek before sunset was the young Italian man from whom I bought my new camera. I had forgotten that sometimes what we wish for comes from unexpected quarters.

My fear had been that if I let go of my expectations of others I would also lose all the excitement of anticipation, particularly for special events. Would my special days just turn into bland non-events? Would I be closing the door on so many things that were important to me? I didn't want that to happen. I like the feeling of excitement. But, that one action by a total stranger in a white goods store sparked a realisation. By closing one or two doors on expectations and perhaps losing some specific excitement, I was actually opening infinite doors to infinite other possibilities. I would be open to so many more and unexpected ways of receiving that which I dreamed of and wished for. Wasn't that what I learnt from Mike Dooley in San Diego? Wasn't that the message of so many books I've read and courses I've done? To get to the point of truly understanding this has taken a lot more thinking and a few more years and quite a few sleepless nights. I've had to flip my thinking, turn everything I had learned in my early years on its head and open my mind to other ways of being. The work is never done, the thinking is never done for I am evolving. Here were the lessons that I needed to have understood back in my 20s when I thought that only my then-husband could make me happy. It has taken close on fifty years to start getting beyond the ingrained fairytale beliefs that were instilled in childhood. Perhaps I'm a slow learner, or perhaps this was exactly how things were meant to be.

Having been struck by the understanding about expectations, the next challenge to resolve was that of purpose. That eternal question asked by so many 'why am I here?' It was a thread back to San Diego that set me on the path toward an answer. It lay within my psychic friend Rona's book 'The Education of Hoot, A Spiritual- Journey', Ronalafae (Hoot) published by Amazon, July 2020. Through the story of her life and near-death experiences, I began pondering the question. I am beginning to understand that my purpose is just to be here. Yes, you read that correctly, just to be here. That although I may only be one person amongst seven billion and only one tiny speck in this vast universe, I am an important speck. For without me the lacework of this amazing universe would not be complete. Just at it wouldn't be complete if you weren't here, or my sons weren't here or my neighbours and your family, neighbours and friends. We are all connected by fine threads, we are all co-creating our lives and without each of us and each living thing our planet and our Universe wouldn't be complete. I am beginning to understand that the elusive 'purpose' so many are searching for is not an earthly one. It is our soul's purpose to be here, to learn. The only way to even touch that is by following our intuition, our internal guidance. I no longer have to search for some amazing earth-shattering purpose, sit on mountain tops, roam the deserts or waste my time asking 'why'. I just have to live a good life and whatever else I do or achieve may, or may not, be part of that life purpose. I am on my way. I miss my mum terribly, but I know she is in a good place and I know that she is never far away. My nights have improved and the adders have been banished.

The journeys with my mother's ashes ended at 1.45pm on Monday the eleventh July 2016; five years, eight months and 12 days after her passing, when three generations of her family laid the last of her ashes to rest amongst the roses at the crematorium in Canberra.

Three generations laying my Mum to rest. From the right– Ginski, Nikolai, Mum's first great-grandchild RoXi, and Me.

Epilogue

The journey with Mum's ashes may have ended but my journey to my true self continues with the help of meditation, reading and more travel as well as continuing to chat with all my angels and family who have passed on.

2018 found me on a three-week road trip with my wonderful friend Shirlee to the spiritual heart of Australia (Uluru) to experience the full moon over 'the rock'. What began as 'just a trip to get away' has become a huge part of my new quest to the heart of me. The massive red, ancient sandstone formation changes colours and shades with each rising and setting sun. Legends and stories from our first peoples abound and the deep sound of a didgeridoo greets the pre-dawn. The domes of the nearby Kata Tjuta whisper their secrets through the winds and the surrounding desert speaks in a language that does not need words. Something indescribable fluttered through my soul as the sun set in the west behind me and the full moon rose above the rock on 28 July 2018.

Where the Desert Oak Grows

Where do you go when your heart needs mending
And your soul needs the freedom to flow?
Out to the centre where red dust abounds
Where the ancient Desert Oaks grow,

To the place where the Seven Sisters ran
And reached where their sky-home now glows
While Wati Nyiru still chases them,
Above where the Desert Oak grows,

Where Kuniya woman carried her eggs
From the place where Erldunda now lies,
Where the didgeridoo greets the dawn's eclipse
And the Uluru spirit sighs,

Where the red moon glows and the soul expands
When the soft early breeze gently blows
Breathing the spirit of indigenous lands
In the place where the Desert Oak grows,

To tales of evil, jealousy, love
Of the Eagle, Cockatoo, Crow
In the country so dry with red-ochre dust
Where the swaying Desert Oaks grow,

There's a feeling there you can't find in streets
Of cities where constant horns blow,
Where the rush and the scurry swallow Earth's sounds
And the Desert Oak simply can't grow.

Jermolajew, Helene, 19 August 2018.

Remember the two gentlemen with whom I kept a coffee appointment on my return from the Grand Gap Year? The most caring father and son team I had ever witnessed, both poets and writers. Bede, the dad, survived the horrors of the frontline on the Kokoda Track in WWII. A poet and a man with a cheeky sense of humour and quick wit, I was honoured to call him 'friend'. Sadly, he has since left Earth and his soul has travelled to where they call home. My friendship with his son Garry continues.

2019 arrived, Carolyn a childhood friend, tracked me down and that meant another road trip, this time to the Central Coast to meet up with her. It had been 55 years since she and I played together on the farm. Something told me to invite Garry to join me and I am grateful that I have his permission to include this part of my ongoing story.

Our road trip to the Central Coast has stayed with me wrapped in warm memories of one of the easiest travel experiences with a male friend. The ease with which we conversed, travelled and experienced our surroundings was touching. The ability of two people to just 'be' discovering and sharing history and surroundings, smoothly moving from churches and cemeteries to beaches, cafes and throwing chips for seagulls. That which proved to be impossible to achieve thanks to high tides was not complained about we just moved on. In conversations since then, we have lamented the ongoing destruction of Stockton beach where we shared lunch in the green café and walked on the sand, where there are historical military relics that relate to his father and the protection of Australia during WWII. The beach is now almost entirely eaten away by high tides and all buildings including the green café have had to close down for fear of falling off the edge. It was refreshing to experience a good, honest friendship understanding each other as individuals rather than coming from assumptions, fear and stereotypes.

It was such a pleasure to engage in conversations and interests that flowed smoothly. Although we were friends before I travelled overseas and are still friends there was something about that road trip that I have yet to fathom. There seems to be much to think about as a result of both of those recent trips. I'm not sure what it is yet, possibly aspects of myself to understand and appreciate, aspects of others, aspects of trust and caring.

The trip with Garry emphasised the possibility of males and females getting along and understanding each other as individuals without the fear of judgement or the need to defend oneself. It took me two emotionally destructive marriages, a long term emotionally abusive relationship and countless courses, books and seminars to finally, truly let go of the childhood training that 'men are the head of the house'. Have you seen those TV advertisements and etiquette books for housewives from the 1950s? Although these days they raise a laugh those underlying beliefs are still around. Throughout my life on the outside, I was fighting for my 'equality' but on the inside, I was pandering to the male ego just as I was trained by both family and society. While we girls were being taught to accept our secondary role in society and our own homes, most boys of my era were being taught that 'boys don't cry,' 'the man is the boss' and so on. Perhaps that is why my Central Coast trip is so memorable, there was no evidence of such behaviours. After some slight nervousness on both our parts, not knowing how this would work, we settled into a wonderful easy-going time exploring our surroundings. I certainly needed to exercise trust and acceptance. I also needed to learn how to receive kindness, I wasn't very used to that. Past negative experiences at the hands of others had left me with more layers of fear and insecurity. Lifelong independence and stoic survival also have a tendency to build impenetrable walls. But, when you have astounding people in your life, those who hold you up rather than tear you down, people who don't judge you for your looks, who accept you as you are, those protective independence walls melt. Then you take the time to look into your own heart and see who really resides there, the ugly duckling or the swan. I'm voting for the swan. She may need a little more time before she fully appears, feathers fluffed and proud head held high. Little by little it is possible to heal almost anything or at least to reduce it to a manageable level. For me it started with healing deep grief and is continuing with healing my heart and mind. My grief is now safely tucked away in a soft feathered corner of my heart, a little sanctuary where I can visit whenever I need to, where I can express my love and sadness and be gentle on myself. I now know that I will never again allow anyone to abuse or misuse me. With that knowledge I feel my heart opening to all Life's infinite possibilities.

How amazing the world would be if we all worked together with our similarities and celebrated our differences. Then perhaps, friendships and relationships would be happier. People accepting each other's differences, rejoicing in the learning from each other instead of forcing change upon each other through abuse, mistreatment and lies. What a joyful world we could have. I guess my inner journey will continue until I also will be called home.

And now, the pandemic is throwing multiple spanners in all our works and testing our love for ourselves, our people and our planet. Giving us so many opportunities to care and learn, will we use it well? I am so glad that I managed to regain my strength and sense of humour in time to deal with this new challenge.

As I continue my life's journey I wish you light, love and great joy in yours.

I'm OK now, but I wasn't...

Into the future
Helene Jermolajew – October 2020

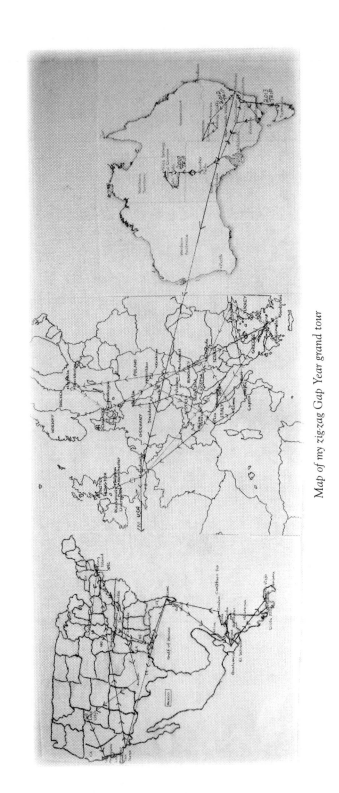

Map of my zig-zag Gap Year grand tour

List of Places Visited in Order

30 April 2013 -Australia to England
Canberra -Sydney -London
2 May 2013-England to Croatia
Split
Omis
Hvar
Croatia to Italy
Ancona-Bari
Naples
Capri
Naples to Belgrade via Istanbul
Belgrade
Fruska Gora
Novi Sad
Kikinda
Bela Crkva
Belgrade to Slovenia via Croatia
Ljubljana
Hrastovec
Lake Bled
Lake Bohinj
Slovenia to Austria
Vienna
Austria to Germany
Dresden
Berlin
Germany to Poland
Wroclaw
Krakow
Wroclaw
Poland to Italy
Venice
Pisa
Rome
Italy to Serbia
Belgrade
Serbia to Hungary
Budapest
Return to Serbia

Belgrade
Serbia to Sweden via Hungary
Stockholm
Uppsala
Sweden to Denmark
Copenhagen
Denmark to
Santorini (via Athens)
Turkey
Istanbul
Return to Greece
Kalamata
Ancient Messene
Athens
Italy
Milan
England
London
Liverpool
Wigan
Blackpool
Skipton
Pendle Hill
Wigan
Manchester
London
England to USA
New York
Springfield MO
Branson
Memphis
Clarksdale
New Orleans
Miami
USA to Guatemala
Antigua
Lake Atitlan - San Pedro
Flores
Guatemala to Costa Rica

Printed in the United States
By Bookmasters